PENGUIN BOOKS

979

MAIDEN VOYAGE

DENTON WELCH

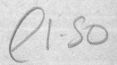

Maiden Voyage

DENTON WELCH

PENGUIN BOOKS

MELBOURNE · LONDON · BALTIMORE

First published April 1943
Published in Penguin Books 1954

Made and printed in Great Britain
for Penguin Books Ltd
Harmondsworth, Middlesex
by Wyman & Sons Ltd
London, Reading, and Fakenham

A FOREWORD
BY EDITH SITWELL

This is a very moving and remarkable first book, and the author appears to be that very rare being, a born writer. I have not seen a first book that produces this impression more strongly – a single phrase (and a perfectly natural one, there is no affectation of writing), and one sees the central point of the person described. In the touching very youthful creature who is the central character, with his curious young wisdom and his occasional young silliness, his longing for affection and hatred of falsehood, his adventurousness, his inquiring nature, his courage, his fright, his shyness and agonies of mind, his youthful clumsiness, his warm kindness, and his pathos, we live again in our own youth. For we are inside that boy's heart and mind, and the whole book has a moving and youthful quality. Mr Welch uses words as only a born writer uses them. He never fumbles. In two episodes of the book, he produces, with absolute restraint, a feeling of overwhelming horror, for all that youthfulness. In another, the parting between this young being and his greatest friend, the writing is extraordinarily touching, real, and true. I feel that Mr Welch may easily prove to be, not only a born writer, but a very considerable one.

Part One

CHAPTER 1

AFTER I had run away from school, no one knew what to do with me. I sat in my cousin's London drawing-room, listening to my relations as they talked. I did not know what was going to happen to me.

The week before, instead of catching the train to Derbyshire, where I was at school, I had taken a bus in the opposite direction.

Sitting upstairs on the bus I felt light, as if I were hollow and empty. Something was churning inside me too, like sea-sickness.

I stared down at the crowds and the traffic, but I did not really see them. Only half of me seemed to be on top of the bus.

When the conductor called out 'Waterloo' I ran down the steps and stood for a moment in the road. A carthorse was pouring out a golden jet of water. I watched it bubbling and hissing into the gutter, then I began to climb the stone stairs between the fat statues.

The trains inside the station was lying close together like big worms. I saw that one was going to Salisbury. I thought, I'll go there. I had seen it once with my mother ; we had been to look at the cathedral. She was dead now. I ran to buy my ticket.

I was small, so I took off my hat, ruffled my hair and asked for a half-fare. The clerk's glasses glistened and his mouth snapped, 'How old are you?' I lied very firmly, and at last he pushed the green ticket through the little window.

I walked past the barrier and up the platform. It was a corridor train, and as it pulled out I went to the lavatory and locked myself in. I knew that nobody could be looking for me yet, but I felt safer there.

I thought of my brother Paul waiting at St Pancras, then going without me at last.

We had come to London in the morning, from our grandfather's house in Sussex. We always spent the holidays there. We had both wanted to do different things, so we parted, arranging to meet again at the station in the afternoon.

He was eighteen, two years older than I was. I wondered what he would think if he knew that I was in a train going the opposite way.

I suddenly felt terribly glad. I looked at my face in the glass. I was so anxious and happy that I thought I looked mad. I pulled my hat this way and that, wondering how to disguise myself. I thought I might dress up as a woman if I could get any clothes. I knocked the dent out of my hat, making it look like a girl's riding-hat. I was so excited that my face was red, with sweat on it.

I sat on the commode lid and began to count my money. I had about five pounds, which was to have been for pocket money and house subscription. I felt rich, but I knew that it wouldn't last long.

My thoughts got mixed up with the jogging of the train. They hammered along the rails and my head felt hot and seething and cut off from my body.

It was evening when the train arrived at Salisbury. The September light was melting and heavy, making everything look a little blurred.

I found my way to the cathedral and stood staring at it. When I had seen it with my mother she had worn some woollen flowers on her tweed coat and they had got mixed up in my mind with the black marble pillars and the arches.

I tried to go in, but the doors were locked, so I wandered along a narrow path, under the brown trees, and thought of Repton: the calling and the shouting and the feet moving over the scrubbed boards in the passages.

Those boards were so worn that they had a soft, dull fur on them, like suède leather. The red blankets in the dormitories and the white chambers gleaming underneath. Every morning when I woke up and remembered where I was, I felt something draining out of me, leaving me weak.

A rush of gladness ran through me at the thought of what I had escaped. I sat down under a tree and looked at the spire of the cathedral. The sun had gone down and the air was getting cold. I thought of the people who wrapped themselves up in newspapers and slept on benches. I lay down on the bench to see what it was like, but some people passed, so I quickly sat up again. I knew that I could not stay there.

When my mother was with me we had stayed at the George. I got up to go in search of it. I wondered if I would dare go in even if I did find it.

I stood outside for a long time looking at the curtained windows. I wished that my mother was there again so that we could go in together.

At last I swung the door open and walked up to the little lighted office. There was a quiet woman there with soft, mousy hair. I asked her quickly for a room for one night. My cheeks were going red and I saw her eyes begin to look curious.

'Have you any luggage, sir?' she asked.

'No, it hasn't come yet,' I lied quickly.

'Then perhaps you'll pay now. Bed and breakfast twelve and six, and dinner to-night five shillings.'

I pulled out my new pocket-book. It was warm and smelt very leathery. I gave her a pound note and then she led me upstairs to my room.

There was a small sprigged paper, and furniture made out of imitation linen-fold panels. When she left me, it was so still that I ran the water in the basin to make a noise. I combed my hair with my fingers and washed my face. It was still very hot and red.

Excitement and fear had taken away my appetite, but I went down to dinner when I heard the gong ring, and sat at a little table by the door.

There were some husbands and wives sitting together, and a larger party who I thought were American. I drank the thick soup, ate the white fish and the roast meat, and when I had finished, went into the hotel lounge and sat in a deep corner of the sofa.

I tried to look at *Country Life*, and the waiter brought me coffee. As I sipped it I wondered what I would do when my money ran out. I noticed that an old lady was looking at me. When I raised my eyes she smiled and said, 'Salisbury is a charming place, isn't it? Are you staying here long?'

I felt very confused but managed to say, 'I think I shall be going to-morrow.'

'Are you all alone, then?' she asked, looking interested.

'Yes, but my mother's picking me up here and we're going on to Devonshire.' I was suddenly able to lie very easily. It made itself up almost as I talked.

The old lady was still smiling very sweetly and I thought for a moment that I would tell her what had happened, but the next moment I knew that I could not, so, after looking about the old room for some time, I got up and said good night.

I climbed the dark stairs and switched the light on in my bedroom; its pink shade was warm and depressing. As I undressed I wondered what I should sleep in. My shirt seemed the only thing, but I did not know when I would have a clean one. I remembered that my nurse had once told me to clean my teeth with soap if I had nothing else. I tried it now and spat out quickly, hating the taste.

Then I got into the white bed and lay down to sleep. It was a horrible night. I kept on waking up so that my dreams were mixed up with the wallpaper, and somehow the Virgin Mary appeared and disappeared, dressed all in Reckitt's blue.

I was glad when the morning came, even though it brought the shock of knowing what I had done. I dressed quickly and went down to breakfast. I ate almost joyfully, and then began to wonder about the tips. When at last I had decided, I ran from the hotel towards the cathedral.

It was light and vast inside, and the organ was playing and people were walking about. I felt the black marble pillars and looked at the broken bits of stained glass framed in the windows.

The Lady Chapel was dark and glittering; the brown and yellow Victorian tiles shone like a wet bathroom floor. I sat down on one of the oak chairs and started to pray. I grew more and more unhappy; there was nothing that I could do. I could not go back and I could not stay away for long, my money would run out. I felt hopeless and very lonely; I longed for someone to talk to me but nobody did, they were all too busy looking at the sights or praying.

I suddenly decided to go. I jumped up and walked down the nave and out of the west door. I looked back once and saw the pinnacles and saints for the last time, then I found my way to the station and bought a ticket for Exeter.

When I got on the train I discovered that it was full of boys going back to Sherborne. There were so many that some had to stand in the corridors. I made my way between them, feeling very self-conscious. As I passed a group of three one called out to the others in a mocking voice, 'There's a pretty boy for you!' I almost ran so that I should not hear any more, then I locked myself into the lavatory, and although the door was tried many times I would not come out till the end of the journey.

CHAPTER 2

I SAT on a low wall in the Close. The sun was full on the burnt-gold cathedral and it warmed me through my clothes. I was writing a postcard to my aunt.

I hope you have not been worrying about me. I am quite all right but I will never go back to school. I have a very nice room here with hot and cold water. The cathedral is lovely, I have been wandering all over it.

DENTON

On the other side of the postcard was a picture of the Royal Clarence Hotel, where I had taken a room. I had found the asking a little easier this time. The housekeeper had seen me as I came in and had stopped to talk to me. She was a thin woman with small bones and tight grey hair. She seemed amused by me and I was able to lie easily.

'But what about your luggage?' she suddenly asked.

'Oh, my mother's bringing that in the car to-morrow.'

'Then what are you going to sleep in to-night?' Her eyes lighted up. She watched my face turning red, then said with relish:

'I don't suppose it'll hurt you to sleep in your skin!'

I grinned, feeling ashamed, and she led me to my bedroom. It was called Abbotsford. The name was in white Gothic letters on the shiny brown door. She left me there. I was pleased when she had gone. I was flattered but revolted by her.

I sat down on the bed to count my money; it was dwindling rapidly. I had had to leave seventeen and six at the office downstairs. I knew that I ought to have found cheaper lodgings, but the dread of squalor was too strong. I did not even go in search of them.

When I had posted the card I stood by the box, wondering if I had been foolish, but then I decided that sooner or later my aunt and grandfather would have to know where I was.

I went into a chemist's shop to buy a toothbrush and some paste, then I looked into the windows in the High Street. I found the antique-shops I had first seen with my mother. In the window of one, the same cracked Worcester salmon-scale plate was still there. The Dartmoor Pixies stared out at me drearily from the souvenir shop, so I turned and walked slowly back to the hotel.

In the high dining-room upstairs the chandelier was already lighted. I sat down in the warm yellow room and began to eat. It was a long meal, and with each mouthful I kept asking, 'What am I going to do to-morrow? What am I going to do to-morrow?'

I slept again that night in my shirt. It was getting tousled and dirty now. I felt old and dirty too, as if I had never been young and fresh. When at last the morning came, I got up and bathed, and then rubbed the cuffs and collar of my shirt with a wet corner of the towel. It was lucky that I did not need to shave yet; there was only a little golden hair on my upper lip. The hair on my head was matted, for two days it had only been combed with my fingers.

I wanted to leave the hotel as quickly as possible in case my aunt should ring up when she got my postcard. I decided to go for a long walk, and made my way out of the town until at last I came into the green fields. I sat down under some trees near a pond. It was a damp, misty day and I felt I wanted to die. Nobody else was about, I was all alone in the fields.

A bit of newspaper was lying on the ground in front of me, so I took it up and began to read. There was a recipe for red cabbage pickle. I thought of it tasting cold and acid on my tongue, and it made me feel sick. I wondered if I would feel better if I had something hot to drink. I got up and walked wearily up the steep hill into the town again.

I saw a small café called the Blue Bird. It was steamy inside, with a smell of vegetables. The waitresses were dressed in flowered pinafores and there were sticky cakes on wire trays. I went upstairs and sat underneath a copper warming-pan. One of the waitresses came up to me and I ordered hot chocolate. I turned my blue plate over and saw that it had 'Old Spode' written on the bottom. The people outside were walking up and down the narrow passage that led into the Close. I felt miserable and the chocolate seemed to weigh me down inside instead of comforting me.

I began to hate Exeter so much that I decided to leave. Standing outside the café I tried to remember the way to Budleigh Salterton where we had once spent a summer.

I would walk to save money. My thoughts were more peaceful when I walked too.

I dodged down the High Street, crossing the road whenever I saw a policeman; I thought that they were all probably searching for me by now.

As I walked I felt the money in my pocket banging against my leg. I had less than a pound now. If only I could get a job! But I felt that I was not good for anything.

Passing a farm-yard I tried to go in and ask for work, but knew that I could not. A young labourer came out sitting high up on a cartload of steaming manure. The sun just caught him and I thought how splendid he looked. I wanted to help him fork the stinking manure out of the cart, but instead I just walked on.

I was so tired when at last I reached Budleigh Salterton that I went into the first inn I saw. I waited under the gas-light in the hall until a maid led me up narrow stairs and down a long corridor to a little room. It was high-ceilinged and the wallpaper was old, with a big green pattern of scrolls on it.

I pulled off my clothes and got into bed. The feel of the dirty rug on my bare feet was horrible. I had eaten nothing since lunch-time, but I was not hungry.

Soon I realized that my room was over the bar. The sound of talking and of glasses being knocked came up through the floor. It maddened me, I could not go to sleep. I lay awake long after the noises had stopped, watching the faint square of light from the window and listening to the sea rustling the stones on the beach.

The next morning I hurried through my breakfast, leaving the thick rashers and the remains of the egg on my plate.

Outside the sun was strong, and I walked along trying to decide what to do.

As I thought, I turned down a narrow lane and found myself in front of a comfortable thatched house. There swam into my mind the words of some people I had known in Switzerland:

'We live in the thatched house at Budleigh Salterton.'

A car was waiting outside the gate and I suddenly felt bold. I walked up the stone path between the neat flower-beds and rang the bell. Mrs Brandon herself came to the door. She recognized me and shouted, 'Denton, what are you doing here?'

I lied very quickly, and she led me into the shiny chintz drawing-room.

I was staying with an aunt in Exeter and had come to Budleigh Salterton to revisit it. We talked of Switzerland and my brothers. I was gaining confidence; her children were away at school and I had been asked no difficult questions.

Two love-birds in the bay window were chattering and

kissing and losing their feathers while we talked. I wondered what was going to happen next.

When her husband came in, I started. He said he was ready to go. She turned to me and said, 'We're just driving in to Exeter. Would you like to come back with us?'

I thought quickly and answered, 'Yes.'

We all got into the old car. Mr and Mrs Brandon were large and noisy, and I prayed that they would not ask to see my aunt when they got to Exeter. As we climbed the hill I asked them to leave me at the top, then, waving good-bye, I disappeared down a side street.

I was in a fever. I had no money left. I thought of writing for some, but I could not wait three days until I had an answer.

I knew that I must go back to London, and I was almost glad.

I had come now to a poorer part of the town and, looking up, I saw three golden balls. I passed them and then went back, but still I could not go in.

At last I pushed the door open and quickly went up to the counter. I had taken my watch off, and held it out now to the man. It had cost five pounds. I wondered what he would give me. He took it under a little light at the back of the dark shop and then, looking up, offered me six shillings.

I did not know what to do; six shillings would only just pay my half-fare to Salisbury. I wanted to get to London. I looked up at the man's steel glasses and knew that I would get no more, so I took the little ticket and left.

I wandered about Exeter all that afternoon. I stood in the Close and watched some soldiers march into the cathedral. The band was playing and I saw the sun flash on the brass and on the sweaty faces. Everything was brown, green-brown khaki and red-brown faces and hands.

I went to the hotel; I had decided to ask if there was any message for me. The reception clerk's pale hair rippled as she looked up at me.

'They've been asking about you,' she said, 'wanted to know if you were still here. I said you left yesterday morning.'

I did not wait to ask who 'they' were. I said 'Thank you, that's all I wanted to know,' and left quickly.

Outside again I felt hot and cold with fear. It was not until late that night that I decided to go back to Salisbury. I did not know what I should do after that.

The station clerk was difficult; he wanted to know when I was born and if I was travelling with anyone. I thought for one moment that I would not get through, but the gloomy dark station spurred me on to lie successfully; I could not stay there all night.

I looked at my change as I waited on the windy platform.

I had just tenpence left.

CHAPTER 3

THE streets of Salisbury were empty and still; I heard a clock striking and looked at my left wrist, then I remembered what had happened to my watch. I tried to count the strokes and decided that it must be midnight. Standing on the bridge I looked into the black river which was so clear in daytime, then I moved on towards the Market, and soon the curved shape of the Butter Cross loomed in front of me.

I went under its dark shadows and sat at its core, against the fat central pillar. I was very tired. I shut my eyes, wondering if I could sleep there.

When I opened them I saw two figures standing at the corner. They seemed to be talking and I felt that they were watching me. Soon one came slowly towards me and I saw that he was a policeman. As he came nearer and nearer I tried to arrange my thoughts.

'Well, what's wrong?' he asked suspiciously, not knowing what to make of me.

I took a deep breath and began to talk very quickly:

'Can you tell me where I can get a bed for tenpence? I'm travelling up to London from Devonshire and I've lost a ten-shilling note.'

He looked at me again and said, 'Where's your family?'

'They're in London; I'm travelling alone.'

He moved his weight from one foot to another, looked over his shoulder and then said slowly, as if he were not quite sure of himself:

'I don't know where you could get a bed for tenpence, but you could come back to the station with me if you like.'

For a moment I thought that he meant to lock me up, then I realized that he was being kind, so I walked with him through the dark streets. As we walked he talked to me, saying that in the morning he would get in touch with my family. I knew that I must stop that. Suddenly the name Day flew into my mind; I knew that they lived somewhere in Salisbury. I said hurriedly that in the morning I would go to see a friend called Mr Day who would lend me some money.

In the warm police station the Sergeant was sitting on a high stool with his jacket off. His braces gleamed and his shirt was made rosy by the fire.

The policeman explained about me and then looked for the name Day in the Telephone Book. I helped, and we found what I thought was the right address.

Then I was led into a wide stone passage and down some broad steps to the cells. The policeman opened the door of one and, turning on the light, said, 'You'll be all right in here, I won't lock you in.'

When he had left I looked round me. There were smooth walls painted dark green half-way up, the door had no lock or handle inside. In one corner was a water-closet with scrubbed oak seat and brass screws. The shock of seeing it exposed there made me want to laugh. I saw that there was no chain to pull; I supposed that the policeman worked it from outside. High up on one wall was a small square window with thick iron bars. A thrill of excitement went through me; then I looked down at the low bed and saw the broad arrows on the blankets. They were dark blankets sewn with red binding wool, and each one was marked in the corner.

I sat down on the bed to look at the broad arrows closely; I had only read about them in books. The straw mattress crackled dustily as I sat down, and I started, not expecting any noise.

I did not undress but lay down as I was, pulling the blankets over me. The bed was very hard and the straw felt sharp through the canvas, but I was almost happy. I enjoyed sleeping in a prison cell.

I woke up in the very early morning to hear loud shouts and heavy banging on the wall. Someone in the next cell was shouting, 'Bloody well let me out, you bastards. Bloody well let me out!'

He was kicking his door violently and screaming like a madman. I began to wish that I had been locked in; I could not do it myself. I heard someone walking heavily down the passage in stockinged feet, and then the policeman telling the man to be quiet. There was more abuse, very violent and obscene, then there was singing that began and tailed off into nothing, until at last the drunk man was too tired to make any noise.

I was awake when the grey light came into my cell from the high window. I lay thinking for a little while, wondering what would happen to me to-day; then I got up and tried to straighten my clothes. My shoes felt hard and stiff as I put them on, and my eyes were puffy and swollen.

I wanted to leave the police station before I was asked any more questions.

I folded the blankets and gave one last look at the lavatory pan, which I had not liked to use as there was no plug. As I walked down the passage I wondered if the drunk was still in the next cell; it was quite still now.

The policeman met me at the top of the stairs with a cup of strong tea.

'I was just going to bring this to you,' he said. I suddenly felt very pleased, and drank the tea while he looked up Mr Day's address again. Then, after he had told me which way to go, I thanked him and said good-bye.

I lost my way several times, but at last, after going under a railway bridge with gaudy posters pasted on the walls, I came to the street. As I stood in front of the number we had looked up, I wondered if the family I knew lived there or not.

I walked up through the mean little rockery and rang the bell. The door was in two shades of brown, like a bar of milk and plain chocolate. When it opened I saw Mrs Day standing in front of me. She had a dark skin and was timid; she just blinked at me and said nothing. Then she recovered a little and I began a long string of explanations.

She led me through the house to the dining-room, where Mr Day and the baby were eating boiled eggs. The baby stared at me from his high chair, letting a long ribbon of egg roll down on to his towel bib. Mr Day was staring at me too; I could tell how curious and surprised his blue eyes were in his dried-up, rather boyish face.

I was glad that I knew my story so well, I did not want to confess anything to these people.

I asked Mr Day to lend me ten shillings to pay for my ticket to London, explaining that I had lost some money.

'Oh, but you must have a pound,' he answered.

I said that ten shillings would do, but hoped that he would give me the pound; then I was asked to sit down and have breakfast with them.

We talked of Switzerland, where I had first met them, as I had the Brandons, and I told them about my night in a prison cell, hoping that it would keep them from asking dangerous questions.

Afterwards I was shown Mr Day's antique furniture, the very polished oak and walnut that he liked. I was told about the rings the dealers made at auctions so that amateurs could not buy anything.

It was comfortable to be with a family again; although I did not really like the Days at all, I felt almost safe; not alone in a strange town with no money.

Mr Day took me to the station before he drove to his office. I thanked him again very much and went to the booking-office to pay my full fare to London. I was tired of lying and contriving.

The carriage I got into was nearly full. There was a

plump, youngish man correcting exercise books, a mother and her baby, and several others. They did not sit, as usual, in stolid silence, but soon began a lively argument.

It is strange that they chose the public schools to talk about. My heart jumped; I wanted to tell my story, I was vain about it, but my good sense told me not and I only made ordinary remarks.

The man with the exercise books was a schoolmaster and he hated the system, but the mother with the baby thought it a very good start in life for most boys. The conversation shifted to snobbery, and it stayed there for the rest of the journey. Everyone seemed to have something to say.

At last the schoolmaster got up, saying that he was going to the restaurant car for a cup of tea. He turned to me and asked me to go with him. I was delighted, but I did not go; I wondered if he really wanted to pay for me.

Instead, I sat in my corner and thought. I suddenly realized what was waiting for me at the other end.

I would have to face my family.

The schoolmaster came back and went on with the conversation, but I could not talk, I was too anxious.

I decided at last to go to a friend's flat and to explain everything to her. She would understand, she would tell my family.

When the train arrived I quickly got a taxi. I did not want to think; I knew that my resolution would grow weak. I would walk about the streets, not daring to go anywhere.

As I climbed the stone steps to her flat I tried desperately to frame my words. There was no need. The bell rang hollow in the empty flat.

I stood looking blindly at her front door, wondering what to do next. My eldest brother was my only near relation in London, but I did not like him. Then I remembered my second cousin May. I knew she was the right person. She had Edwardianly dressed white hair, and had done much work for charity. When asked if she would like to be made a Dame she had refused, saying that she had many better things to spend twenty-five pounds on than the insignia which she would need for the ceremony.

Although I knew her so little I felt that she must be clever and wise. I hailed another taxi and drove to the Boltons.

As I walked up between the two stucco lions that guarded her door I was almost too frightened to think. Wills opened the door. She had the sour, grudging look that faithful maids often have. I asked hurriedly if my cousin was in. She nodded and disappeared into the dining-room, leaving me still standing in the hall, seething and trembling inside. I heard her talking to my cousin, and then the rather high, metallic answer, 'Please ask him to come in.'

The door was held open for me. I steeled myself as well as I could, and walked in.

My cousin was sitting at the table with an auburn-haired woman. Papers were spread out in front of them; they were evidently busy.

'What a surprise to see you, Denton!' my cousin said. 'This is nice, but why aren't you at school? Hasn't term begun yet?'

I gave her a desperate look. I knew what I had to say. There was no escape now.

'I didn't go back to school. I took the train to Salisbury instead, and I've been away nearly five days.'

The auburn-haired woman looked at me, and I was angry because I thought her eyes twinkled. My cousin's face had gone blank.

At last she said quietly, 'But, Denton, why did you do it?'

'I don't know, I felt I couldn't go back. I've always

25

hated it. But what's going to happen now?' I asked anxiously.

My cousin was still bewildered. 'I must let your aunt and brother know that you're safe,' she said slowly.

It was the auburn-haired woman who relieved the tension.

'Let's all have lunch and think afterwards,' she said gaily.

I smiled at her nervously and thankfully, and my cousin rang the bell.

We talked through lunch as naturally as we could, but there were long pauses. I could not eat much; the food seemed to stick and get coated on the sides of my throat.

Afterwards, while we were drinking our coffee by the fire, my cousin wrote out two telegrams. Both said,

'Denton safe with me. May.'

Wills went out to send them off. From the window I saw her going down the steps in her tight navy-blue hat and her narrow fur collar.

That'll bring them all down on me, I thought. I turned away and got ready to go out myself to buy the things my cousin suggested that I needed.

The Kensington streets were grey and blurred and the lights were already on in the little chemist's shop. I bought a face-flannel and a comb, and then wandered farther down the street. At the corner there was a flower-booth covered with cornflowers and those pink shop roses which have such long stalks and seem always to be smothered in dew. Next to it was an antique-shop. I looked at all the worthless little things and then walked on. I was almost light-hearted. I had no problem to solve before night came. I knew where I was going to sleep.

I did not go back until tea-time. My cousin was in the drawing-room. She handed me a cup and I sat down on the sofa. Queen Alexandra had sat on it, I had been told when I first came to visit my cousin. I remembered it now and thought of the Queen's high jewelled collars and her complexion, perfect as one of her own imitation roses.

My cousin was asking me what I wanted to do in life. I said that I was interested in history and architecture, and that I liked drawing and painting. The words made me feel embarrassed.

She listened quietly, then said: 'To-morrow we'll get Miss Billings to drive us to some of the art schools.'

I felt very grateful; my cousin seemed to be taking it for granted that I should not go back to school.

We began to talk about the things in her room. She despised the white marble mantelpiece, saying that the carved plants were ugly and unnatural. In a rosewood cabinet there were Dresden cups and saucers, but they were not very old; they had been used by her mother. On one side of the fireplace was a signed photograph of Queen Alexandra, and on the other a pretty, old engraving of Queen Victoria with roses in her hair. She looked like a ballet dancer with her wide eyes, pointed chin and bare shoulders.

I was told that Wills would make up a bed for me here, in the drawing-room, as the spare room was being used by my cousin's brother Stanley.

I was glad; I thought how comfortable it would be by the fire, amongst all the drawing-room things.

I tried not to think of to-morrow when my aunt and brother would arrive.

I went upstairs to wash, and spent a little time trying to make myself as clean as possible. I had worn my clothes for nearly a week now and felt very dirty. When I came down again to wait for dinner there was another man in the drawing-room. I had never met Stanley before, he was a soldier in India. He was very polite, but he did not understand why I was there. I sat down, not knowing what to say, while he drank whisky-and-soda.

My cousin May arrived, and being much too kind and

tactful to explain in front of me, only said, 'Stanley, this is Denton; he's come to spend a few days with us.'

Dinner was constrained. We none of us knew what to talk about. Afterwards I retreated upstairs and hoped that my cousin would tell her brother about me.

When I came down again I heard him laughing softly. I hated it. I knew he was laughing at me. It was like laughing at someone who had tried to commit suicide, I thought.

CHAPTER 4

Wills woke me in the morning, bringing with her a
cup of weak tea.

'It's eight o'clock, Master Denton, the bath is quite
free and I shall want to do this room,' she said, all in one
breath. I could not ignore such a hint. I drank the tea
quickly and got up.

Stanley's pyjamas dragged on the floor and I had
drooping sleeves, like a Chinese court lady, but I liked
the fine pale blue wool and the dark red initials on the
pocket.

The drawing-room was looking rather outraged. A
heap of tousled bed-clothes on Queen Alexandra's sofa
seemed somehow insulting. I left it and walked up the
white stairs. The bathroom was still steaming from someone else's bath. The pink and black fittings were frosted
over. I ran the water and threw in big handfuls of my
cousin's bath salts. I felt sick; my inside was upset by
fear and excitement.

There were a lot of medicines in the mirrored cupboard. I took some Milk of Magnesia and some liquid
paraffin, pouring them into the cup of my hand; then I
drank. They made me feel worse.

I lay in the bath recovering, then I dried and put on
my clothes. They had sucked up the steam from the bath
and were clammy, like rubber, but I could not have
dressed in the drawing-room because of Wills.

My cousin was already having breakfast when I came
down.

'I can face the day much better after my first cup of
coffee,' she said as I sat down at the white cloth. There
was a mother-of-pearl tea-caddy and a spirit-kettle by

29

Stanley's place. He was not down yet. I was glad, I did not know what to say to him.

When we had finished, my cousin went upstairs to put on her hat and coat; then Miss Billings brought the car round and we set off to see the art schools.

Miss Billings's skirt came as a surprise after the peaked cap and jacket which were all that could be seen from the outside of the car.

I was thinking about her and the cruel long hatpins my cousin still wore, until we drew up at the first school. We went to Chelsea, to Gower Street, to Southampton Row, to Westminster. We visited them all, ending up at South Kensington on our way home.

At Chelsea I looked into the basement and saw two girls doing dumb-bell exercises. They did not look at all like art students. It was lunch-time when we got to the Royal College. The students were streaming down the stairs. Some of them were strangely dressed and dirty, and I was impressed.

Lunch was like the meal before execution to me. My aunt and brother were arriving afterwards to discuss what was to be done with me.

Before they came I was very restless, wandering in and out of the rooms upstairs although they were other people's bedrooms. Wills's was small. I expected to see a hair-tidy, but there was nothing: only a doggy calendar and a few pins. My cousin's room was dark and quiet. The white furniture gleamed from dark corners, and the pink eiderdown seemed like a soft patch of rouge on someone's white cheek. In Stanley's room I found a lot of medicines on the marble washstand. I read the labels and tasted some of them. I hoped they would make me feel better.

At last I heard the front-door bell and knew that one of them had come. I looked over the banisters and saw my aunt going into the drawing-room. I came down quickly, wanting to get the meeting over, but I waited in the hall some time, not daring to go in.

Then I opened the door and walked quickly towards her. She got up and gave me a strange, heavy kiss. Her voice was bewildered and childish.

'Why did you do it, Denton?' she said. 'Why did you do it?' Her anger was overlaid with bewilderment, but I knew that she was judging me.

I grew very red and found nothing to say except, 'I'm never going back to school.'

'But you must.' Her voice was almost desperate. She seemed frightened by my obstinacy. 'Everyone expects you to go back.'

At this moment Wills opened the door for my brother. He came in, hat in hand, smart and civilized. He shook my hand extravagantly, saying, 'I never thought you had it in you,' and then he laughed breathlessly. He sat down and I stared at the brown wing of hair brushed smoothly from his temple to his ear. I felt ashamed that these people had power over me. I could not drive the blood from my face. It was burning my cheeks and drying up my skin.

They began to talk about me as if I were not there.

'I certainly think he ought to go back,' my brother said.

I sat stiffly on the sofa, saying that I would never go back.

'What'll he do if he doesn't?' my aunt burst out, looking wildly towards my cousin. 'He's far too young to leave school.'

I was angry that they talked about me in the third person. 'Tell them,' I said, turning to my cousin as if she were an interpreter, 'that I've decided never to go back.'

She looked into space, saying nothing for a moment; then she asked quietly, 'Would you go back just for this term, Denton?'

I suddenly felt cornered. I knew that my cousin expected me to be reasonable.

'There isn't any point in going back just for this term,' I said, still fighting. 'Why can't I leave now?'

'Because they'd think you were afraid,' she answered softly; and as she spoke, the words 'Harmless as doves and wise as serpents' sprang up in my mind. I saw them spelt out as if they were written round the walls of a chapel. I felt that I had been betrayed, that I had to do right against my will. Slowly and miserably I said that I would go back till the end of the term. I did not know how I would do it, but I said it. I could not argue any more.

My aunt sighed and decided to stay the night. She seemed to be almost enjoying her trip to London. When I left the house with my brother, Wills was already moving out of the dressing-room to make room for her.

My brother was taking me to tea with some friends. I suppose in his way he wanted to cheer me up.

We climbed the narrow stairs to the mews flat and found our hostess sitting by the fire. She was like a fat little bird in her tight black hat. She hopped round my brother asking questions. She wanted to know why I was not at school. My brother frowned.

'Denton hasn't been well, but he's all right now. He's going back to-morrow.' This was not done for my sake, but to flout her.

As they talked, I took in the gay little 'Victorian' room. Big white china dogs stood in the hearth, and on the mantelpiece, over their heads, cut-glass prisms dangled round black candles. The walls were covered with white and silver ceiling paper, and the curtains were deep purple satin with white fringes.

Mrs Estridge was in mourning for her husband, and the money he had lost before he died. She was asking my brother where she could sell his guns and fishing-rods. Her daughter Mary would not be in just yet, as she had got a job as mannequin at five pounds a week.

When the tea-tray was set down in front of her she poured out like a starling pecking at a bird bath. I do not think she liked me very much – I was not manly enough;

but she saw that I had a scone and jam to eat, and then went on talking to my brother. I could see that he was annoyed because Mary was not there. We left early and walked out on to the oily cobblestones of the mews.

'I would have told the old bitch about you if she hadn't asked,' my brother said.

I was thankful that she had. For once I was glad that my brother was so perverse. I was almost fond of him. He took hold of my arm when we crossed the street, and we walked like this back to my cousin's house.

He left soon after dinner and, seeing that I was tired, my cousin took my aunt into the dining-room so that my bed could be made up on the sofa.

Wills was more silent than ever now that she had been turned out of her room. Her grudging looks seemed to say, 'I have been personal maid and a good many other things all these years, and now I'm turned out of my room and the drawing-room's ruined by people who are hardly even relations!' She would not smile. She made me feel that I was hindering, not helping, as I tried to tuck in the bedclothes.

When she had gone and I was alone by the fire, I took up my cousin's novel and began to read. It was about rich people in Mexico who built a sort of baroque palace and had a chapel full of rococo saints. The mother of the family liked oak beams and warming-pans and copper kettles, but her children would not let her have any of these. They made her have a bedroom with salmon-pink velvet curtains, silver-framed mirrors all over the walls, and ostrich plumes on the canopy over her bed. They built imitation classical ruins in the garden.

I put the book down and began to undress. I did not feel at all well. The medicines had upset me even more, and I was terrified at the thought of going back to school. I watched the firelight playing on the ceiling. The heavy curtains were drawn back and I could see the red-dark glow of London through the chink. Sometimes a taxi passed in the street. I tried not to think.

My aunt had brought some of my clothes with her from the country, so that I was able to change in the morning. I buttoned up the trousers of my blue suit. Soon I would have to change again, into tails and a butterfly collar. I could not bear to think of it. There seemed no fear in anyone's mind that I would run away again, and I knew they were right. It could never happen again.

My cousin was nice to me at breakfast, seeing how unhappy I was. She said comforting things and told me how short the term would seem.

My aunt asked for Mr Day's address so that she could return the pound, and I also gave her the ticket to redeem my watch from the pawnshop.

I did not leave until after lunch, when Miss Billings drove me to St Pancras alone. I was thankful that no one else had come with me. I sat next to her in the front of the car and watched her knees. Just hidden by the dark blue skirt, they shifted and rustled like animals in a wood.

A Frenchwoman was buying a basket of fruit inside the station. She was annoyed because the girl behind the counter could not understand her. She gave me an imploring look and I wanted to help, but I suddenly thought that she might be a prostitute, so I hurried away.

Not many people seemed to be going to Derbyshire. The two others in my compartment spoke with Midland accents. They were going home.

I tried to let the jogging of the train send me to sleep. I sat in my corner, only half conscious, until we reached Derby. Something had contracted inside me by now. I changed trains mechanically, like an empty ball, rolling from one place to another.

As I moved along the platform I suddenly caught sight of Taylour, who had been at school and had left to learn engineering. He was working with the railway company, and he came up to me now and told me how he hated it.

'What a lucky devil you are,' he said, 'to be going back!'

I would have given almost anything to change places with him. A part of me suddenly whispered, 'Why not run away again?' but I put it away and got into the carriage.

As it moved out of the station I looked back and saw Taylour standing forlornly amongst the trucks and engines.

The platform at Willington was drowned in rain. I walked down the sloping ramp, carrying my suitcase and wondering whether to take a taxi to Repton or to walk. I looked at the ancient Rolls Royce which was always there, and then decided to walk. It would take so much longer.

The rain was already trickling off my hair and down my neck. I turned up my collar and set off. I could see the spire of Repton Church across the fields. It seemed as slender as a sharpened pencil.

I stopped on the toll-bridge and tried to read the names so many people had scratched on the parapet; then I looked over and watched the Trent seething between the piers. The paths of white foam where the water divided looked evil and dangerous.

On the straight, flat road in front of me the telegraph wires hummed as they always had done. Some of the fields were flooded.

Six years before, my mother and I had been travelling along this road, but in the opposite direction. We had just said good-bye to my eldest brother. My mother was crying and I did not know what to do; then I looked out of the back window of the taxi and saw all our clothes scattered along the road. I shouted to the driver and we stopped. Laughing and crying, my mother and I ran back to pick up all we could find.

It was unbearable to think of it now. I walked on, counting my footsteps to blot out the picture.

I was getting near the school. The red brick Gymnasium glowed through the trees, and across the way the Hall loomed up in all its muddle of Medieval, Eighteenth-Century and Victorian architecture.

As I walked up the gentle hill a boy came out of the entrance to the Gym, and I saw that it was Peach. His big mouth opened wide when he saw me.

'Good God, Welch, have you come back? I heard that you'd got hold of forty pounds and had gone off to France, and someone else told me that Iliffe had taken you to Italy.'

Iliffe had shown a frank interest in people younger than himself. He had left at the end of last term.

I suddenly laughed at the extravagant stories, but I realized that Peach still thought they might be true, so I tried to tell him everything that he wanted to know.

Every step was taking me nearer to my own House. I walked slowly past the church, the dripping thatched cottage, the one remaining arch of the medieval gatehouse and the strange village cross, high up on its circle of steps. I could hear the pianos from the Music Schools. They chimed and jangled like an exciting orchestra of lunatics.

As I drew nearer I could not decide whether to go in at the housemaster's entrance or the boys'. I tried to imagine which would be worst.

I opened the garden gate, and in desperation went up to the front door. The porch was covered with ivy. The leaves stood out, waving and nodding all together, like a regiment. I rang the brass bell and stood staring at the frosted glass panels, waiting for the door to open.

Clarence, the house-boy, let me in. He looked pale and unwholesome, with spots round his chin. I waited in the hall while he went to report that I had arrived.

Upstairs, in the study, I heard a deep voice say, 'Show him up here.'

I screwed up all my courage. My movements were not well joined together. I made a plunge for the door and stood in front of my housemaster, smiling, but feeling burnt out and gutted inside.

He was a small man with a manly voice and dog's lips. His head was thick and round. He began to talk.

'Look here, Welch, I'm never going to mention this again. You've had a brainstorm, that's all, and there's no reason why we shouldn't carry on just as if nothing had ever happened. I shall never hold it against you.'

I was told to sit down on one of the slippery leather chairs, and he went on talking to me about living in a community and not ruining my career. I sat very still, saying over to myself, 'How funny! He thinks I've had a brainstorm.'

The high, childish voice of Mrs Bird broke in. She was calling from the landing, 'Rwobert, has Denton come yet?' She could never say Rs properly, and she often used my Christian name.

She came in without waiting for an answer, and began to talk at once. Under her grey wiry hair her flat glasses winked as she smiled.

'Cadbury's has sent everyone a sample box of chocolates, and I've kept yours for you. You must eat them, and then write down which you like best.'

I was grateful for her warmth and for the chocolates. I looked down, not knowing what to say.

When I lifted my eyes again, Mrs Bird was staring at me.

'You don't look well,' she said. 'Are you very tired? I'll ask Matron to take your temperature.'

I think Bird was glad of the excuse, for he said, 'I don't need you any more, Welch; you'd better go along to Matron.'

I passed through the double doors from the master's to

the boys' part of the House and knocked on the Matron's door.

'Mrs Bird wants you to take my temperature,' I said. She did not answer, but began:

'You naughty boy, where have you been?' as if I were five years old. Then she went to the wooden hanging-cupboard and fetched the thermometer in the little glass jar. I tasted the disinfectant as she put the glass rod under my tongue. She stared at her yellow-faced clock and felt my pulse with her dry fingers. Her face was the colour of dry earth against the whiteness of her cap.

'It's nearly a hundred,' she said unprofessionally. 'I'd better go and tell Mrs Bird. You wait here.'

She rustled out and I was left looking at a picture called 'Cherry Ripe.' When she came back with Mrs Bird I was still staring at the oleograph.

'Would you like to go to the San., Denton?' Mrs Bird asked. I was very surprised and delighted, but I felt I had to say, 'I'm not really ill, Mrs Bird. I'm just a bit tired.'

'I think it would do you good to go up there and have a rest.'

I said nothing. I was too happy to contradict her. Matron was already looking on the shelves for my clothes, and Mrs Bird went to order the taxi.

So I left the House again without speaking to a single boy.

CHAPTER 5

As the heavy maid led me along the passage I felt
anxious. Sister might not be friendly; she might also be
very inquisitive.

I clutched the handle of my suitcase tightly when I
caught sight of her small white figure at the end of the
corridor. She came forward, very businesslike, her head
pushed forward like a greedy bird. 'Oh, here you are,
Welch! I've put you in No. 5, quite near me. I must say
you don't look very ill, with that colour.'

I was blushing and trying to appear at ease. She led
me into one of the smallest wards, where there were only
two beds. One was unmade. I was glad that I was going
to be alone. It was too early in the term for many pa-
tients. Sister told me to undress and then left me.

A fire was burning in one corner. The grate was built
three or four feet off the ground so that one could see the
flames when lying down. A small print of Botticelli's
Nativity hung over the bedside cupboard, which held two
Bibles and two chambers.

After I had undressed and got into bed, I took the picture down and looked at the angels uniting and kissing
with such love. The ones on the roof were singing. Sister
came in and wanted to know what I was doing with the
picture. When she had hung it up again, she took my
clothes and suitcase away and then came back with
someone else.

'This is Nurse Robins,' she said, 'who's going to look
after you.'

I looked at Nurse Robins. She was small too, but much
thinner than Sister. She had a pointed face with round
red cheeks, and her hair was hot brown. She smiled at

me shyly and suddenly looked like a fox. Then Sister went out and left us alone.

I had my temperature taken again, but this time I was not told what it was. A dot was put down on the chart which hung inside the door.

Nurse Robins said very little. I wondered if Sister had told her about me. She took away the water I had washed in and came back with a glass of hot milk and some bread and butter. I was hungry by now and wished she had brought more.

I wanted to read; I had nothing, so I opened the cupboard and looked on the top shelf for one of the Bibles. The chambers loomed like horrible wells underneath, and a smell of carbolic and paper and pinewood came out. .

'O Lord, there is no god like unto thee,' I read, and then, 'As thou knowest not what is the way of the spirit, nor how the bones do grow in the womb of her that is with child; even so thou knowest not the works of God who maketh all.'

I read sentences, turning over large lumps of the book. They made a strange picture in my mind.

I let the Bible drop and just lay back thinking. London seemed far off and I could hardly believe that I had gone to Devonshire. I was docile enough now.

After I had cleaned my teeth and Nurse Robins had switched off the light, I stared into the fire. It glinted on the shiny walls and ceiling. The open window made the blind billow and swell. I clutched at the peace. I would be safe here for one more night.

The maid woke me with her loud knocking. She lumbered into the room with pail and broom and began to rake out the fire. Soon the room was filled with dust and her smell.

I longed for her to go. When at last she had finished I ran over the empty bed and pushed the window up at the bottom. Cold, bright air came rushing in. I drank it up, and was only just able to get back to my bed before Nurse Robins opened the door.

She made me wash, then brought me bread and butter and marmalade and tea.

I lay in bed all that morning, doing nothing, feeling bored, but thankful I was there. The doctor came before lunch to look at me. He had queer, pale eyes, and his red face clashed with his red hair. He breathed heavily through his nose. He looked right into me and smiled, but all he said was, 'You can get up this afternoon as your temperature's down, but stay inside, don't go out.'

Nurse Robins brought my clothes after lunch. She said that Sister had invited me to have tea with her. It was early yet, so I went into the Common Room and sat reading by the fire until four o'clock.

I had never been in Sister's private sitting-room. The maid showed me where it was. Sister was still upstairs, so I looked round freely. The room was white, with a small bay window, and it was filled with the relics of some other house. The blue Nankin cups on the mantel-piece were the last remains of an old tea-set. There were flowers in a Victorian, ruby glass jug. Over the rosewood work-table hung two silhouettes; I was bending to look at these when Sister opened the door.

I think she was pleased to see my interest in her things. She told me about them and I listened quietly. Then, when the tray had been brought and I had admired her silver teapot and spoons, she turned to me, twinkling, and said, 'You're a funny boy: visiting cathedrals instead of coming back to school. Tell me why you did it and what happened to you.'

Her command disintegrated me. I smiled redly.

'I don't know. I didn't want to come back to school much.' I could not say any more. I think she saw how uncomfortable I was.

41

'Which cathedral do you like best?' I asked in a strangled voice, trying hard to be natural.

'Winchester, I think,' she said promptly. 'I love Norman architecture. Do you know Romsey Abbey?'

I felt safe. I could discuss architecture all afternoon, but I could not tell her one reason why I ran away from school.

The Common Room seemed cold and lonely after I had left her, but I did not have to wait there long. Nurse Robins came and told me to go to bed. She never seemed to talk for pleasure.

The next day I felt sure that I would be sent back to the House. I had not really been ill; only worried and tired. I looked out of the window and hoped that the doctor would be late. I could not go back before he had seen me. Outside it was fine and windy. Over the stiffly moving privet hedge I saw boys with books under their arms, holding their straw hats tightly to their heads.

While I was still standing there the doctor's car drove up. I heard him talking to Sister in the corridor, and I waited, uncomfortable inside with anxiety. He came in alone, wearing his strange smile as usual. He brought a smell of tobacco, and perhaps beer, with him.

'Well, how are you?' he asked. He held a stethoscope in his hands. 'Pull up your shirt, I want to try this.'

I unbuttoned my braces and dragged my shirt up. He moved the cold feeler about on my chest, then he gave my stomach a little slap and said, 'That'll do.' His hand felt hard against that part of me which had always worn clothes. I pulled down my crumpled shirt and tried to tuck it in again but could not, so had to undo my flys. He watched me until I felt embarrassed, then he gave a deep, chuckling laugh and went out.

I heard his footsteps growing fainter, then the slam of the front door and the tyres on the gravel. Sister came in. I gulped and waited to hear the verdict. 'You're to stay here till to-morrow,' she said. I was too glad to speak, I only smiled. She went on busily, 'Nurse Robins will take you out for a walk after lunch.'

The maid was laying the table while Sister was talking. When they had both gone out, I walked up and down the room in my excitement. I stopped at the table and looked down. Most of the things were electro-plate, but two spoons had caught my eyes. I turned them over. They had large hall-marks on the thin part of the stem and I knew that they were early Georgian. They belonged to Sister, I supposed, and had got muddled with the others. I thought how easy it would be to steal them. I would like to have had them for myself very much.

Nurse Robins was already dressed for walking when she came in after lunch. Her coat and hat were of green tweed and there was a little strip of moleskin round each. She had put powder on her cheeks so that they looked like frosted red lamps. I wondered what the walk with her would be like.

The red Sanatorium ribbon was pinned round my straw hat, over my House colours, and we set off down the hill. Not many people were about; they were all playing games. We heard fives balls smacking against the courts and, farther away, whistles being blown, and shouting from the football fields.

Nurse Robins said nothing except, 'It's a lovely day, isn't it?'

I looked at the flying clouds and the last leaves still trying to cling to the branches, and agreed. The sun was making all the decay rich and lovely. Only the stream we crossed seemed cruel, still. The cold scum whirled under the bridge and reappeared with evil bubbles pushing through it.

At Milton, the house on the corner was crimson. The Virginia creeper had got over the eaves and was climbing up the roof, straining to reach the chimney-stack. We walked over the little footbridge next to the ford and went into the fields.

Nurse Robins seemed to be coming to life. Her cheeks were redder than ever and she was making little, impulsive movements with her body. Suddenly she skipped and then jumped over a mole-hill. She put out her hand and caught mine, saying, 'Let's run to the end of the field!'

We raced over the spongy grass, swollen with mole-hills, until I fell, bringing her down with me. We lay there laughing; then I felt the soft fur on her collar press against my neck. I started as if a bat had flown against me. I got up quickly and left her still lying there with her hair matted on her cheek, like lines scribbled on paper. 'Don't tell Sister we've been running about like this. She'll think I'm mad,' she said weakly.

We got as much mud as we could off our clothes and walked on.

'People think that because you're grown up you don't want any fun.'

'Yes, isn't it silly?' I said politely.

'Shut up all day in that uniform, you need a little freedom when you can get it,' she mused as if talking to herself.

Now I knew why Nurse Robins was so quiet. She hated her uniform. She wanted to run in the fields, to trip over mole-hills and sprawl in the mud. She was a Peter Pan to herself.

We did not run any more, but we talked. Nurse Robins told me about her life in hospital, but she said that she liked nursing boys most.

By this time we had climbed Askew Hill. We stood on the vague outline of the earthwork and looked across the Trent Valley. Far away at Willington we heard the trains shunting.

The footpath had been ploughed up on the other side of the hill and we sank ankle-deep into the clinging earth. It was dotted with silvery oyster shells. We sat on the stile and scraped the heavy mud-clogs off with sticks.

44

'What a long time you've been out!' Sister said when we got back. 'Your tea's waiting for you in the Common Room, Welch.'

I went in and found Sister's dog by the fire. I played with its ears until it gave me a little nip, then I turned it over and rubbed its stomach, and it stretched out its paws as if it were hung up dead in a butcher's shop.

As I drank my tea I turned over the pages of the book I had chosen off the shelf. On the flyleaf someone had written, 'Sister expects that every man this day will do his duty.'

I laughed although I knew how old the joke must be. Every night Sister would come round and ask, 'Have you done your duty to-day?' She never varied her words, just as hospital nurses always say, 'Have your had your bowels opened?'

I tried to make the most of my last night, but the thought of going back to the House was gnawing at me.

I walked about the room and wandered in the passage. I even went upstairs, which was forbidden, and looked in all the empty rooms just as I had done at my cousin's house.

The wards were very bleak in the half-light. They were like modern milking-sheds with rows of four-legged iron bedsteads instead of cows.

As I crept down again the dull maid saw me, but she did not say anything. I wondered if she would tell Sister.

No taxi came for me in the morning. The red band was taken off my hat and I left the Sanatorium, carrying my suitcase. I took the footpath through the fields behind New House so that I should meet as few people as possible. No one passed me. I walked very slowly. The House was empty when I arrived; morning school was not yet over.

I went quickly up to the notice-board to find out which study and which dormitory I was in, then I reported to

45

Matron and stayed talking to her until the lunch bell rang.

The House had been gradually filling up. Feet stampeded in the passages and voices rang out. I was thankful that I had arrived early. It would be much better to meet at lunch when there was the business of eating to occupy everyone.

There were smiles and nods as I joined the long line streaming into the dining-room, but talking was not allowed until after Grace.

Haltingly at first the conversation flowed all over the room; then it gathered volume until it had reached a steady throb. I imagined that everyone was talking about me, and I expect they were. I tried not to look at anyone, but to smile and be natural.

'Be natural!' I told myself fiercely, 'be natural.'

Watson was the first to speak to me directly.

'What have you been up to, Welch?' he asked.

'Oh, nothing.' I tried to be casual. 'I was fed up, so I thought I'd go to Devonshire instead of coming back here.'

I could see his eyes behind the slightly tinted glasses that he wore. They did not look dangerous.

'Tell us about it,' he said. 'All sorts of rumours have been going about here.'

'About Iliffe taking me to Italy?' I asked.

'That was one; then there was something about you getting fifty pounds and going to Paris.'

So the money had grown to fifty pounds! I wondered who could have invented these stories. Other people were listening by now and questions were being passed down the table to me. Nobody seemed at all unfriendly and I tried to answer everything, only pretending that I felt adventurous and not desperate.

Across the room, at the prefects' table, I could see the back of my brother's head. His hair was so fair it seemed almost white. I wondered what he thought about it all.

46

There was a shuffling, then a silence as we all waited for Mr Bird to thank God again for the food we had just eaten. The room gradually emptied, and Clarence and the maids began to clear the tables.

My brother was waiting for me in the passage. He was smiling.

'You are a bloody fool, Denton. I couldn't think what had happened to you. When I turned up here without you Bird was furious. He sent me back the next morning to look for you, and I had three days in London with Bill, so I didn't mind. We rang up all the hospitals, and told the police; we thought you might have been run over. You were a sod, to disappear like that!'

I was glad that he had had three days' holiday because of me. We went into the changing-room and walked up and down while I told him all I could remember. I finished up by saying, 'When you leave at the end of this term I'm going to leave too.'

'Don't be a fool, you're not seventeen yet,' he answered impatiently.

'I only agreed to come back for this term.'

'Oh well, don't let's bother about it now. You'd soon settle down if you stopped worrying.'

I left him and went up to my study. This would be my first term free of fagging; that, at least, was one relief. When I opened the door I found Wilks making faces at Bradbourne. He was always making strange faces and sounds to attract attention.

'Hullo, Welch, have you decided to come back after all?' he asked.

I nodded and tried to look bold. Bradbourne saw my face twitch, so he jumped up and pulled me on to his knee.

'Come and tell your uncle all about it,' he said soothingly, bumping me up and down as if I were a baby.

I felt silly, but I did not try to get off. Bradbourne was much stronger than I was; besides, I liked him. He said he was going to be a doctor, and one of his front teeth had been broken by a cricket ball.

'You bold, bad boy,' he pronounced after I had finished my story. 'You deserve to be beaten.'

He turned me over on his knees and beat me playfully with a ruler. He hit hard and I felt the ruler biting into me. My body twitched and jerked until I fell on to the floor; then I quickly got up and ran out of the room. Bradbourne's laugh and Wilks's strange noises flowed after me down the passage.

I put on my straw hat and went to the Music Schools.

CHAPTER 6

GETTING used to school again in those first days was strange. Everyone thought that I had run away for a different reason and so they all treated me differently. Thus I found that I had been moved up two forms because I was supposed to be frightened of Dr Thorne.

I had been very unpopular with him the term before when I had been in his French class. He had made me sit at a special desk away from the others, and had become so furious when I signed my name Denton Welch instead of D. Welch that he had purposely trodden on the dark glasses he always wore in summer.

I was glad that I had missed his form, but fear of him had not made me run away.

The Remove where I now found myself was quite peaceful. Mr Ward's flat face dominated it like a placid, soapstone sphinx. His eyes had a sphinx's far-away look too.

He would tell us strange stories about food. How the rich had eaten vermin cooked in liqueurs during the Siege of Paris. Rats, stewed in Green Chartreuse; mice, swimming in Benedictine.

His eyes would sparkle as he imitated a newly created duchess imploring her guests to begin.

He told us how, as a child, he had once eaten swan for dinner. We asked him greedily what it tasted like.

I imagined the Ward family sitting round the gas-lit table with the baroque bird in front of them, redecked in all her plucked feathers. Then I imagined the fishy taste of her meat.

Everywhere I met with more tolerance than I had ever known before.

When I went to Miss Fenwick to arrange my music lessons with her, I found Major Willett there. I thought he would show his disapproval very openly, but there was no sign. He only smiled and said, 'The wanderer returned!' Then, when Miss Fenwick had gone out of the room to fetch her time-table, he came up and gave me a playful punch, adding, 'You're a sly one, taking the bit between your teeth like that!'

I suddenly liked him enormously. Whenever we met after that he always paid me some attention.

In the Art School I found Mr Williams still secure behind his wall of sarcasm.

'Had a good holiday, Welch? Do you prefer Salisbury to Exeter? What's so lovely about Salisbury is its setting. Take away the Close and half the beauty's gone.'

I knew his manner so well.

I smiled at him and went out again into the School Yard.

I tried to settle down for the next two and a half months, and the days were not really unhappy.

Every Sunday morning a few of us would go to Miss Fenwick's room to sing. Her sister was the Headmaster's wife and she lived with them at the Hall. It was a lovely old house with an ugly upper storey and wing built on to it, but nothing could quite spoil its fine doorway and sash windows.

The atmosphere was freer here than anywhere else in the school. We were all of different ages and from different Houses, and the caste system was broken down.

I was happy, singing in that white panelled room.

Sunday was the most civilized day of all. In the afternoon I would generally go for a walk with Geoffrey Forbes. If we were going towards Milton, we would knock on the door of a grim-looking cottage near the stream, and buy large pieces of cake from the woman who lived there. The passage was so dark and stale-smelling that I often wondered about the cake, but I would soon be hungry enough to break large lumps off and eat them with Geoffrey.

As we had both been at school for two years we were allowed to carry umbrellas. I never had one, but Geoffrey always flourished his. He would wave it and recite to me as we walked along. Suddenly he would stop in the middle of the road and ask me if I had enjoyed Hamlet's speech. If I showed no pleasure he would begin to shout, 'You little sissy, you can't think about anything but yourself.' He would poke me with the umbrella, and once he tried to tie me to a tree with my scarf.

When he was tired of trying to punish my vanity he would say, 'I'll sing to you.' He set his face very carefully, then began, 'Hark, hark, the lark at Heaven's Gate sings,' or 'Who is Sylvia, what is she?' It always seemed to be Schubert.

One day he came to me while I was in the lavatory (all the doors had been removed from the compartments) and told me that his mother was dead.

He leant forward as I sat there and said, 'She's dead, Bird's just told me.' He spoke in an excited way and his eyes sparkled. It was strange; I knew how fond he was of her. He was always telling me how pretty she was and how hard he would work when he left school so that she could have everything she wanted. He had no father; he had been killed in the first war, just after Geoffrey was born.

I murmured how sorry I was, but he was still grinning and smiling.

'I missed school this morning,' he said. 'Mavis took me to see the point-to-point.'

Mavis was the daughter of our housemaster. I remembered seeing her that morning dressed in breeches and bowler hat. I did not know why she had put them on since she was only going to watch, not to ride.

Suddenly he burst out, 'O God, I felt awful half-way through it, but now I'm all right again. I don't realize it at all.' He smiled all over his face.

We left the lavatory together and, as it was a half-holiday, I suggested that we should go for a walk.

'All right,' he agreed. 'But we must be back when Aunt Janet arrives. She'll be here about four. I'll take you to tea with her.'

'Won't she want to see you all alone?' I asked nervously.

'I don't know whether she will or not, but I couldn't stand being left with her, so you'll have to come.'

I nodded my head, but said nothing. I was feeling very uncomfortable, but wanted to help as much as possible.

We walked up the hill into the woods. The autumn leaves were clotted into great coloured lumps all over our path. The rain had stuck them together. The corners of Geoffrey's eyes and mouth twitched as they often did, and he looked at nothing long, moving his head about in little jerks. The stream we crossed was swollen; with scum and bubbles bursting behind rocks in a secret way.

Geoffrey beat at the leaves with his umbrella, raking them into giant's confetti.

Suddenly he poked at a dark thing on the path. We did not know what it was. The ferrule skewered it and Geoffrey ran, waving it in the air.

Then we both gave piercing screams. Geoffrey had skewered a frog. He flung it from him madly and it fell in the grass. I felt sick, but I rushed up to it, trying to decide how to kill it in the least revolting way to myself.

But I saw that it was an old, dead frog, dry and hard as leather. I told Geoffrey and we both lay against a smooth beech trunk laughing and recovering. It had been a disgusting moment. Geoffrey dug the ferrule into the ground and then wiped it on the leaves.

He looked at his watch. 'We must be quick,' he said. 'Aunt Janet will be there.'

The lights were shining in the windows as we went back into the village. They made the daylight seem blue. A mist was rising and the red roofs shone through it, bright as orange-peel.

We came to the stone guest-house where Aunt Janet had arranged to stay. It was small and we walked straight into the sitting-room. Little tables covered in Japanese crêpe tablecloths were dotted about and there were some arm-chairs round the fire.

We looked in the glass over the mantelpiece and smoothed our hair; then we waited for Aunt Janet.

At last the door opened and she appeared. She wore a tight little turban and she looked like a monkey. She kissed Geoffrey and grinned at me with her wide, prehistoric mouth.

The tea was brought in and we sat down at one of the little tables. Large scones, black-currant jam and fruit cake were spread in front of us. The tea was in a bright, silver lustre pot. I said to Aunt Janet, to make conversation, 'What a nice lustre pot!' I felt Geoffrey trying to kick me under the table and I wondered what I had said or done wrong.

It was a dull tea. None of us were able to talk for long, but in spite of the gloom I enjoyed it. It was a respite.

We ended up by talking about chess, although none of us played it. Then Geoffrey left the room, and while he was gone Aunt Janet turned to me and said:

'You are Geoffrey's friend. I think it would be so nice if you suggested that he should be confirmed this term. I know his mother has brought him up to be a Roman Catholic, but it would be so much nicer if he were like the rest of us, don't you think?'

I was dumb. To try to make me influence Geoffrey against the wishes of his mother who was just dead seemed horrible. I felt insulted. Aunt Janet must think me very simple and stupid.

I smirked at her, said something vague; then Geoffrey came back. We took up our straw hats and said good-bye.

'Isn't she like a monkey?' he said, as we walked down the dark High Street.

'Yes, she is.' I smiled inwardly. I was going to take a delight in influencing him as strongly as I could against changing his religion. So I began bluntly:

'While you were out of the room she tried to get me to say that I'd persuade you not to be a Catholic.'

He looked at me and his face went hard. 'The bitch!' was all he said; then he burst out:

'But why did you talk to her about lust at tea-time? I thought you were mad – muttering something about lust.'

For a moment I could not think what he meant, then I realized, and laughed.

'I was only talking about the lustre teapot.'

'What's lustre?' he asked.

'It's shiny stuff – like metal, only china.'

'Oh!' he answered blankly, and I wondered where his thoughts were.

I watched him that night as we did our prep in the study. We had our supper and prayers came. Then we went up to bed.

I lay awake after the lights were out, wondering if Geoffrey was very unhappy. I could just see his bed in the corner, but there was no sign from it. The cold air swept round the floor and the iron beds creaked.

I fell asleep after the last person had stopped talking, and did not wake till several hours later. It was still dark; nothing could be heard but the trains shunting, two miles away. Suddenly I thought I heard deep intakes of breath from the corner where Geoffrey's bed was. He must be snoring, I thought. Then I imagined that he was crying under the bed-clothes. I listened for some time, trying to decide.

CHAPTER 7

THE big dormitory was the grimmest part of the House.
It was so lofty and cold that it seemed to make people
heartless.

Two lips had been painted on one of the beams
and all new boys had to pull themselves up by
their arms, to kiss them. I remember straining up,
and at last reaching the yellow pitch pine and the two
crimson lips. They looked indecent, for some reason;
as if they were the drawing of another part of the
body.

When I kissed them, the taste of varnish and dust
came as a shock. I imagined that they would somehow
be scented.

I thought of this now as I watched other people trying
to kiss them. If they were not quick or could not reach
them, they were flicked with wet towels as an encourage-
ment.

I had been told that you could lift the skin off someone's back in this way. I always waited, half in horror,
to see a ribbon of flesh come off.

All the handles had been broken off the chambers so
that we could play bowls. Being hollow, they looked like
white skulls as they spun towards you across the dark
linoleum.

The head of the dormitory this term was Woods. He
was tall and heavy, and he sometimes wore a pair of
black pyjamas which had, at first, created a sensation.
He would lie in bed, looking frowsty, the black pyjamas
open so that you saw the little black hairs sprouting on
his chest.

He used to tell loud stories about his aunt who wanted

to be a débutante at forty-three, and insisted on being presented at Court.

Anyone who was going to be beaten had to stay downstairs after prayers. When they came up to the dormitory Woods would say, 'Show us your marks.' Then we would all crowd round and look at the purple marks on the white behind.

If I hated the dormitory, the Gym was one of the places I liked most. It always seemed fresh and strange. The sergeant was extraordinary; everyone said he was muscle-bound. I did not know what this meant, but afterwards, whenever I looked at his thick chest and swelling arms, under the white jersey, I thought of them as 'muscle-bound'.

We did not see him when we first came in. He lurked in his little office until we had finished changing, then he came out, dignified and ceremonious, like a penguin.

He marched us round, intoning to himself, 'Up down, up down,' as if we were horses and he were teaching imaginary people to ride on our backs.

Suddenly he would break the rhythm of his drone with an order and we would be thrown into confusion, not understanding a word of it. Then he would pick on the slowest person and shot, 'Eintz peintz, I'd like to slash your bum with a sabre!' or 'Sissy Boy, you've got no more sense than when your mother dropped you!'

Once when I was squatting down, doing a knee-bending exercise, he yelled out:

'Get up, Welch, else I'll take a piece of paper to you!'

These remarks excited us. We were more unruly in the changing-room after Gym than anywhere else.

I split a seam in my trousers one day as I jumped over the horse. Geoffrey heard it go, and laughed. When the class was over he dashed at me and tore at the place, making a gaping hole where the trouser legs should join.

Other people helped him, and I was soon struggling

on the floor with each seam split open from top to bottom.

At last I stood up again in the flapping, divided skirt they had made for me. The laughter was wild and I was very excited myself. Somebody unbuttoned my braces from behind and then I was on the floor again in a tangle of legs and arms, with everything torn off me.

I sat up, naked, and suddenly realized that I had to go back to the House in the ruined trousers. It would be almost as bad as going back to the House in no trousers at all.

Geoffrey realized my difficulty and found two pins. We fastened the flaps round my legs at the knees, but large cracks of pink flesh still showed.

Geoffrey and some others walked closely round me and we made our way over the playing-fields, hoping to meet as few people as possible.

I reached the House safely, but once inside I could conceal my state no longer. My legs and arms were seized and I was swung into the big rubbish-box and then covered with waste paper; for decency's sake, I was told.

On Saturday evenings I would get an 'exeat' from the prefect on duty so that I could go to the Art School.

When the 'exeat' was signed and I was out in the road, I felt free; as if I were not at school at all. The dark village street seemed full of excitement. I stared hungrily into all the lighted rooms where the curtains had not been drawn.

Once a drunk man lurched off a bus and made in my direction. A little thrill of horror ran through me, I thought he was going to attack me; but he suddenly fell down and lay on the ground vomiting. I went up to him furtively. His shoulders were trembling and he was lying in his vomit. I wondered what I could do to help, but at that moment he swore so fiercely that I took fright and fled.

The lights of the Art School were blue and high up, amongst the rafters. The building had been the ox stable when Repton was a priory.

Now, in the evening, it was sombre and mysterious with casts of the Elgin Marbles floating on the gloom and partitions of heavy drapery thrown over the beams. There was a huge sink where the taps dripped, and next to it a cupboard stuffed with paint-boxes, dead singing birds, owls, brushes, milk-jugs, drawing-boards, plaster noses, ears and eyes, flower-bowls, pencils, saucers and shells.

In the far corner, on a dais, sat the portrait model, nearly always an old man or woman from the village. His or her face seemed falling to pieces under the disintegrating blue lights.

Only the more senior of us painted the model. The rest chose something to copy, from the long line of shelves.

Mr Williams passed in and out amongst the stools, cracking jokes. We were all a little afraid of what he might say next, but he was malicious about the masters as well, which delighted us.

There were rare evenings when he took us back to his rooms and showed us pictures on his magic-lantern. He never worried about the time, and once someone was sent from the House to fetch me back to supper.

'Is Mr Bird's supper worth going back for, Welch?' Mr Williams drawled out wickedly.

There was a pause, and then a shamefaced titter from all of us. We liked his malice but we knew that it was dog eating dog.

One Saturday afternoon, towards the middle of the term, he took a small party of us to Chatsworth. We went in the O.T.C. bus. The change from football was intoxicating. As we jolted over the little stone bridges in the khaki ambulance I began to feel more alive. After the dark, rocky hills, Chatsworth, standing in its park, looked pale and delicate in spite of its huge size. The grass all round it was dry and tow-coloured, and the stone of the building the colour of smoky honey.

The librarian met us on the doorstep. His glasses flashed in the sun as he bent towards us, smiling. With him was a young painter whom the Duke had befriended. They were the only two people in the house except for the servants.

We were led into the dark hall, and there the painter left us – to wash his brushes, as he explained. When he had gone the librarian turned to us and said:

'That's a most remarkable man. He used to work in a laundry, but he carried on through thick and thin with his painting and now he's staying here and painting subjects in the house and park.'

We passed the footman's high-winged draught-chair and stood at the foot of the great staircase.

The librarian walked in front, leading us through the great chain of state-rooms. He told us about the pictures and the furniture. The sun shone weakly through the plate-glass windows and dust motes swam in the light. The scent was warmed out of some dried rose-leaves and I bent down over the blue bowl to smell them.

The painter joined us again as the librarian was showing us some Chinese Chippendale chairs. The door opened just as he was saying, 'The Duchess is thinking of putting these somewhere else.' I remember the look the painter gave the librarian, as if he hated all this talk of duchesses and Chinese Chippendale.

After the state-rooms we went into the long library. The librarian climbed up the early Victorian, cast-iron spiral staircase and brought down books for our wonder and admiration. We all remarked on the brightness of the gold, but the librarian said:

'There's nothing to go wrong with the gold, it's the

brightness of the colours that is so marvellous in these old manuscripts.' Then he locked them up again behind the gilt, open-trelliswork doors.

Next, he moved towards a picture on an easel. It was covered with a little curtain of grey velvet and we crowded round, waiting for him to show it to us. When the little triptych was sparkling like precious stones in front of us, he described the specially constructed box it fitted into; so that it could be thrown out of the window in case of fire and yet arrive unharmed in the fountain or on the flower-bed below.

On the desk near the door was a lovely Greek bronze head. Its empty eye-sockets made it look blind and as if it were crying. The librarian showed us how the inlaid eyes would have fitted, and where tufts of hair were inserted in the holes on the scalp.

We left the library and went into the tiny private dining-room. A sticky-looking, empty medicine bottle was on the sideboard.

'The mixture. To be taken three times a day. His Grace the Duke of Devonshire,' I read. I wondered what it had tasted like and what it was for. If I had been alone I would have smelt the bottle.

The librarian was pointing out the beauties of the little wax pictures on the walls. I lifted one up to get a better light on it, and immediately there was an outcry.

'Don't touch the things, Welch,' Mr Williams ordered harshly, and the librarian added more mildly:

'It would be better not to, as one of them has just come back from being mended. A maid knocked it down while dusting.'

I was annoyed and humiliated. I felt, arrogantly, that I could appreciate and take care of the things in the room better than the whole lot of them put together.

The librarian led us into a book-lined study. When the door was shut we were completely surrounded with books. There seemed to be no doors; they were covered with dummy bindings. The fat chairs were upholstered with buttoned red morocco, and the whole room reminded me of brandy and soda and cigars.

Before we left we were taken round the gardens. We were shown where the huge conservatory had stood. I imagined all the glass splintering in the air when it was blown up. I did not know what to expect as we stood round the leaden willow tree. I knew that there was something strange about it. When it began to spurt water from its delicate twigs and branches we all jumped back laughing and shouting. The librarian turned the tap off and the mysterious rain suddenly stopped.

We walked back to the khaki ambulance. We said good-bye and got in. As it drove off we all waved to the librarian. He stood like a small black rod in front of the huge lion-coloured building. The fading light just caught his glasses and they glinted again as they had when we arrived.

I noticed two large paper bags that Mr Williams had taken from under the seat. One held Swiss buns and the other doughnuts. We all began to eat and talk gaily. I was happy and contented although the fried cakes tasted of cloves and lard and made me feel slightly sick.

Evening school had begun by the time we got back, so Mr Williams had to write an explanation for each of us to take to our form masters.

'Unavoidably detained at the Duke's,' was what he wrote for me. As I went through the cloisters I wondered what Ward would think about it.

His eyes lit up and became more questioning still.

'What does this mean, Welch?'

'Mr Williams took us to Chatsworth and we were rather long in getting back, sir.'

'So it seems. You'd better go to your place and try to catch up with the rest of the form.'

No more than that, but I could tell how annoyed he was.

More trouble was waiting for me when I got back to the House. I had forgotten to ask the Captain of House Games for permission to go to Chatsworth. He had put me down to play in the Third Eleven and was very annoyed that I had not been there.

He told me to go and see him after prayers. This meant a beating.

The blood tingled all over my body as I left the room. I kept saying, 'Come and see me after prayers,' to myself, until the words had no meaning at all. I wondered if I should tell my brother about it or whether I should leave the House and run away again so that nobody could touch me, but I did nothing.

I watched supper being eaten and then being cleared away. The fag on duty put the hymn-books on the tables, opening them at the right place for Mr Bird and the prefects. Whitney was practising the tune on the walnut piano. Soon prayers would begin.

The last words had fallen off Mr Bird's tongue and I knew that I had no more time to wait. When everyone had gone upstairs Newman would be ready for me. I went to the study to wait for him.

There was a book about Disraeli lying on the table. I opened it and began to read about his red-heeled shoes, his chains and black ringlets. I thought of the dazzling Jew Boy.

Then the door opened and Newman came in.

He looked nice really, with his powerful body and springy, uncoloured hair. He had a bandage round his neck because of a boil. Together with his collar it looked like a high cravat.

'Why the devil didn't you let me know before you went to Chatsworth, Welch?' he began.

'I didn't think I had to. I had Bird's permission,' I answered anxiously.

'How can I make the games lists out if I don't know who's available?'

'I'm afraid I forgot that.'

'Well, it's no good forgetting. You've got to learn that. Bend over the desk, please.'

The moment had come. I held my tongue between my teeth, biting on it, trying to make it hurt; then I put my hands over my eyes and burrowed inwards to myself, shutting everything outside away. My eyes bored down long passages of glittering darkness as I waited.

I heard Newman's feet shuffle lightly on the boards, then the faint whine of the cane in the air.

There were two bars of fire eating into ice, then nothing. Only two strokes, but the room was quite different when I opened my eyes. The light was thick like milk and it seemed to float cloudily about the room.

Newman was saying good night to me ceremoniously and I knew that I must reply. My voice seemed blurred too, and I felt angry that I could not control it; then my feet took me to the door and I was outside.

Through the pain that was biting into me I felt a surge of admiration for Newman, yet I hated myself for liking him. The other part of me wanted to smash his face into pulp. My mind was rocking about like a cart on a rough road.

I was scowling deeply by the time I reached the dormitory. Woods saw it and called out gaily, 'Had a nice beating, Welch? Show us your marks.'

I made no answer, but went quickly to my bed and began to undress. I kept my back to the wall and pulled my pyjama trousers on, tying them tightly before I took my shirt off.

I thought I would be forced to show my marks, but I meant to fight.

For some reason I was left alone; so I got into bed and lay, hot and sore, between the cold sheets.

CHAPTER 8

I CAME in from games one afternoon to find a letter from my father waiting for me. He wrote so seldom that his letters were always an event.

I wanted to read it quietly, by myself, so after I had changed I took it with me, still unopened, into the fields.

The path I took must once have been a road. There was an old inn half-way down, now stranded in the fields. The banks were high and crumbling, with Old Man's Beard creeping like mildew over them.

I spread the skirts of my raincoat on the ground and sat down to read the letter.

Via Siberia was written in the top left-hand corner. Then there was my name and address. I looked at everything, including the Chinese postmark and stamp. I did not want to open the letter and see inside what my father said about my running away.

At last I tore it along the top and quickly pulled the letter out.

He did not say much; only that he was sorry, not annoyed, that I had run away and, as I seemed to be unhappy at school, he thought it would be a good plan if I went to Shanghai with Paul, who was going to join him at the end of the term.

He finished up with the words, 'Write and tell me what you think of this.'

I leapt up and walked about, giving small jumps and screwing up my eyes as climaxes of excitement swept over me. I could not believe that my father was suggesting that I should leave school and go to China.

I was so full of joy that I ran down the lane and over the fields until I was exhausted. I felt like a person full of power and skill. I was no longer a part of the dead old system. I could bear anything now till the end of term.

Back in the house, I snatched up my books for evening school and hurried out into the street again, for I was a little late.

The hum of the waiting class reached me as I mounted the stone steps of the Science Block. The master had not opened the laboratory yet. Geoffrey was there, fooling noisily with some others. All around us were cases of fascinating, coloured crystals.

I wanted to tell him about my letter at once, but I had to wait until we were inside. We both stood at the same bench and I managed to whisper my news while we were making sulphuric acid.

'Lucky sod!' he muttered. 'You get everything you want just because you run away.' But I knew that he was glad for me. We dabbed some of the sulphuric acid on to a piece of blotting-paper and watched it burning brownly and wetly into it; then he flapped it at me as if he would get it on my hands or clothes.

I started back, frightened. I hated the stuff, remembering the stories of vitriol throwing I had heard. He made a laughing noise by breathing out in little gasps, then he said between his rigid teeth, 'So Cyril's frightened, is he? Perhaps the horrid stuff might spoil his beauty.' He was often silly and theatrical like this.

I blushed hotly and would not talk to him again. But at the end of the lesson, as we were collecting our books, I looked in my pockets and saw that I had a little money; so I asked Geoffrey to come and have tea with me at the school shop.

The fire-light was jigging on the floor and on the tables in the little tea-room. We sat down in a corner and ordered poached eggs on crumpets spread with anchovy paste. Geoffrey still seemed to be dwelling on his mother's death, but he listened to me.

We enjoyed the fire and the hot tea as long as we could; then, when the time for prep came, we walked slowly back to the House, down the damp blue-black street.

After this letter the term began gradually to melt away. It was no longer a great lump of time which nothing seemed able to dissolve. When the foreboding, senseless bell woke me up each morning in the bleak dormitory, I was content to live that day and not to worry. Now that I could see the end in sight everything was different.

Geoffrey and I did most things together although we often disagreed. His aunt, as I have said, wanted him to be confirmed. He had given in at last and was having instruction twice a week.

Most people of our age were being confirmed that term, but I refused to be. I think it was my obscure answer to Geoffrey's aunt. I wanted her to be cheated somewhere.

She came down, of course, for the ceremony. I saw her through the bars of the visitors' chapel, the Bird Cage, as we called it. Sitting with the other parents and relations behind the bars, she looked more like a bright monkey than ever.

I forgot to watch her when the Bishop came in. I had never seen one with mitre and crozier before. I stared at his frilled cuffs and the great boat-shaped ring on his finger, as he laid his hand on each head.

The Chapel rang with the repetition of names. Apart from Geoffrey's, I only remember Peter Cherry Partingdon, because it tripped off the Bishop's tongue so gaily.

I was glad to be out in the sun again after the service was over. I saw Geoffrey hurrying towards the Bird Cage to meet his aunt. She came down the steps showing all her teeth in a primitive smile.

As they passed me she nodded her head and said, 'How are you, Welch?' I hated the use of my surname by a so-called friend who was a woman. She should not have used any name if she did not want to call me Denton.

'I should have liked you to come back with us, Welch, but Geoffrey and I have so much to talk about that I'm afraid you would be bored,' she went on.

I knew what she meant; I felt angry and pleasantly martyred. This was the cross I had to bear for not helping Aunt Janet and for not being confirmed myself. She had had her way with Geoffrey, that ought to content her.

I raised my straw hat awkwardly. I hated being chivalrous to anyone, let alone Aunt Janet. As I turned back to the House I thought of Geoffrey between the paws of his monkey aunt.

I had to walk alone that afternoon. The early winter rains had soaked the ground until it was like squelching seaweed.

I decided to try to get into Foremark Church. It had always been locked before, but on a Sunday it might be open. If not, there was an Anchorite's cave near by for me to explore again. Its doors and windows and columns had been dug out of the cliff-side, I suppose, for some 'ornamental' hermit, for it was in the grounds of Foremark Hall, a huge grey stone mansion brooding on the other side of a weed-grown lake.

The church was locked when I got there. I pulled and turned the big iron handles, feeling exasperated. The small doors were locked too, which made me determined to get in. I walked down the green avenue which led from the church to the house.

The gardens were well kept, but the windows of the house were all shuttered. There was a small door under the stairs of the great portico. I rang the bell and waited. Footsteps rang in the stone passage and then a youngish woman appeared. Her hair was untidy and she seemed to have very little on under her brown overall, but she willingly went to get the key for me.

When she came back I asked her if the house was empty and whether she would show me over it.

'The housekeeper's out and there's nobody here, so I will if you like,' she answered.

I was delighted. She led me down the dark passage and then up a spiral staircase to the next floor.

'Nobody has lived here for twenty years, but it's all been kept up,' she said, opening some shutters so that the afternoon sun fell on the wide-boarded floor and the slightly discoloured walls. I did not know what to look at at first. There were lovely old portraits and mirrors and dark cupboards full of china.

We went from room to room, letting in the light. There was a gilded harpsichord in the long drawing-room, but it was locked and covered with a rug. The floor here must have been fairly new, for it was parquet, like a hotel. Sometimes there was a lighter-coloured square on the wall and then the woman would tell me that the picture had been taken to the owner's other house.

I saw everything, including the bathrooms and the water-closets. The baths were raised up on steps and had wide rims of polished mahogany. The water-closets had blue flowers printed inside the pans and cut-glass handles, the shot, golden-green colour of lubricating oil.

At last we reached the attics, which were divided into three parts: for the servants, the children and the bachelors. Most of the windows were oval. I looked down at the green, slimy lake and at the grey fields beyond. I felt as if I were in a giant's head, staring out of his eye-socket.

We went down through the house, closing the shutters until each room was swallowed up and dead again. There was only one more thing to see: the smoking-room in the basement.

I did not expect anything so strange. There was a large

seat of stuffed and buttoned leather round the central pillar, and built into the walls were divans framed in alcoves of Arabian fretwork. Palm fronds stood in the corners and groups of dusty pink electric-light shades hung from the ceiling. There were some pictures of Edwardian young men playing billards. There were jokes written underneath each scene.

I tried to take everything in, to remember it as a perfect period piece. I wondered what I should give the woman or whether I should give her anything at all.

When I said good-bye, I held my hand out with a shilling in it. The woman, thinking I meant to shake hands, grasped mine and I left the coin in her palm. She gave a start, saying, 'What's this?' then she said 'Oh' as if she had been insulted, but she did not give the shilling back.

I smiled, feeling awkward and rude. Then I left. It was too late to go on to the church, so I passed over the balustraded bridge and out of the main gates.

The tip of a rotten punt stuck out of the mossy boathouse.

The week after the confirmation an 'old boy' arrived with a pack of beagles. We all collected round the village cross, dressed in our vests and running shorts. The huntsmen, or whatever they are called, wore green velvet coats, black caps and snow-white breeches. I enjoyed looking at them as they walked in and out amongst the squat little beagles, talking to them and keeping them in order.

I grew cold listening to the little speech on the glory of the sport, and was glad when the beagles streamed out across the fields in front of the Priory, and we followed. I was running alone and so could race or go slowly as I wished.

When we got to the stream, some people boldly dashed in, getting wet up to the waist. Others took the footbridge. I did, but wished afterwards that I had splashed through the water. Couples tore by, looking as if they were being hunted themselves, but I was content to be left behind. There was a feeling of licence in the air and I enjoyed being free and alone.

Soon we were ploughing up a hill. We had spread out now, like a jet of water. The beagles were worrying round in circles in the copse at the top. The huntsman yelled and the air was full of excitement. People broke through the bushes with a cracking, tearing sound. Everyone was tense. Something was hidden in the heart of the wood.

I sat down on a stile to wait and rest. Hot, panting groups ran by, their faces shining with sweat. I looked down and saw something bright on the ground. It was a sixpence. I picked it up, feeling delighted. There was no possible chance of finding its owner in all this crowd.

When I looked up again, I saw someone tearing a way through a thick tangle of branches. He was older than I was, and in a different House, but I had often seen him at the Art School on Saturday evenings.

He had a large rent in his shirt and I could see his bare shoulder through it. He stopped when he saw me and said, 'Is anything sticking in my shoulder, Welch? It hurts like hell.'

I jumped off the stile and went up to him. He was as big as a man and I suddenly felt very puny. He turned his back to me and pulled the shirt off his shoulder. There was a long, red scratch on the white flesh. Beads of blood were dropping from it, so I wiped it with my handkerchief and then tried to look into it.

I found two broken-off thorn heads and gradually worked them out. I held on to his other shoulder and he bent down so that I could reach. He was still trembling from running and his breath came in gasps.

'There, I've got them out!' I said at last.

He swung round quickly and pressed hard against me, rubbing his cheek against mine. I could feel how warm and moist his body was, and the touch of his eyelashes was like feathers. He spoke harshly and yearningly and shut his eyes.

I was suddenly alarmed and made a movement away from him, but he grasped me tightly and dug his fingers into my flesh until I gave a short gasp of pain. When he heard it he dropped his hands to his sides and laughed softly.

'Was I suffocating you?' he asked. Then he hitched up his shorts and ran on.

The glory of our beagling was that we never caught a hare. We just ran on and on. No sport could be more harmless.

In the steaming changing-room afterwards I felt happy about life. The room was full of the nice smell of bodies, and gay shouts rang out. I sank down into the hot bath which twenty other people had already used. The thick, muddy water stroked my flesh.

When we were told that a band of Negroes was coming to sing to us, we all laughed and wondered if the music would be hot swing. Piers Hall seemed such a strange place for Negroes. It had a pine hammer-beam roof and enormous windows filled with stained-glass pictures of school worthies and their coats of arms. The only lovely thing was a seventeenth-century Flemish tapestry hung high up in the organ loft, well out of sight.

Geoffrey and I, like all the rest, waited impatiently for the singers to file on to the stage.

Then the lovely music began. The light was concentrated on the black faces so that the songs seemed to come from a lighted cave. The words floated over the lumpy field of heads.

'Little David, play your harp. Hallelujah, Hallelujah.'

'I went to the rocks to hide my face, but the rocks they said,"No hiding place, no hiding place down here."'

'Who's that a-calling. Who's that calling so sweet?'

71

I knew that in future I would not have only Schubert from Geoffrey. He was listening with a furious look of concentration on his face, and as we walked back to the House afterwards he kept prodding me with his umbrella, telling me to listen to him.

CHAPTER 9

ONE cold morning, the whole School stood on the field where the monks had once had their tile kiln. We were waiting to be marched off in companies to Willington. We were going to have a Field Day. I looked to see what my rations were. I found an apple, a pork pie and a bar of chocolate.

The shouted commands rang out excitingly in the clear, biting air and I felt suddenly thrilled, as if our pretence at soldiering were serious and heroic.

There was nothing serious about our railway journey. Some people expressed themselves by ordering coffee, with two lumps of sugar wrapped in paper, as if they were independent citizens and not schoolboys; but others seemed to want more scope.

One unfortunate in my carriage had his trousers taken off and chewing-gum rubbed in his pubic hair. He screamed a lot but I think he really enjoyed the publicity.

I sat very still in my corner, drinking my coffee and hoping that nothing like this would happen to me.

I was supposed to be a Lewis gun. To make a convincing noise, I had a large wooden rattle. I was pleased, as this meant that I did not have to carry a rifle.

When we got to the end of our journey, I think it was somewhere near the Wrekin, we were lined up in the station yard and then marched to the foot of a smooth, round hill.

My water-bottle bounced against my side and gurgled, and the webbing of my equipment cut into my shoulders. Our uniforms smelt, just as the real Army's do. It was very realistic.

I think that some people had soaped their socks. I did

not mind about my feet, I only wished that I had long pants on underneath, to stop the chafing of the harsh khaki between my legs.

I suppose that when we stopped marching we were all ordered to do different things. I know that sergeants and officers looked blankly into the crowns of their caps where they kept a plan of operations. As the day wore on, a little circle of grease and sweat formed in the middle of these plans.

Suddenly I found myself rushing up-hill sounding my rattle madly, while blank cartridges went off all round. After that I was completely lost. I wandered along the edge of a field, close to the hedge, wondering what to do and giving my rattle an aimless twist now and then. I liked the noise. It was like a croaking wooden bird.

A head appeared over the hedge.

'Shut up, else we'll be captured,' it said.

'I'm lost,' I answered.

'So am I.'

'What are you?' I asked.

'I'm a bugler.' He waved his bugle at me.

'I'm a Lewis gun.' I started to twist my rattle again.

'Stop it, you fool!' he shouted.

'Shall we sit down here and eat our lunch?' I suggested peaceably. 'I'll come round to your side if you like.'

I scrambled through the hedge and sat down beside the bugler. I did not know him. We were in different Houses. His hair was dark and already you could see the smudge of his upper lip where he shaved.

We unpacked our pork pies and began to eat. They were very good but they had a flavour of grease-proof paper, and the water in our bottles was all churned up and warm. It tasted of corks and rust and the dead old smell that lives in thermos flasks.

The chocolate was lovely. I nibbled it very slowly while I listened to the bugler talking of music and philosophy.

He was very serious and seemed to think the Field Day a waste of time. I agreed, although I think I enjoyed it all, especially getting lost.

We sat huddled up under the hedge for some time ; then we heard shouts coming nearer and nearer. We got up and walked by the side of the hedge until we came to a dried-up pool, and there three 'enemies' burst out on us. They had been running down the hill and were hot and red.

They seized us, yelling, 'You're captured!'

We thought them very uncouth. We felt outraged and embarrassed because we knew that they would tear off all our fly buttons. This always happened to prisoners.

They were triumphing over us in a most disgusting way and were just about to wrench off our buttons when all the bugles blew. The Field Day was over.

The relief made me draw in a deep breath, then I ran as hard as I could, not trusting our enemies although the Field Day was ended.

We all sang as we marched back, and some of the sergeants and corporals, in outbursts of chivalry, carried the younger boys' rifles as well as their own. I was delighted – it was like Knights and Squires or the Theban Band.

It was such fun to sing, 'Down came a ruddy or bloody or any-other-adjective blackbird and pecked off her nose' to the tune of *Venite Adoremus*. Nobody could mind what words you used on the way home.

People were too tired to be troublesome on the train. A few electric-light bulbs were thrown out of the windows to burst on the line like small bombs – that was all. I noticed many cap badges stolen from the prisoners of the other school. The pillagers seemed very fond of their treasures. They rubbed them against their trousers to polish them. Others had pockets full of loose buttons which they jingled contentedly. I turned away and was thankful that the Field Day had ended when it did.

I lay in bed that night wishing that everyone would stop talking. There was some discussion which never seemed to end. At last I could stand it no longer; I let out a sort of groan, and someone hearing it said, 'What's wrong with Welch, is he talking in his sleep?'

I was so tired that I caught at this idea. I pretended that a battle was going on in my dream and that I was shouting out warnings and war-cries. It must have sounded convincing, for soon the whole dormitory was listening and there were suppressed chuckles and long, smothered laughs. Nobody wanted to wake me up; they wanted to hear the end of the dream.

I began to enjoy myself as I sensed how amused they were. Gradually, as my invention failed, I became silent. I tried to make it appear that I had sunk to a deeper layer of unconsciousness.

In the morning everyone asked me if I had slept well – if I had not been disturbed by bad dreams.

'No, I don't think so,' I said, trying to appear as innocent as possible. Then they all laughed and told me about my noises and the battle I had fought in my sleep.

I felt rather guilty; it seemed so easy to hoax people. But I knew I must never confess. It would make them feel such fools, and they would rightly want to punish my trickery.

The Gym became my refuge on free afternoons when I did not have to play games. I used to go down and let myself in quietly. Nobody was there at this time. It seemed to me a sort of temple of freedom.

After I had taken off my hateful butterfly collar, tail coat and straw hat, I would run round, jumping over the horse, climbing up the wall bars, trying everything in turn. When at last I had reached the top of the rope, a climax of excitement would pass through me – to be swinging up amongst the rafters after so much pulling and straining with arms and legs.

Then I would slide down, worn out with clutching the rope, my arms and thighs aching and my hands scraped and burning.

There was a grand piano standing in the corner. It was old and never used. I would sit down and play one of the three pieces I knew by heart, the Bach gigue, the Mozart waltz or the Beethoven sonatina.

It always sounded better here than anywhere else – grander, fuller, more exciting. I would exaggerate the louds and softs and play very staccato when I could.

I hated putting my ugly clothes on again. If there was time before evening school I would branch off into the fields, behind the Gym where the Witches' Cauldrons were. These were deep holes in the ground with brambles growing over and almost roofing them sometimes. They were along a ridge with a footpath running beside them. The ground was always churned up by the cows.

I used to climb down into one of the cauldrons and sit there thinking. Only a small sheet of sky appeared above. People used once to come here for a quiet smoke, but there had been a great scandal the term before, when all our lockers were searched and several boys beaten because of the cigarettes found there.

Nobody came here now. I had it all to myself.

When the snow came everyone went tobogganing. One of the masters put on the skis he had brought from Switzerland, but the snow was too thin and he fell on his head and was knocked unconscious. We all laughed about it for days.

I had no toboggan and I did not want to share one, so I used to go for walks with Brophy.

He wore a small truss under his clothes, and his face was rather puce-coloured. He was always eating sweets and seemed to be ashamed of it. We had both come the same term, so there was some bond between us.

We decided one afternoon to try and catch a glimpse

of the famous 'Findern Fillies,' not because we were at all attracted to girls but because, I think, we wanted to appear knowing and vicious.

These three women would sweep by every Sunday evening as we went into chapel. Their eyes seemed to take in the whole four hundred and fifty of us at once. One was rather fatter than the others, with fluffy hair and a fluttering scarf. I think she was the favourite.

No one was ever seen talking to them; they only boldly stared at us as they went on their way.

It was said that they lived at Findern.

Brophy and I made no real plan, we just decided to walk to Findern in the hope of seeing them. The snow had half melted and then frozen again, so we had the deserted road to ourselves. We walked along, Brophy swinging his umbrella and sucking an icicle. We had seen them glistening in the sun, hanging from the roof of a cowshed, and Brophy had scythed one down.

He began to tell me about his family, who lived at Purley. It was not exactly London, it was not exactly the country, and it wasn't exactly a suburb. He told me about his sister and about their telephone which was red, not black. You had to pay a little more for this.

My eyes wandered over the white fields. Brophy was being very dull. He was not at all like Geoffrey, who was always singing or being violent. I had to think of something that would interest us both.

Suddenly I burst out, 'O London, London! Just think, Brophy, of leaving all this in a few weeks' time and going back to civilization!'

You could do this sort of thing with Brophy; he was too sluggish to be irritated by affectation. All he said was:

'You sounded just like an actor, Welch, in a play, saying, "O my country, the country!"'

We could not stop talking after this, about the end of term. My fingers and toes were being bitten, but I felt very warm inside.

Leaving the road, we went down to the river-bank. I walked on to the ice and then tried to entice Brophy, but just as he was about to follow me I took fright, thinking how terrible it would be if he fell in and was not able to save himself because of his truss.

I had a religious fear of his truss. I told him how dangerous the ice was. It might give way at any moment. He looked rather puzzled at my change of front, but followed me up to the road again.

I went on talking, not caring what I said.

'I can't believe, Brophy, that I shall never come back here again. After two years of being a fag and being beaten and hustled about, it seems too good to be true. I know I shall never send any of my children to a public school. Not that I shall marry or have any children,' I added as an afterthought.

'Don't you ever want to marry, Welch?' he asked.

'Not unless I found a very old woman with plenty of money.'

'What a swine you are, Welch. Besides, you'd have to go to bed with her.'

'No, I shouldn't. There'd be an agreement that we only met at meals or when other people were there.'

'Then what do you think she'd marry you for?' he jeered.

'She might like to have young life about the place,' I answered weakly.

We had nearly reached Findern by now, but we had quite forgotten about the Fillies. The village street was deserted. Fine, dusty snow blew round the whitened doorsteps, making them look dirty. It was getting darker, the clouds seemed to be sinking down like a press.

We hurried through the village, Brophy still telling me about his idea of marriage. The homeward journey was depressing. It was getting so dark that we both began to hurry. I thought of tea and jam. I don't know what Brophy thought about. His face had gone a deeper puce and there was a crystal drop at the end of his nose.

Geoffrey saw us as we came in through the yard-gate. He was still in his tobogganing clothes – dirty white sweater, enormous scarf and blue shorts.

'What have you sissies been up to?' he screamed hysterically, rolling his eyes. 'Why don't you go tobogganing?'

'We've been looking for the Findern Fillies,' I answered. I thought the wickedness of it might satisfy him.

'A lot of good they'd be to you!' he sneered. Then he chased me into the drying-room, which was full of steaming, muddy, sweaty clothes. I ran behind the boiler and pressed hard against the wall to get away from him; but it was too hot and I had to come out. He was ready for me.

'You can pretend I'm one of your Findern Fillies,' he shouted as he pounced on me and knocked me down. When he had me on the floor his head swooped down like a bird and he slobbered on me, biting my ear viciously in his pretended kiss. I pushed my hand in his face and he bit my finger; then he got up and trod on me, knocking all the air out of me.

The days were being eaten up. I wriggled in my clothes, feeling my body separate itself from the wool of my vest and pants. Soon I would put these tails and striped trousers away and would never look at them again unless, perhaps, I were going to a wedding.

Although I had always hated their tightness and blackness, I had never felt so conscious of myself as I had in them. To wear clothes you hate makes you concentrate inside yourself, away from your surroundings.

The rain had melted my straw hat into soft curves. Although I had pressed it with books it would never quite regain its shape. I hated it most of all. I wanted to wear soft, loose, bright clothes with no hat at all.

I thought of the clothes I would have for China, but I

knew that my aunt would supervise everything. I would not be able to choose for myself.

She had written to my brother lately, and I had opened the letter as I often did. My aunt did not know this. She said how glad she was that I was soon to be removed from the bad influence of my friends. She mentioned one who had been very good to me; often having me to stay.

A delightful feeling of rage seethed and bubbled over me as I read the letter. I was trembling a little and my palms felt sticky. Righteous indignation must be the cheapest emotion in the world.

I rushed up to the study, and sat down at my table with its ink-stained green table-cloth. I rummaged for paper and pen and then began to write. It must have been a silly letter. When I had finished I felt quite soothed and chastened. I put on my hat and ran to the pillar-box before I could change my mind.

The result of this letter was that my aunt told my brother that she refused to have any more to do with me until I apologized.

I had not apologized, and never dreamt of doing so. I wondered what would happen when I went back for the holidays.

CHAPTER 10

I BEGAN to collect my things together. All the school books had to be left in a big pile on my table. I took my games clothes up to the dormitory to be packed. Geoffrey and I went together to the Armoury to return our uniforms. The long, thin sergeant called 'Pull Through' was there. I smelt the oil rags and metal for the last time. We made jokes about someone's initials which were F. L.

In school that afternoon we each had to write a chapter of a ghost story. This is the only lesson I have ever enjoyed or remembered.

Borrowing from the Bible, I wrote, 'The hair of my flesh stood up.' How everyone laughed when it was read out! I described the red damask walls, the silver sconces, and the great bed crowned with mouldy ostrich feathers. It was very romantic.

When the marks for the term were read out I was four-teenth, a not very distinguished place. Geoffrey was a little above me, and right at the top of the form was someone we both looked on as simple. Either we were quite wrong or very lazy.

On our way back to the House I stopped at the Art School to collect my drawings and say good-bye to Mr Williams. He was in a corner, bending over someone's drawing, giving it a big, grey wash. The boy was hating it. His work was being spoilt for him. Masters never understand this.

When Williams saw me he pushed his round shoulders back and said, 'Well, good-bye, Welch. Go on with your drawing. Don't let them make you do anything else.'

I felt flattered. I decided that I wanted to be a painter.

I collected my drawings and went out feeling warm and comfortable.

Geoffrey was annoyed because I had kept him waiting. He knocked off my hat and trod on it. It looked like a big, crushed egg, pale and fragile in the darkness. For a moment I was horrified, then I remembered that to-morrow was the last day.

We ate all we could at tea so that we should have nothing left in our lockers.

The next day the House began to fill up with 'old boys'. They were everywhere, standing in the corridors and studies, smoking pipes and cigarettes. Two even followed me down to the lavatory and asked me for a first-hand account of my adventures when I ran away.

I was pleased that my fame had spread so far, but embarrassed that I should have to answer questions while standing uncomfortably in that Jeyes' Fluid smelling place. So I did not do my story justice.

There was a football match in the afternoon between the 'old boys' and the First Eleven. Geoffrey and I watched contentedly as we munched our chocolate, but after that we began to feel cold and soon Geoffrey decided to quarrel with our neighbours. I did not want to bicker, so I said, 'Let's go round to the other side of the field.'

When we got there, we stood next to someone who had a little naked woman in the palm of his hand. He told us he had modelled it himself out of candle wax. His eyes glistened and he was 'lusting over it', to use his own words.

I had repaired my hat somehow but it looked rather disreputable. I was to go to the Headmaster after tea, for my farewell lecture, and my face was twitching with nervousness.

At six o'clock I rang the bell at the Hall and then stood in the dark, pillared room, waiting to go into his study. I smoothed my hair and ran the palms of my hands down my trousers. I wanted to be calm when he saw me, not mad with anxiety, like a cat let out of a basket.

I wiped the sweat from my upper lip and felt how hot my face was against my cold hand. I looked at the old bindings on the shelves. A smell came from them – an embalmed, enduring smell.

Someone passed me quickly and whispered maliciously, 'Your turn!'

I opened the door swiftly and stood on the threshold of the brightly lit study. He was writing. There was only a gleam from the top of his spectacles as he said, 'Sit down, Welch, I won't be a minute.'

I looked round at the room; I had never seen it before. It was in the medieval tower round which the Hall had been built. The walls were newly and roughly plastered, and little coats of arms had been fastened to the bosses of the ceiling. Two new wrought-iron fire-dogs held up the logs in the worn Tudor brick fireplace. Wine-coloured carpet, studded leather chairs and leaping flames completed the clubland 'luxury.'

When I had made my inventory, my eyes came back to the man at the desk. He was soon to be a famous bishop, but I would never have suspected it. In spite of his dog collar, I never thought of him as clerical. He lifted his head and I saw the little piece of cotton-wool stuck on his chin to staunch a shaving cut. The skin round it seemed purply black and uneven like rusticated granite.

'So you're the one who went to visit cathedrals instead of coming back to school!' he began. He knew me slightly; he had seen me sketching the Priory ruins and had noticed that I was left-handed. He seemed amused now. I blushed. To have my escape explained as an architectural holiday sounded silly. I said nothing, so he went on talking.

'My experience is that one must accept one's environ-

84

ment and fit into it as best one can; otherwise life is nothing but beating one's head against a brick wall.'

I felt his sincerity apart from his ordinary words. Schoolmasters generally never show it. I had never had three words of deeply felt advice before. It had always been argument or parrot-rule. I knew the difference now. I got up, warm inside and admiring.

'Good-bye, Welch. You ought to have an interesting time in China.' He shook my hand; my fingers curled round and I felt the black hairs at his wrist.

I was in the dark hall again, then out of the front door, running across the school-yard between the Norman priory and the church.

The house was alive with excitement when I got back. Everyone was getting ready for the House supper.

Those who were leaving had to make a speech at the end of the meal. I did not know what to do. I had nothing to say and I had no confidence. I went from person to person, asking them to think of something for me.

At last an 'old boy' came up to me. He had a strange cast in his eye and was handsome.

'I'll tell you what to say.' Then he made a little speech. 'Everything I wanted to say has been said, so like the humble onion I will not repeat myself, since brevity is the soul of wit.'

It was horrible, but I learnt it by heart. I was a drowning man clutching at anything.

I ate the turkey, the plum pudding, the mince pies, the tangerines and dates, saying over to myself, 'Since brevity is the soul of wit – I will not repeat myself – like the humble onion – Everything has been said –'

The phrases had grown meaningless by the time Mr Bird had risen from his chair. He began ponderously enough, but an 'old boy' who had had too much to drink kept interrupting with 'Hear, hear!' in the wrong places. Mr Bird rebuked him with great dignity but it was no good; the speech had to end abruptly.

For a moment I was pleased, then I felt sorry. We had been less bored, but the time for my own speech was brought nearer.

We rose in order of seniority. My brother made a suitable speech, and one person made us laugh. I, being the youngest, was the last to speak. Just as I was about to get up I saw Mr Bird rise, evidently to say Grace.

I sat down quickly, confusion and relief racing through me, and somewhere, the remotest resentment that he should have ignored me.

But I was not to escape. The Head of the House was bending towards Mr Bird, whispering something to him, and louder voices were saying:

'We haven't heard Young Welch yet, Sir!'

Mr Bird smiled patronizingly and waved his hand at me with a shade of impatience.

I stood up and began the speech, very falsely and loudly. I tried to imagine that I was alone in a wood, miles from anywhere. I dissociated myself from my words.

At the mention of the 'humble onion' I saw Mr Bird's face crumple up, like an affected music master's when his pupil plays a discord.

I knew the dreary, matey vulgarity of my speech. It was sickening; but I resented his face.

People were clapping and laughing, and I was pulled down on to the bench again by my neighbours and fed with dates and raisins. They hit me on the back and shouted, 'Well done, Welch, well done!'

I felt comforted. They at least knew what I had been through.

The room was emptying now and the actors were getting ready for their play. The rest of us went into the passages and studies and waited about expectantly.

We returned to sit in crowded darkness. I saw Clarence and the maids troop in behind us just before the play began. When the curtain was drawn I saw my brother on the stage, dressed as a pretty girl with cherries on her hat. The soft grey dress hung down to the ground and I thought we were going to have a sort of Pinero-Oscar-Wilde scene. I was disappointed when it turned into a farce with my brother and the hero hiding under the garden table.

The next sketch was more promising. The judge and the escaped prisoner confront each other; but that too began to be funny when the prisoner became so impassioned that he tore at his shirt until a pink nipple peeped out.

There was smothered laughter. It looked so funny, winking there.

We all sang 'God save the King' at the end of the evening. It swelled excitingly as we bawled out, 'Send him victorious, happy and glorious.'

As we went out of the door we said good night to Mr and Mrs Bird and their guests. I remember that one of them was in a fur coat. Each separate, glistening hair seemed alive, as if some animal had just been skinned.

There was not much sleep to be had that night. I was so tired that I wished everyone would go to bed, but instead, they sat up in their studies, talking and making hot drinks. I lay in bed listening to it all unwillingly, then towards dawn I left the cold dormitory and went downstairs.

The House was bubbling with voices and laughter and the sound of restless feet. The light in the study glared down on to Wilks and Bradbourne and the fire, turning them all to a grey white. The stale air smelt of chestnuts and smoked saucepans. I threw my clothes down on a chair and stood in front of the fire, letting it warm me through my pyjamas.

I wondered if I should shave in celebration of to-morrow, but I had no razor. I looked at Bradbourne and then asked him if I could borrow his.

'No, you can't, but I'll shave you myself if you like,' he answered. 'Go and get some water in this saucepan.'

When I came back he was stropping his razor and feeling its edge against his thumb in a workmanlike fashion.

'I didn't know it was a "cut-throat",' I said.

'It's all right, I won't hurt you,' he sneered comfortingly. 'Sit on this chair and take off your jacket, else I'll mess it up.'

He pulled it open at the neck and then over my shoulders so that I felt the fire on my chest and arms. Then he tilted my head and held it firmly, saying, 'Don't squirm, else I'll cut you.'

I sat there rigidly while Bradbourne lathered my face. He began to scrape my cheeks gently. He was intent and professional, his tongue wandering round his mouth in concentration. If I twitched or moved in any way he would press his elbow into my chest and say, 'For God's sake keep still!'

I enjoyed being shaved; I trusted him. When he had finished I stretched forward and thanked him.

'There was nothing much there,' he muttered.

My smooth upper lip pleased me. I put on my pyjama jacket again, but left it unbuttoned as I liked the glow of the fire on my skin. Wilks made some chocolate and we sat down to enjoy it quietly.

If anyone tried to come in, we shouted all together, 'Get out!' At last Geoffrey came in search of me. He took no notice of our automatic shout but strode up to the old wicker chair where Bradbourne and I were sitting and yelled out above our din:

'Put some clothes on, you lazy beast!'

It was not yet light. Wedged against Bradbourne in the creaking chair, and lulled by his breathing and the warmth of the fire, I felt half asleep.

'I think I'll stay here, it's too cold outside,' I answered weakly.

'No, you won't!' He got hold of my arm and tried to pull me across the room, but Bradbourne held one of my legs and ordered Geoffrey to let go. For answer he only pulled harder. I yelled as one of my joints cracked. Seeing that I was being hurt, Bradbourne let go himself, and I flew across the room, landing against Geoffrey's legs. He picked me up, pulling my pyjamas off as he did so and thrusting my shirt over my head.

So I was dressed unwillingly and bundled out into the clammy High Street. The sky was deep, navy blue. Our feet skimmed through the sticky layers of leaves but we could scarcely see them. We began to walk towards Crew's Pond. In the utter stillness we could hear the ticking of a clock or the sound of deep breathing from open cottage windows.

Geoffrey beat about as usual with his umbrella and talked excitedly about the holidays. Although his mother was dead and everything would be different, yet he seemed to be reconciled to the idea of living with Aunt Janet.

We went through the gate across the road and skirted Crew's Pond until we came to the clump of hissing pines on the hillside. We left the road and made for these, jumping the freezing, bubbling stream and climbing the high bank. When we stood in the circle of pines I suddenly felt like a Druid stone – as if part of me were buried in the ground – as if I had stood there for centuries, seeing the trees grow and die around me.

There was a strange smell in the air, it overlay the dusty, pine-needle smell. It was filthy and disgusting. We made noises in our throats.

'Do you think there's something dead near here?' I asked.

'God, isn't it awful!' Geoffrey said.

We rooted about with our feet and Geoffrey poked with his umbrella. It was too horrible to be left alone. I even began to imagine that it was the smell of a ghost; linking it up with my sudden thought that I was a Druid stone.

Then my foot slid on something slimy. I felt sick and

revolted. I wanted to rush down the bank and wash my shoe in the stream. Geoffrey came over to me, and in the strengthening light we saw that it was some horrible, spongy fungus. A Stink Horn. What had not been broken stood erect like a naked, aggressive phallus. It was white as if it had never been uncovered before.

I was fascinated by it. I pulled at it and it came away soggily, like a joint rotting in its socket. I put it to my nose and breathed in its filthiness deeply. Waves of sickness passed over me but I drew more into my lungs. Then I threw it down into the dark grass and it lay there looking like a great, white, helpless grub.

The smell was so overpowering by now that Geoffrey could stand it no longer. He rushed at the growth and, skewering it on his umbrella, he lifted it up and tossed it high over the tree-tops. We heard it plop at last into the stream below.

We ran along the ridge and down into the thickets where the waterlogged earth sucked at our feet. Twigs flicked in our faces, stinging like whips, but we did not stop until we reached the other bank of the pond. And there, by the water's edge, near the ruined stables, we sat down and watched the sun rise.

It came slowly, turning the water to mercury and separating the black tangle of trees. It showed us that the noise of plums being dropped into people's mouths came from the dripping of the choked-up weir. We walked towards it and saw all the refuse caught between the iron teeth of the grating. Paper and fruit peel, leaves, twigs and an old shoe were all stuck together with scum and bubbles.

Geoffrey and I linked arms and began to sing carols through the noise of the dropping water. 'Venite adoremus, venite adoremus; venite adoremus, Dominum!' The heathen woods took no notice at all, except to return a silly echo from across the lake.

Pleased by this freak we shouted again. Soon the air

was full of past and present noises calling to each other like spirits and spiritualists at a séance. When we grew tired of it we took the footpath that followed the stream. We wobbled and jostled under the willows, trying to walk two abreast. The path was so narrow that we nearly fell into the water. We were saved by throwing ourselves against the bank. I laughed and gasped and was thankful that only one foot had gone into the bitter water.

The House was cheerless when we got back. After having stayed in all night, the fires were choked with white ash and nearly dead. The studies looked squalid and dirty.

We ate our breakfast flippantly, knowing that we would have our real meal on the train. My brother, with four others, had chartered the ancient Rolls Royce to take us to the station. It swayed rakishly, like an enormous perambulator. I looked out from its dark felt and leather interior and said good-bye to everything at once – to the houses, the trees, the hills, the boys, the masters. To the lovely church and the sore, red Gymnasium.

As we rocked past the village cross we saw with amazement that the ball had been broken off the top. It lay at the foot of the steps amongst thick white pieces of broken crockery.

Someone had evidently tried to crown the cross with a chamber and the top had broken off. We gave mock groans to show what a dreary old joke we thought it was. I secretly thought it very daring, but was furious that the ball had been broken off the cross. I was glad to know afterwards that it had fallen on the toes of the vandal and had crushed them black and blue.

It was thrilling to be in your own clothes again; to feel the softness of the collar and to be hatless.

When we changed trains at Derby, Geoffrey left us, as he was going to Scotland. He said good-bye with mock sentimentality, putting his arms round me while we were in the great station lavatory, and trying to thrust his tongue right down my throat. He screamed with laughter when I ran away, rubbing my face with my handkerchief.

He was still waiting for the Edinburgh train when the London one moved out. I waved to him and he made a terrible face in return, sticking his umbrella between his legs like a battering-ram. Then he turned his back and I saw him, broad and not very tall, moving indifferently towards the bookstall.

Breakfast was already being served when at last I turned away from the window. I had everything : grapefruit, porridge, eggs, toast and marmalade, and coffee in the thick-lipped, ball-shaped cups. People were reading newspapers and smoking briar pipes and exotic-smelling cigarettes. The air was full of emancipation. The suffragette movement must have been like this! I thought.

CHAPTER 11

THE train journey was too happy to be remembered well. I only know that it was the most delightful feeling of escape that I have ever had.

Paul and I looked at each other excitedly in the dark station at St Pancras.

'Where shall we go?' we asked each other. It would soon be lunch-time. In spite of our breakfast we jumped into a taxi, and told the man to drive to Scott's. It was expensive and greedy, but we knew that nothing else would satisfy us.

We passed down side streets where young men with strong, blue chins and with red handkerchiefs round their necks sold vegetables and fruit from barrows. They seemed to belong to a different nation. The passers-by looked tame in comparison.

We sat upstairs at Scott's, near the mahogany and mirrored wall. We ordered hors-d'œuvre, steak-and-kidney pudding, and green figs with cream. I found oysters in the pudding and told Paul to look for them too. He ordered lager beer and I tasted some but left it. I did not like anything bitter.

It was pleasant to talk and eat with my brother again. At school there was a great gulf set between us. He was a prefect and two years my senior. Now we could think about our journey to China and discuss it for as long as we wished.

We left Scott's when we had talked and eaten to our heart's content. We stood on the pavement outside, wondering what to do next. We did not want to leave for Sussex until the evening. Paul suggested going to see our eldest brother, and I agreed without much enthusiasm.

We drove to his rooms and found him sitting by the fire in the small, fresh sitting-room, staring at a bottle of old brandy. Somebody had just given it to him for Christmas. He smiled when he saw us and began to pull the cork out with a soft, sucking noise. He poured it into little glasses and we were about to drink, when the door opened and a ripe, handsome woman with soft red mouth and dark eyes came in. My brother gave her one of the glasses of brandy and she laughed. It sounded like a deep, melodious organ-stop being pulled out.

'What, brandy at half-past three!'

She lay back on the divan and undid her fur coat, for she had only just come in from the street.

'I really came to ask if Billy would have tea with us. We live in the flat above,' she explained, turning to Paul and myself. 'Now that you're all here you must come too.'

We thanked her and sat quietly in the hot room, listening to her gay, deep voice. I hated the taste of my brandy but I loved the idea of drinking it.

We would have to have tea early as we were catching the five o'clock train from Victoria. The brandy bottle was put away and we climbed the stairs to the handsome woman's flat.

It had grey walls and golden-peach net curtains, making the light into a rosy-mist. A gilded flying angel hung from the ceiling, carrying a torch in its arms. Its rounded, sensual cheeks were worn, but bright paint still clung to its hair and mouth.

She saw me staring at it.

'Do you like my angel?' she asked.

She lit it up, switching the light on and off as if she were a spy signalling to the enemy.

Having been brought up to like 'artistic' Tudor cottages, I thought it rather vulgar.

'It's very nice,' I said. 'How old is it?'

'It came out of a Spanish church,' was her only answer.

We left the angel and were taken to see her bedroom. The bed was in an alcove draped and curtained with yellow and white striped satin. While we were still looking at it, her husband walked in. He had just taken off his hat and there was a subdued ring round his damp-looking hair. I suddenly thought of them both getting into the great striped bed at night. His pyjamas would be striped too, I supposed.

For tea, there were little marzipan cakes shaped like fruit and flowers. They seemed to me to be exactly the sort of food that the baroque angel would eat, if it were alive. The palms of my hands began to feel sticky as I sat near the fire and drank the hot tea.

When we had finished, Mrs Graham searched in the bag she was still carrying and brought out a lipstick; she pressed it on her upper lip, which dinted like a ripe medlar. Her flesh seemed unnaturally soft.

'I wish someone could play the piano,' she said, 'I'd love some music.'

'Denton can,' my brothers shouted, pushing me towards the lumpy, glistening object.

I sat down, showing my self-conscious back to them, not knowing what to play. I did not think of my Bach or Mozart pieces. The angel, or something, had made me pretentious. I began a Brahms waltz and then gave up at the difficult piece just before the end.

I left the piano, feeling very red and angry. I wanted to go at once. I turned to my brother. 'If we don't hurry we'll be late for the train,' I said.

Mrs Graham looked at us indolently, from her chair. Perhaps she was wondering what we would be like in five years' time. Then she rose to her feet, saying:

'You must come and see me again when you're visiting Billy.'

We thanked her, and our brother led us down the

warm, dark stairs to the street. He saw us into a taxi, then I heard the clang of the front door and I imagined him mounting the stairs again and spending the rest of the evening in the grey and peach room.

Victoria seemed like a dark, cloudy aquarium where great black eels wriggled swiftly in to swallow up mouthfuls of small, eddying fishes. From the crowd, faces glanced up, pale and floating, like spirit pictures.

There was a soldier in our compartment who picked his nose, looking at the find between his fingers afterwards. He did not talk. Nobody talked.

We had to change trains at Horsham. We drank coffee, for something to do while we waited. The urns hissed and the waitress stared at us with flat eyes, as if she were drugged.

From the road, we saw the light burning in our grandfather's hall. We crunched over the gravel to the front door. Our aunt must have heard us coming, for she was there to meet us, at the foot of the stairs. She held her glasses in one hand and her book in the other. She kissed us quickly, her lips seemed rather dry and cracked, then she led us into the drawing-room where our grandfather was sitting by the fire. He wore his thin, oval spectacles and was reading Herodotus.

'What a liar this man is! What an imagination!' he ejaculated. Then he saw us and said:

'Well, how are you? Neither of you seems to have changed much.'

He never mentioned my running away, nor did my aunt. I realized that it was to be forgotten and not talked about.

Just as usual, the brass cans, swaddled in towels, were waiting for us in our bedrooms. I was pleased that my grandfather's house was so old-fashioned; it gave me a feeling of experience, of having lived longer than I had.

I poured the water into the flowered basin and began

96

to wash. The scent of the lavender soap came as a shock. I still expected the carbolic of school.

There was macaroni cheese for supper and crème caramel. My grandfather drank two glasses of claret and my aunt sipped a little. I did not like her dress at all. It was made of blue and brown silk stockinette.

Afterwards, I sat next to her on the drawing-room sofa and looked at the *Sussex County Magazine* while she embroidered a bag in Florentine stitch. I looked after the coffee machine when it was brought in; watching until the water bubbled up from the glass bulb into the coffee grounds. I passed the cups round and sat down to drink my own. I, as the youngest, always fetched and carried. My grandfather would say with mock ceremony, 'Will the youngest bachelor ring the bell' or 'shut the door', 'open the window' or whatever it was he wanted.

I sucked the sugar candy in the bottom of my cup and looked at my apostle spoon. It was fifty or sixty years old, hall-marked and mass-produced. My aunt gave me some silk to unravel. I worried my fingers through the coloured tangle until I got it into some sort of order; then I said good night and got up to go to bed.

CHAPTER 12

IT was Christmas time, so we went to parties at the houses where there were sons and daughters of our own age.

On Christmas Eve we went to the Blakeneys'. It was depressing. We played paper games, and one of the girls, who was training to be a ballet dancer, tried to give us a little demonstration. Unfortunately she was sadly hampered by her dress, a black velvet sheath with a fish-tail train; and although it was split to the knee in front, it was so tight round that part of her, that her legs might have been tied together there with a stout piece of rope.

Our hostess stood up after this and began to sing 'Parlez-moi d'Amour.' Her gestures and the shape of her mouth made us all feel very uncomfortable.

Soon after half-past eleven we decided to leave. As I stood on the frosty gravel outside the front door I did not want to go home. I turned to my brother and said, 'I'm going to the Midnight Mass.' Then I ran, not wanting to be asked questions or to be late for the service.

'Leave the front door open for me,' I shouted before I disappeared.

The wooden chapel was nearly full when I arrived. I had never been to a Roman Catholic service before, and felt anxious about my behaviour. I was shown into a seat at the back, next to a plump girl and under the statue of a saint. Just above my head were artificial flowers and a little brass lamp. The Stations of the Cross were photographs of sculpture in Oxford frames. My eyes followed them up to the altar where the priest and the acolytes were. It was all a maze of lighted candles, frothing lace and incense smoke.

I was thrilled by the deadness and silence before the birth of Christ, and then by the coming to life of the congregation again as they moved about uneasily on their hassocks and made coughing, human noises.

I stood or knelt through the service, copying the plump girl beside me. When it was over and I had just passed through the varnished doors, an Irish voice spoke to me softly from the darkness:

'That was lovely, wasn't it?'

'Yes, I've never been before,' I answered.

'Why; aren't you a Catholic?' Her voice sounded quick with interest.

'No, I'm nothing,' I said.

'Well then, you're going to be one, aren't you?' Her question was urgent. I felt flattered.

'I suppose I'd have to know a lot more about it before I could become a Catholic.'

'That's easy; I'll tell the priest and he'll give you instruction.'

I took fright. I thought she was going back there and then to find the priest. She stood, almost barring my way, waiting for my answer.

'I will think about it,' I said hurriedly, 'but I must go home now.'

I felt the plump warmth of her hand as she grabbed mine. 'Good night', 'Good night' we said, and I ran back by the field path and let myself into the house as quietly as I could.

I opened my window and leant out. The frost had made the white paint glisten. It is Christmas Morning, I thought; and I've just run away from the first person who's ever shown any interest in my soul.

The days and weeks passed and we did little things. We went for a paper-chase organized by some friends for the boys at the near-by crammers'. I ran with one of them, over sodden fields and through hedges, following the trail of paper until at last we both fell into a dyke which we had tried to jump.

It felt like being cut in half. One part seemed living flesh and the other frozen. The wet shorts clung to our thighs.

We were the last to get back. The others were all having tea in the big Georgian dining-room when we arrived. Everyone laughed at us, and the beefy women made jokes about taking off our trousers, which made us blush.

I drank some hot tea and bit into a thick sandwich to cover my confusion. To add to my shame I saw, when I got up to go, that I had left a deep stain of damp on the red morocco seat of the chair. I hoped that the sporting women would be too delicate to make remarks about this too.

As I ran home I thought of the boys settling down to their work, cramming to pass some examination. I jumped and ran faster at the thought of escaping from it.

I poured a whole tin of mustard into my bath. It made the water look yellow and sticky and it stung a scratch on my finger, but I enjoyed it because it reminded me, for some reason, of the *Ingoldsby Legends*.

It was raining and I was alone. My aunt and my brother were out. I sat on the settle in the dining-room and watched the rain soaking into the lawn. My aunt's dog was with me. He was practising half-hearted perversion on the white Persian cat. I watched them for a little and then told Scamp to stop. He looked up and wagged his tail as if he were inviting me to join in.

I went to the sideboard and opened one of the cupboards. A breath of salt, pepper, mustard, green baize, jeweller's rouge, wine and spirits escaped. The whisky decanter glistened from the bottom shelf, as prickly as a prison wall. The prisms and roses seemed too sharp to touch and the glittering stopper was like a diadem. I pulled it up with the soft crunch and squeak of glass on glass, and smelt the whisky.

Then I ran upstairs to fetch my tooth-glass. I wanted to leave no evidence of my experiment.

I more than half filled the glass with whisky and went to the tap in the flower-room to pour a little water on top. The water made the whisky look greasy, like syrup.

I took the glass back to the dining-room and sat down under the window. I held my drink up to the light, then I drank very quickly, trying not to taste the horrible stuff. I felt a churning inside me, and heat left in my throat. I waited, expecting every moment to feel suddenly drunk.

Very gradually I heard a drumming in my ears. My head began to feel heavy, so I leant it on the back of the settle. I gave a little gurgling laugh and Scamp came running to me. He jumped up, thrusting his paws into my lap, and I put my arms round him and kissed him. I went on kissing him and gurgling until I lurched forward and rolled on to the floor.

It was then that I heard footsteps in the hall. I sat up quickly. My head was rocking and singing. The door opened and Kate looked in. 'I've taken the tea into the drawing-room, Master Denton,' she said.

I nodded my head seriously and she shut the door again. I was appalled. I did not think I could sit through tea with my grandfather, in this state. I got up very uncertainly and made for the flower-room. I filled the basin with cold water and dipped my face in it. I had stopped giggling but I could not control my movements.

I opened the drawing-room door and walked hurriedly to the sofa, praying that I would not lose my footing. My grandfather poured out a cup of tea for me and I had to get up to fetch it. I held on to the arm of the sofa and reached forward. I had to get up several times after that, to pass things to my grandfather. I remember it as a nightmare. I felt that at any moment I would fall, to wreck the tea-tray or the cake-stand.

I spoke as little as possible, only answering his questions. He did not seem to notice anything strange about me. I made my escape when the last cup of tea had been drunk. I clung to the banisters and pulled myself up to my room. I lay face downwards on the bed, feeling utterly miserable, crying into the pillow until it was wet and clammy. Then I went to the slop-basin wreathed with roses, and tried to make myself sick by pushing my fingers fiercely down my throat.

My aunt took me to see the old house on the Common which was being sold up. The dead farmer's daughter let us in. She told us how her parents had lived there for fifty years. All the china and glasses had been put in the dark dining-room. Blue Nankin cups with no handles and glasses engraved with barley-corns shone and glittered there. They stood on old tin trays still bright with birds and flowers and pagodas. There was every kind of household utensil of a hundred years ago.

I supposed that all these things had been brought from an earlier home and that almost nothing had been added. There were little corner washstands in the bleak bedrooms. A wall-clock in a perished case of black and gold lacquer ticked in the hall.

I wanted my aunt to buy me something. I knew that she was going to give me a present before I went to China.

We got nearer and nearer to the front door, until at last we were saying good-bye and walking through the ragged garden. My aunt was moving briskly. 'I didn't ask the price of anything,' she said, 'as I thought that there was nothing you would like.'

I was startled. I had never been in a house where I had liked so much.

'I wouldn't have known what to choose,' I found myself saying, 'and the things were a bit big, weren't they?'

I thought of the sale next week, when the dealers and local families would divide everything. And I was envious and fiercely sorry that the things could not be left together.

They would be dull in antique-shops, robbed of the years crusted on them. The furniture would be varnished and polished and the wooden knobs would be replaced by 'period' brass handles.

It snowed again in late January. Paul and I took the rusty toboggan out of the stable and sandpapered the runners. Then we set out for the slopes near the old sand-pit. I sat on the toboggan and Paul pulled me across the Common. The sun was shining and I began to sing and feel very happy.

We heard shouts and saw the flick of a coloured scarf before we reached the top of the slope. The scene on the other side was exciting. Sitting people or people flat on their stomachs tore down the hill, narrowly missing the frozen pond and the tangle of black hedges at the bottom.

They were mostly young men and boys. The snow brought colour to them and made them look more lusty and strong. Hot breathing and pipe-smoke made little clouds in the air, and mouths opened wide and teeth flashed when jokes were told. Some of these were not to be understood by strangers. I shall never know what 'Take care of your scruples, Jim!' or 'Don't forget to insert a table' meant.

Paul and I tobogganed till the sun went down. It burnt into the ground like a red poker sinking into wood. The air was deep blue and we could not see the others until they had run into us. We left reluctantly, dragging our toboggan and puffing at the cigarettes a man had given us. We had told him that we did not smoke, but he said, 'Well, why not try?' and had stuffed them into our mouths and lighted them.

After the excitement of the day, the stillness by the fire was oppressive. I slipped out after supper into the garden. The leaves and bushes smelt strong and aromatic.

I felt the light film of dust on the laurels under my fingers. I walked over the bricks in the stable-yard and stood by the gate. A young man passed me with a cigarette between his lips. I walked behind him up the road and saw him climb over a stile. It only led into the fields and down to a spring. I wondered what he was going to do; I decided to follow.

When he stopped underneath the elms I hid behind the corner of a shed. The little red tip of his cigarette still glowed like a button on a switchboard. His shoulders were very broad as he hunched them. He seemed to be holding his hands in his pockets, against his thighs. He hummed a little tune and threw his weight from one foot to another. Then he stopped suddenly and came forward. Someone else had arrived from across the snowy fields.

He drew her underneath the trees and I saw him throw down the cigarette impatiently, so that it fell like a small rocket. Then his arms went round her and I saw them moving nervously up and down her back like black shadows on a wall. He bent her backwards, curving her like a bridge until he lost his balance and fell and lay on her, a long, dark, trembling line in the snow.

I left them to their bliss, running away with my face on fire. Back in the lighted drawing-room, I could not concentrate on the pictures in the *Illustrated London News*. I went to bed and lay in the dark, thinking of what I had seen.

The next morning I climbed over the stile again and walked up to the clump of trees. I bent down and looked at the shape their two bodies had made in the snow; then I saw the sickly, yellow patch of his cigarette, where it had melted and stained the snow.

I took the remains of it up in my fingers. The paper was grey and wet now, falling away from the sodden strands of tobacco. I thought of it lighted and glowing, stuck between his teeth the night before.

Part Two

CHAPTER 13

I FELT our journey had begun the day we went to London to order our clothes for China. In the upstairs room in Hanover Street we were measured for grey flannel and Palm Beach suits. I hated standing in front of the great cheval-glass without my trousers while the tailor measured between my legs. He pressed the cold little tab against me, so that I could feel it through my pants.

My aunt made me buy another hat. When we went out of the shop I thought that everyone must be looking at me. My head felt big and clumsy like a doll's. I hated hats and never wore them willingly. I took the thing off and carried it. My aunt frowned.

'Why don't you wear your hat, Denton?' she asked.

'Because it makes my head ache,' I answered loudly and rudely.

'What nonsense!' she said, and we walked on in silence to the next shop.

That night, when we were home again, I started to collect my things for packing. I wanted to take everything I possessed.

The next day I rode about the country on my bicycle, visiting the places I might not see again for a long time. The lanes and forgotten roads through the fields were rutted and slimy. The mud clogged my wheels and sometimes I had to walk. I tried to get to what had once been a bishop's palace, but it was so lost in the floods that I would have needed a boat to reach it. It was a labourer's cottage now, standing near the railway line. Only one enormous chimney-stack with decorated shafts showed what it had once been. I looked across the water to it, while a dog belonging to a near-by cottage tugged and danced on its chain, barking furiously at me.

I arrived back late for tea. I made excuses and took the piece of clammy toast that lay unhappily in the bottom of the dish.

Everything was the same and yet everything was changed. I was going away.

The hotel where we slept the night before we sailed was politely fly-blown. My aunt had a talent for finding such places. The echoes in the passages were muffled by doubtful, unpleasant carpets. I hated it.

My eldest brother had dinner with us; then Paul and I were sent to bed early so that we should be ready for the next day. I did not sleep well. I heard strangers talking and floorboards creaking until the early morning.

The maid who brought us tea revolted me a little. She was pale and puffy like a blown-up bladder.

Bill appeared again after breakfast and we began the long taxi-ride to the docks.

I had never been through that part of London. It horrified me. It was like the back-cloth of an early pantomime with all the colour left out. There were the same meat shops and chemists' shops. The same loutish sense of brooding squalor lay over the scene.

The paint-smelling cleanness of the ship was such a contrast that for a moment I stood not thinking, only smelling the brass, the coiled ropes and the pitch between the scrubbed boards of the deck.

The gangway, springy as a diving-board, rose and fell, and I saw our light luggage being dragged up through the forest of legs.

Our cabin had two portholes looking on to the deck, but was rather dark. We sat down on the bunks and talked.

'God, how I envy you,' Bill said to us. I saw my aunt turn her head slightly. I knew that she did not like God to be mentioned.

'Think of leaving this filthy place and getting into the sun!' my brother added.

The siren blew and we all stood up convulsively. I looked at my aunt and she kissed me very quickly. It was a sort of sincere peck. I suddenly hated leaving England. I wished impatiently for them to go. I felt that I was going to cry.

The ship came to life and began to throb its way out of the river-mouth. Paul splashed water into the bright metal basin and made me wash my face; then he led me down the companion-way to the dining saloon. The things on the table all shivered gently in rhythm with the ship's vibration. I looked at the man in front of me. He was middle-aged, with a very fine nose. It was small and straight with no lumps. The skin was thick, not delicate, so that no veins and blood showed underneath. I sat and looked at it while he and his wife talked politely to us.

After some time I began to listen to what they were saying. They also were going to Shanghai. Their name was MacDonald. I stirred my coffee and looked at the other tables. The ship was very small. I saw the edge of a piano jutting out of an alcove. There were chintz-covered seats under the portholes, and at the head of the companion-way hung a great picture of a Scottish glen. It looked very incongruous, as if it had been looted from Glasgow; as the ornaments of Rome were snatched up by the barbarians.

After the meal we went up to our cabin to talk and unpack; then we walked round and round the deck while the light faded. Someone came out after us and leant against the rail. I recognized him as the only other passenger of about our own age. He was smoking. He blew the smoke in our direction, wanting to talk to us but not knowing how to begin. At last he said, 'Do you think it's going to get rough to-night?'

We stopped walking and stood beside him. He was

taller than either of us and his face seemed flat and long. I could see that his straight, thick hair was dark. We soon learnt that, like ourselves, he was going out to China to join his parents. He had just left Marlborough.

There was a lull after we had in turn explained ourselves. Suddenly my brother said quite unexpectedly, 'God, I've got frightful indigestion.' It was not the sort of thing he usually had, and I imagined that he was just saying it for something to say, but Fleming took it seriously.

'Come back to my cabin; I've got some Yeast-Vite tablets,' he said.

The patent medicine sounded very ugly, but he was so eager that we went.

It was then that I saw the colouring of his face. As he switched on the light I saw the red-brick glow of his cheeks. Together with his shining black hair they gave him a heated look; as if he were about to sweat.

He pointed nonchalantly to a photograph in a silver frame above the washstand, saying, 'That's my mother.'

Feeling rather surprised, I looked at the picture of a woman dressed in the fashion of 1919 with osprey-trimmed hat and wired Elizabethan collar. She had what are known as regular features. I imagine the thick layer of powder that lay over them in real life. Her clothes would smell of violent scent.

'She's very good looking,' I said, wondering as I spoke what she looked like now.

We sat on the bunks and Paul was given two tablets and told to chase them down his throat with a drink from the tooth-glass. The little electric bulb glared down on our heads and I began to feel restless. Fleming did most of the talking. He ended up by asking us if we knew the definition of a gentleman. He waited and then said slowly:

'A gentleman is a person who uses the butter-knife when he's alone.'

He looked at us triumphantly and we tried to force a laugh. My growing dislike crystallized. It was degrading to have to laugh at anything so suburban and B.B.C. It wasn't even improper, and I'd been preparing my face for something dirty!

I turned to Paul, saying that it was time to get ready for dinner.

The next morning I began to draw. I sat in a corner of the deck and drew the coiled ropes, the lifeboats, the ventilators and any other strangely shaped thing. It made me happy and contented. I did not think about myself at all. When other passengers came up I held my board very close and frowned as if I were deep in thought. They usually muttered something like, 'I won't disturb you, I see you're concentrating,' and then moved on, but one woman would not leave me. She was between fifty and sixty and the ends of her silk scarves fluttered in the wind. Her head and neck were like the Roman symbol of an axe embedded in a bundle of sticks. The neck was all broken up into wrinkled skin and corded muscles, and the head jutted out at the top.

I could see from the colour of the scarves that fluttered and slapped against her that she was 'interested in Art.' They were puce and peacock-blue. She was persistent as a bird, swooping down to peck at my drawing every moment. At last I gave it up and leaned back against the side of the ship while she talked.

She was going to India to meet her husband. She had no children of her own, but she had several nephews and nieces who were extremely clever. One of them was going to an Art School. She ended up by telling me her name. It was Mrs Wright.

There was a moment's pause and I felt her eyes on me. I looked up suddenly and caught the glint of curiosity. She dowsed it instantly, but I knew what was coming. She began with more skill than I gave her credit for, and I found myself answering her questions with only slight resentment. She soon knew that I had run away from school, that I was going to China and that I was not quite seventeen.

The reaction came after she had left me. I brooded on my dislike of her. I hated to think that I had satisfied her curiosity. She was like a greedy, sinewy spider.

In the evening I walked round the deck, passing constantly the portholes of Mrs Wright's cabin. On one of my rounds I stopped close to them and leaned against the side to rest. My eye caught something gleaming gold and blue just inside the cabin. It was a still unopened box of chocolate. It lay on the sill of the open porthole.

'The greedy bitch,' I said to myself. I thought of her sitting up in her bunk, wearing, perhaps, a boudoir cap with lace and blue ribbons; reaching for the chocolate without taking her eyes from the page of her novel.

I imagined her face when the groping hand told her that it was not there. I put my hand in, picked up the chocolate and walked on swiftly.

When I reached the stern I leant over and watched the wake disappearing into the collecting darkness. I tore the shiny paper off the chocolate and threw it down so that it was swallowed up in the churning of the propellers; then I began to eat.

It was like a communion feast. I was eating Mrs Wright. Not for love, but for hate, so that later she should be ejected from my body to go swimming down with the rest of the ship's sewage. I put large pieces in my mouth and savoured them deliciously until the whole pound was finished.

At dinner Paul asked me why I ate so little. He asked me if I felt seasick.

As I sat on deck at eleven o'clock, drinking the highly-peppered soup that had just been served, I heard the voice of Mrs Wright, and the next moment she appeared round the corner with one of the ship's officers.

'I don't think it could have been the steward,' she was saying. 'He seems so honest. Perhaps it was one of the sailors who scrub the decks in the early morning.'

I knew at once what she was talking about. My heart gave a little jump of fear, and disgust at her meanness. Before the officer could escape she said, 'I'd like you just to ask them if they know anything about it.'

He answered impatiently and I saw her look of annoyance at his brusqueness. I sat very quietly in my chair, pretending to read my book but secretly exulting. She did not sit by me or interrupt me. She just swept down the deck to her cabin.

The answers she had wrung from me the day before bore fruit a few days later, as I knew they would.

I was sitting in our cabin drawing some objects on the washstand. And as I drew, the sound of voices floated in through the porthole. They grew louder and did not move on. There was a scraping of chairs. It was evident that a group of people had settled on the deck just outside. Mrs Wright's was the only voice I could hear well.

'I think he'll always regret running away from school. He's much too young to be going out to China. He needs a lot more discipline yet.' I could not hear the reply. I crossed the cabin swiftly and noiselessly and lay on the bunk under the porthole so that as little as possible should escape me. I enjoyed eavesdropping. I wanted to hear every word about myself. I did not dream of leaving the cabin or coughing so that they should hear me.

The conversation went on for some minutes, and although they only criticized me I felt strangely flattered.

CHAPTER 14

PAUL and I went on shore at Port Said with Mr and Mrs MacDonald. After we had been persecuted and mobbed and had looked at the shops, we sat down to rest on the hotel terrace. Mr MacDonald ordered drinks. I looked at my parcels. I had bought Turkish Delight studded with bright green pistachio nuts, and a fez. I wanted to wear the fez with a velvet smoking-jacket and be like Disraeli in 1830.

While walking in the town I had expected to be stopped and asked to buy obscene pictures. I had imagined touts plucking my sleeve and suggesting that I should go to see some extraordinary spectacle. I had even feared that there would be whores standing in doorways with red lights above their heads, beckoning to me.

For these reasons I had been nervous, but now that nothing had happened I was somehow disappointed. Port Said, after all, was just a collection of shops which sold Turkish Delight, Egyptian designs on cloth to hang behind the washstand in a boarding-house, and little telescopic pencils, shaped like an obelisk and enamelled with hieroglyphics.

We went back to the ship and I washed my hair in disinfectant, as I suddenly was worried by the idea that bugs had flown into it from the Egyptians.

Then began the long, silent slipping through the Suez Canal, with the soft desert on either side and the water licking and sucking at the banks as we passed. I stayed on deck in the coolness till late at night, staring at the desert and the dark blue sky. Camels passed in the daytime bearing draped, precarious-looking men who sometimes sang or shouted to us in high, keening voices.

Aden was the colour of the bars and firebricks in an empty grate. It was just that dull, bruised purple-brown. We went to see the cisterns hewn out of the side of the hill. They were old and dry and useless like empty honey cells. The barracks which we passed looked like an enormous carcase, clamped to the ground and sheltering under its arched bones all the things that lived on its rottenness.

We were told about the mermaids in glass bottles, but did not go to see them. I imagined horrible little monkey faces and withered torsos joined to disgusting, scaly tails.

In the Red Sea I wrote a poem: I had not thought of doing so since I was nine years old. I was in Switzerland then with my mother, and I showed her my first poem while we stood on the balcony in the sun with the snow gleaming all round us.

She read it through, then wrinkled her eyes and nose slightly in a smile and said, 'Why don't you write about things you know?'

So I didn't write any more until the moment in the Red Sea when I suddenly saw the burnt-up mountains. I had just come on deck with my drawing-book and I saw them crumbling in long lines to the sea. They were like piles of brown sugar, everlasting and fierce, sticking up out of the sea.

I leant on the rail and scribbled in my drawing-book. What I wrote seemed almost perfect. I hugged it to me for the rest of the day, saying it over to myself.

Other poems followed and I thought how good they were, but I told no one that I was a poet. It was nothing to laugh at and I could not trust them to do anything else.

A swimming-bath had been rigged up on the deck, and every day I swam between its canvas sides and tasted the salt water. The sun was so hot that it dried my hair and shoulders in a moment, leaving them sticky with salt. I saw my bathing-suit fading from purple to mauve, my skin darkening to coffee from pink, and my hair bleaching at the ends.

From morning till night the rope quoit flew backwards and forwards against the solid blue sky. The peppered soup was no longer served hot at eleven o'clock; it was iced, with little coins of hard fat floating on the top.

Although they told me that the sun was dangerous, I sometimes lay in it, early or late in the day. I had found a lonely place on top of the apprentices' cabin. I would climb the little metal ladder, and after spreading out my clothes would lie down naked on the hot roof. The heat and the vibration of the ship gave me a strange sensation. I felt as if I were strapped to the back of an enormous animal.

One day as I lay there I heard footsteps on the ladder. I sat up in alarm and saw a pleasant, loutish face looking at me over the edge of the roof. One of the apprentices had evidently had the same idea as myself. There was a pipe between his teeth, and when he climbed up I saw that he wore dirty white trousers and a singlet.

'I hope I'm not trespassing,' I said doubtfully.

'No, that's all right. I've come up here for a bit of peace and quiet myself,' he answered.

He came and sat next to me, and I suddenly saw the hairs on his arms gleam bright gold as the sun caught them. He looked out to sea, puffing at his pipe and saying nothing; then he broke out gently and softly, 'God, what a life! I've been chivvied about all day.'

He told me about the life of the ship and what he had to do. The loutish look on his face grew more intense. I could see now that it was really sullenness; when he smiled it disappeared.

We lay in the sun until our bodies were shiny with sweat. It was too hot. I got up to go. He suggested that we should listen to his gramophone. We climbed down the iron ladder and entered the cabin. He switched on the electric fan, and after fumbling in the drawer under his bunk he drew out a black and white striped box and offered me a cigarette. It was Russian, done up in biege paper. I was flattered. I felt that he only brought them out on special occasions. When he bent forward with a lighted match cupped in his hands, I saw how horny and broad they were. They were nice, and strong, with dirty nails. I wished I had hands like them.

'What would you like me to put on?' he asked.

'Well, what sort of records have you got?'

'There's plenty of swing and I've got some sea-shan-ties, but they're not very good.'

'Let's hear a sea-shanty,' I said. 'I won't know what's wrong with it.'

He put a record on and hung over the turning disc, listening and making a guttural noise which turned at last into, 'God, they're so bloody land-lubberly!'

I wondered if this was done for my benefit, but de-cided that it was not false.

'Apart from a little fancy-work, can you imagine them doing anything while they sing this?' he burst out. 'They're supposed to be sweating about hauling up anchors!'

The song now began to sound too articulated and pedantic, but I imagined that any other attempt by the singers would have ended in British-Broadcasting-Corporation toughness.

I said that imitation heartiness was worse than prig-gishness and he agreed.

'But why don't they get real sailors to sing them?' he asked.

'Do real sailors still sing?'

But he did not answer my question; another apprentice came in at that moment and threw himself down on one of the bunks. His whole body still quivered from some violent work. He put his arm over his eyes, and I got up swiftly to go.

The Captain found me one day in the bows, watching the sea divide as the ship drove forward. Flying-fish darted in and out of the water like nightmarishly big insects, and the iron-deck plates were red with rust and so hot that I felt them through the soles of my shoes. The huge anchor chains had the same dreamlike quantity of enlargement as the flying-fish.

I thought as he came forward that he was going to tell me that I had no right to be there, but instead he stood beside me with a broad-minded grin on his face and began to talk of politics and art. I wanted to escape, but he took me back to his cabin to show me his things.

As I entered the cabin he pressed a switch which immediately lit up two statuettes standing in the corners. They were naked women made out of opaque green glass, standing in bowls of water where artificial lilies floated. He flicked the light on and off, pleased with his vulgar toy.

On his desk was a photograph of a woman with her arms round a child with curly hair. The child in turn had its arms round a very large teddy bear. He saw me looking at it.

'The wife and kid,' he explained, adding, 'Jolly pair, aren't they?'

I looked round for some way of escape. 'I expect you're very busy,' I said. 'Thank you so much for showing me everything.' I moved firmly towards the door.

On the way down I ran into the Chief Engineer.

'The Captain has just been showing me his cabin,' I said. 'I don't like those women that light up.'

'Nor do I,' he answered. 'They're not suitable for a ship.' He paused for a moment, then added: 'Like to come and see my place while you're up here?'

He led me down the passage and opened a door. I caught sight of the Infant Samuel hanging over the bunk. It was a big reproduction and strangely embarrassing. The only other picture was a Japanese print of a huge wave breaking into foam at its crest.

'I don't like that,' he said, pointing to the print. 'They've got no sense of art.'

'Why do you hang it up, then?' I asked.

'Because someone gave it to me.'

'Did someone give you the Infant Samuel?'

'No, I bought that when I first went to sea.'

He suddenly turned to me with deep intensity and said: 'Don't you ever forget to say your prayers at night.'

It was exciting and refreshing to reach Colombo after the long waste of Indian Ocean. Mrs Wright came up to me as I looked towards the land and asked if I could smell the spices mentioned in the hymn. I said that I could smell nothing but brass polish and tarred rope. She turned away abruptly, her scarves fluttering angrily in the breeze. That was the last I saw of her.

I tried to make my brother avoid Fleming, but he would not, so we went on shore together and drove to Mount Lavinia, where we bathed and ate curry. I found cowrie shells. Their little pointed teeth and pink gums grinned up at me from the beach. Catamarans were sailing on the water; others had been dragged up under the palm trees.

We drank our coffee on the terrace, looking out to sea. We did not see the jewel-seller until he stood bowing in front of us. He was wrapped tightly in a long piece of cloth, and the back of his head was surrounded by a curved comb.

He spread his wares on the ground and uncovered them. Moonstones and rubies and sapphires winked at us. I longed to touch them, but I would not as I could not buy. Seeing my interest, he thrust a tray at me.

'Look, Sir, Mister, buy lovely jewel for your lady!'

I took the tray reluctantly and fed my eyes on the coloured frost. I wondered how many of them were real.

'Send him away, Denton. We can't buy anything,' Paul broke in impatiently. He started to talk to the man

in pidgin-English. 'No can buy to-day. No have got – –'
but he was cut short.

'Never mind, Sir, this young master want to see.'

The man was watching me closely. He suddenly opened
his mouth in a mechanical, flashing smile, and I saw that
his teeth were rimmed with red and that his tongue was
a tendril of raw, orange meat. I knew that it was due to
betel-chewing, but I drew back horrified.

I put the tray firmly on the ground and found myself
saying with curious, suburban refinement, 'Not to-day,
thank you.' It was as if I were turning the milkman away.

'But, Sir,' he said hysterically, leaning forward so that
I could smell his dark skin and see each coarse, dull hair
growing out of his scalp. 'But, Sir, buy for your best lady
the beautiful Ceylon stones. No cheat can be detected.'

'I have no "best lady",' I said with emphasis.

He gave me a curious look. 'Then buy for your
mother, your best mother.'

He tailed off hopelessly, like an organ monkey trying
to collect pennies from a crowd.

'I have no mother,' I shouted angrily.

I did not like to see the rubber trees bleeding their
milk into little tins strapped to their trunks. It made me
remember a nightmare.

I once found myself in a narrow, squalid street where
people jostled me and threw their filth into the gutters.
Suddenly I came upon a woman lying on the pavement,
her head propped against a wall. She was crying hopelessly and whining and groaning through her tears.

As I looked down my eyes focused on a great steel
hat-pin. A shock of horror ran through me. The hat-pin
pierced her left breast, the head and point appearing on
each side of the globe of flesh. At her slightest movement
milk spurted from the wounds, splashing her clothes and
falling on her skin in white bubbles. I passed on, too
dazed to think until I had reached the end of the road.

Now in the rubber plantation at Singapore I remembered this dream again. I turned away from the sticky white milk oozing into the cups from the wounded trees. I waited in the car for the others, and when they had seen enough we drove over the red roads to the hotel where we were going to have lunch.

A languid fountain played in the hall. The ex-rubber-planter whose car and services we had hired discreetly withdrew, and Mr MacDonald chased him, imploring him to eat with us, but he refused quietly.

I was asked playfully if I would like a gin-sling, but I saw when the drinks appeared that I had been ordered orange juice in company with Mrs MacDonald. We sipped slowly. Our glasses were wet and frosted on the outside. The ice tinkled, the wicker chairs creaked, and high up in the darkened room electric fans whirred. They were almost silent, but the noise of the rushing air was sinister.

I was glad when we went on to the veranda to eat our lunch. Mr MacDonald decreed that we should have rice tafel. I wondered when the chain of waiters would stop coming to our table. Each bore a different dish, from which I helped myself. On a firm foundation of rice I built a tower of fish and eggs and roasted meat; of nuts and vegetables and fried banana; roofing it all with chutney and hot peppers and condiments whose names I did not know.

I looked at the coloured tower, then I dug into its walls with my spoon and fork. I blessed the Dutchman who had invented this gluttonous dish.

After so much heat, the coolness of coconut milk blended with syrup and tapioca was delicious. I ate the simple pudding gratefully and then sat watching the bathers. In front of us was an enclosed pool, jutting into the sea. There were sharks which had to be kept on the other side of strong steel netting. After so much food, it seemed greedy to begrudge the sharks their share.

CHAPTER 15

A SURPRISE was waiting for us on the ship. Some new passengers had arrived and they were not ordinary. There was an American father, tall and stringy, a French mother, quite deaf, with a fierce, permanently waved look, their son and daughter, together with a red-haired tutor, a young female companion and two round-faced Chinese boys to look after two round-faced Pekingeses.

I could not take my eyes from the fantastic family, and I was pleased when the boy, who was my own age, came up and spoke to me in the graceful, abrupt American way. We leant on the rail and watched the land disappear as we exchanged views and asked polite questions.

Their yacht had broken down and had been left behind for repairs while they went on to Hong Kong. A faint breath of onions hung about him as he spoke, and I began to wonder if I also smelt of onions after eating the rice tafel.

At dinner that night I listened to his mother's conversation. It echoed across the saloon in the queer, ventriloquistic way that some deaf people's voices do.

'Every bit of it is thirteenth-century lacquer,' she was saying.

I wondered what she was talking about; as she went on I realized that she was describing the saloon of their yacht.

'We found the lacquer in a temple fifteen years ago. It was being ruined by neglect. We bought it, but the fun began when we tried to fit it into the saloon. It all had to be specially shaped, because, as you know, a ship is all curves.'

The voice stopped. I had been enjoying its metallic tone and the curious French perversion of each word, but what she described made me angry. It seemed silly and vulgar to tear old Chinese lacquer out of a temple and fit it into a ship's saloon. I tried to visualize it. I saw the saloon shimmering gold and silver and red. I realized suddenly that it would be beautiful. It would be like floating on the water inside a jewel-box. On rough days the ship would groan and creak and the waves would be like glass mountains, but inside the lacquer saloon there would be peace and silence, only broken perhaps by the Pekingeses being sick on the velvet cushions.

The next day I made friends with the daughter and her companion, Miss Swanwick. After walking round and round the deck like mice revolving in a wheel, they stopped behind me as I sat drawing. They had been discussing Esther's education.

'Esther says she wants to go to Oxford,' Miss Swanwick began. 'But I tell her that she hasn't got the guts to stick at anything long enough.'

I looked at Esther and wondered about her guts.

She was pale and round and about eighteen. A profusion of Arab silver ornaments hung at her wrists and round her neck, giving her a barbaric look she would never have had without them.

'Swan always dumps my schemes,' she said, turning to me. 'But I don't care, I'm just going to go right ahead and start studying.'

At that moment the Chinese boys came by, leading the Pekingeses. Esther stopped them and asked what the little dogs had had to eat.

'Have pay he plenty chickung, plenty rice,' one of the boys answered.

The Pekingeses danced about like griffins and lifted their paws. It seemed as if they understood the pidgin-English and were asking for more food.

'I don't believe the poor darlings have had nearly enough,' said Esther, kneeling down and gathering them into a pen made by her arms. They whimpered and yapped very plaintively and she became convinced that they had had no food at all. She turned angrily to the boys. 'I all time talky you must pay plenty chow. What for no can do?'

The boys looked at each other despairingly, knowingly; as if they were exchanging glances before a lunatic.

'Missy; have pay plenty plenty chow,' they chorused wearily.

'Maskee, go pay some more, chop chop,' Esther shouted, driving them along the deck in front of her.

They looked over their shoulders with disgruntled faces, like Adam and Eve being turned out of the Garden of Eden in an old engraving.

The discussion about Oxford began again. I went on with my drawing until Rex came up with his red-haired tutor.

'Say, Bob, what do you think about me going to Oxford?' Esther asked.

'The idea's all right if you can get in,' the tutor answered coolly. He had broad shoulders, a smooth, taut skin and long legs. The sort of body everyone admires.

Esther and Rex treated him with respect and familiarity. He must have been a satisfying person to have in such a capricious household. Rex always obeyed him, and he was careful never to order Esther to do anything.

I shut my paint-box and got up to go, leaving them all still talking about Esther's future.

After this we met every day on the deck and played games or sat together. I felt lonely when they left the ship at Hong Kong.

The last time I saw them was in the hotel at Kowloon. They were sitting on their luggage, grouped round the lift, waiting impatiently to go up to their suite. As usual, some mistake had been made and no rooms were booked.

Bob, looking taller and saner than ever, was taking the situation in hand.

I thought of them muddling round the world year after year in the yacht, with the deaf, French mother, the Pekingeses and the lacquer saloon. I wondered if the children would ever escape.

At last we were in China. We took the mountain-railway up the Peak and had lunch at the top.

Fleming had come with us. After we had eaten, the longing grew in me to be alone. I said that I was going for a walk. Paul ran after me, annoyed, afraid that something might happen to me. I promised to be back in half an hour.

We had left the heat of the tropics. I walked along the mountain paths. The even, damp warmth was like spring. The wind blew gently, breaking up the reflected sunlight which glistened on the bays and inlets far below.

Feeling full of happiness, I began to run along the tarred path. When I was tired I lay down in the grass, under an aromatic bush on the edge of a precipice. I shut my eyes.

When I opened them again an English soldier in khaki shirt and trousers stood over me.

'You ought to be careful,' he said comfortably, 'or you'll be rolling over the edge.'

He was dark and stocky, and the white cigarette in his mouth made his face look dirty.

'Oh, I wasn't asleep,' I said. 'I was just resting.'

'I sometimes lie out here myself,' he added chattily. 'I'm just off duty.'

He sat down beside me and puffed at his cigarette.

'You new here?' he asked.

'I'm just passing through; I'm going to Shanghai to-morrow,' I answered.

'Oh, then it's sort of novel to you. I've been here six months and I'm fed up with it.'

'But it's a lovely place,' I said. 'I think I'd like to live here.'

'It's all right to look at, but what is there to do? In the evening I go and have a drink and then come back to bed. I don't like them Chinese girls.'

'What are they like?' I asked, trying to appear experienced and curious.

He gave me a rather derisive glance.

'What do you want to know for? You keep away from them; all they want is your money.'

'Have you been with them much?' I persisted.

'No bloody fear. Take my tip and leave them alone, else you'll come away with more than you bargained for.'

And with this hygienic warning he got up and walked away. I saw him enter the parched-looking barrack square where two figures in dirty singlets were playing an unending game of tennis.

I had been away for more than half an hour. I ran back to the hotel and was greeted with black looks from Paul and Fleming. We went down the mountain in silence, but once in the streets, we could no longer sulk. We were brought together by the onslaughts of the shopkeepers.

They wheedled and were insolent; flattering and insulting until they had dazed us. I found myself buying a little gourd-shaped ivory bottle. It had two compartments, and one of them still held the ghost of a strange scent. It was like the fragrance from someone's hair, mixed with cinnamon.

I held it in my hand, stroking its worn, yellow sides with my fingers, as the launch took us back to the ship.

When night came a hundred thousand lights broke out all over the mountain.

I thought of the soldier drinking all alone, and having nothing to do with the Chinese girls.

Now that the fantastic family had gone, the ship seemed empty. I had taken Rex's address in America, but I knew that I would never write and that I would never hear of them again.

Paul and I grew feverish over our packing. It was finished at last on the day we steamed up the river. The water was covered with boats. Junks with coloured sails and great eyes painted on their bows were stuck together with sampans and iron-plated steamers, like a pudding of small sago and large tapioca.

The Bund glistened through the masts and funnels. The buildings reminded me of New York, which I had never seen. There were no skyscrapers, only an uneven terrace of buildings looking huge and majestic in the sun.

The wind raced coldly up the legs of my new grey flannel trousers, and made stars tingle in my eyes.

I wiped them and saw my father waiting on the quay to meet us. He looked up and smiled calmly.

He shepherded us through the Customs House and led us to the waiting car.

'There's something important to see to at the office but I shall be back to lunch,' he said. Then he turned to the chauffeur.

'Take young master home; by-and-by come catchy me Shanghai Club,' he ordered.

The pidgin-English sounded fresh and amusing. I was glad that we were going to be alone. I wanted to drink everything in.

The streets were covered with a moving throng of black and light blue figures. Over their heads swung the most elaborate shop-signs I had ever seen. Black, eel-like characters crawled down boards heavy with red and gold carving. Banners with fretted edges fluttered and bellied in the wind.

The houses were a dreary mixture of Western and Eastern styles, but the smells were almost pure Chinese. Once when we stopped near a cook-shop I caught the most complex smell of roasted meat and vegetables.

Looking up I saw a row of glistening ducks. They were varnished with some rich brown sauce.

We nearly ran down a rickshaw coolie and had to stop again. He stood grinning and swearing at us, spreading waves of garlic round him.

We passed through the city and the scene changed. First came the naked race-course, where the grandstand looked like a box empty of chocolates, but still trimmed with the frilly papers. Then there were groups of mid-Victorian houses in red and grey brick with wide, arched verandas. They bore a disreputable look and were being jostled by modern shops. These gave way to Mexican cream stucco with iron grilles, and to sash-windowed 'Georgian' buildings. This was the newer area of private houses. Towering above them here and there were pompous, dignified blocks of flats.

We approached one of these down a long avenue of budding trees. The building was set almost in the country, with the remains of a tiny Chinese village not far away.

The baroque, barley-sugar columns of the porch reminded me of Oxford. I went quickly into the hall and found myself walking on deep blue carpets. Electric candelabra glowed softly against the rough-surfaced walls. Large Botticelli reproductions in silvered frames hung over the two fringed and tasselled Knole settees.

Realizing that this was what was known as 'quiet, good taste,' I made hurriedly for the dull bronze lift where a Chinese admiral took us to the top floor. As is the custom in the East, my father's name on a brass plate was fixed to the front door. We rang the bell and waited. A Chinese Boy opened it and gave us a wide, mechanical, ballerina's smile.

We soon learnt that he was deaf. When we spoke he bent forward, cupping his ear with his hand, saying, 'No can hear, young master.'

The hall was warm and dark, lit only by an elaborate

Chinese lantern. The Boy took our coats and led us into the drawing-room. It was long and low, running the whole length of the building. There were three tall windows at one end and a wide veranda at the other. Persian rugs and an enormous bearskin covered the polished floor, while Korean cabinets and black-wood stands for china stood against the wall. Worn leather armchairs with blue velvet cushions in the seats were grouped round the open stone fireplace.

It was a pleasant room, although a discriminating person would have found much to change. I remembered things I had known as a child; these set me thinking of my mother. I wondered how she would have arranged the room if she had been alive. After my grandfather's dull Sussex rooms, I enjoyed the brilliant surfaces and rich colours.

The Boy was holding open the bedroom door, expecting me to go in.

He had arranged daffodils on the dressing-table in an old pointed champagne-glass of about 1820. I looked out of the window and stepped back at once. The height was alarming. Half the city lay in front of me. The Boy saw me and laughed. 'Young master no liky; he velly fear.'

I turned away angrily and waited until he had taken himself off; then I went into the adjoining bathroom. It was tiled in black and white, and the closet flushed with a smooth, American, sucking sound.

I wanted to explore the flat. I found many of the books and pictures I had known, and in my father's bedroom I recognized the old dressing-case which had once been full of Victorian jewellery. I wondered if it was so, still. I knelt down to see if I could open it, hoping that my father would not return, but before I could undo the leather straps I heard his voice in the hall.

We sat down to lunch at once, as it was late. I noticed that my father poured his second glass of sherry into his soup. I remembered how surprised I had been when I first saw him do it. I wondered if it would be thought rude if I did the same when next I went out to lunch. I wanted to try sherry in my soup. I thought how clever the Chinese cook must be, to make everything taste so delicious.

After lunch, my father went back to his office again, and Paul, to my secret joy, decided to go for a walk. I was alone in the flat. I ran into my father's room and knelt down again to try to open the dressing-case. It was not locked; I only had to unbuckle the perished leather straps.

I pushed up the lid and saw the small boxes still nestling in the space between the ivory brushes and the tarnished silver-topped bottles.

I began to open them with excited fingers. First I discovered two wide, hollow, gold bracelets decorated with the Gothic tracery of 1840. Then from a little, domed ring-box I took a fleur-de-lis made of fire-opals. It looked like a pope's ring, I thought. I put it on, and each petal rippled shot colours when I moved. There were lugubrious, chaste ornaments of jet and pearl for mourning; a spiky coral necklace for a young girl; lumps of turquoise strung together on a gold chain; garnet earrings that would hang in tassels almost to your shoulders; silver buttons for a dress, each one enamelled with a different reptile; and a belt of silver cupids and clouds to fit round a wasp-waist. It was too small for me by two cupids and one cloud.

In a long flat box I found mother-of-pearl and tortoise-shell lorgnons and painted fans that breathed out smells of dust and women and scent.

There were double perfume bottles in jagged blue and amber glass, and tiny vinaigrettes with pieces of withered aromatic sponge still imprisoned behind golden grills. There was a card-case of cut-velvet and another of gold wire, which held two glossy cards engraved with the name 'Miss Sturtevant' in lines as delicate as pin-scratches.

At the very bottom of the case I found three daguerreo-types, a miniature, and a round silver disc bearing this inscription:

'Persevere to higher attainments.'
Awarded to WM PITT DENTON, Dec. 31, 1838.
Fourth Prize. Chauncy Hall School.
'Industry secures its reward.'

Round the edge was a pretty, chased border. I looked at the miniature next. It was of a little boy in a broad white collar and a dark green suit with large buttons. He held a little whip in his hand, and his head was framed in purple-grey storm-clouds.

Against the painting, the daguerreotypes looked sordid and natural. The baby girl had a long-suffering expression, as if she had already given up hope; the young man seemed nervous and supercilious, while the older one looked pouchy and dissipated.

I shut them up, preferring the little boy with the romantic whip and the stormy sky.

I put everything away and went into the drawing-room. There was a radio-gramophone in one corner. I switched it on, not bothering to read the name of the record already there. I knew that it was old by the way it softly grated and scraped before the tune began.

I moved into the kitchen, which I had not seen yet. Through the buzzing of the refrigerator I heard snatches of the song: 'Dream awhile, scheme awhile, we're sure to find, happiness and I guess, all those things you've always –'

I was suddenly filled with depression. I looked out of the window and felt very lonely. The tune was finishing. 'Diamond bracelets, Woolworth doesn't sell, Baby. Till that lucky day you know darn well, Baby, I can't give you anything but Love.'

The jazz-music had worked on me. I looked about me

rather hopelessly; then went back into the drawing-room and tried to comfort myself with tea.

My father had four people to dinner that night. There was an American with his journalist wife and an Englishman with his pretty, fat fiancée.

I got more and more melancholy as they sat drinking cocktails. I hated the way the anchovies, curled up on rounds of hard-boiled eggs, disappeared down their throats. They seemed very worldly and middle-aged to me.

I was put next to the American woman at the table. She started a conversation on the American accent.

'We Americans,' she said, 'pronounce fertile to rhyme with turtle. English people tell me this is quite wrong, but I like the sound of it, don't you?'

But before I could answer she began chanting to herself, 'Myrtle, the fertile turtle, undid her kirtle – ' She stopped to think; then said, 'the only other word to rhyme I know is "hurtle" and I can't fit that in.' She called across to her husband, 'John, can you help me with my new poem? It begins, "Myrtle, the fertile turtle, undid her kirtle – " after that I'm stuck. Can you work in "hurtle" any place?'

Everyone laughed and I felt my face turning red. She saw it and held up her hand, saying through her laughter, 'Stop, Denton's blushing.' Which made me hate her for the rest of the evening.

Part Three

CHAPTER 16

THE next day Paul went with my father to his office. I was alone in the flat in the morning and the early afternoon. I loved the feeling that swiftly settled down on me as the front door clicked behind them. With the servants shut away through double doors, I had every room to myself. The things seemed to be living for me specially. I touched the furniture and china and looked into every cupboard. Hidden behind jars and cracked basins on the top shelf in the kitchen I found two open-work Worcester baskets and two old powder-blue jugs. I took them down and studied them greedily; then I washed them and polished them and put them in my room.

The stillness in the flat seemed enchanted. The noises from the ground below came up as if filtered through water.

When Paul came back, we went to see friends of my father's who wanted to meet us. In the days that followed, while drinking tea or awkwardly sipping sherry, which I hated, I was finding out which people I liked myself. Soon Paul and I each had different sets of friends.

On Sunday we went for a long walk in the country. We collected at the Barbours' house and set off in pairs along the narrow paths through the smooth, bare fields. There were four Barbour girls. Margot, the oldest, walked with a man who wore a dreary-looking signet ring and was related to Hall Caine or Marie Corelli or Rider Haggard – I can't remember which. It was someone of that period. He talked in a fluting voice about history and infuriated us by saying that our ancestors in feudal times were probably villains. The only other man was tall and had a flat, teddy-bear's nose and a name that sounded like Jonquil.

The trees were sprouting with feathery, sickly green. Harsh dry bamboos bristled round the curling grey-black roofs of the villages. The yellow dogs that came, snarling and yapping, to meet us, had no part in the spring. They must have been born old and diseased. I never saw a puppy. The peasants, worn down with exposure like their bleached blue cotton clothes, stared at us with a sort of animal dignity. They were like cows, who look through you cynically. They went on ladling human manure out of huge earthenware crocks. To do this they used wooden buckets fixed to the ends of long bamboo poles. The crocks themselves were half sunken in the ground, so that when you came on them they almost looked like wells or springs; but instead of water, a soft, uneasy mass of half-caked dung rose and fell as great bubbles of gas lazily pushed their way up to the air. There was a singing too from the bubbles, and a liquid plop when they burst. I watched them for as long as I dared: there was something strange and awesome about the sleeping masses of disgustingness.

When we got back to the house at last, we found Mrs Barbour by the fire in the library with an enormous tea spread on little tables round about her.

I slipped into a deep corner of the shabby Chesterfield and lay back. I was tired and the wind had made my face hot and dry. Someone passed me bread-and-butter and I spread it thickly with quince jam.

I set out to find an American woman who had been one of my mother's friends. I had her address in the French Concession, but it was evening before I found the house. It stood on the edge of a wide waterway, the farthest limit of the settlement.

I walked in at the white, English park gates. A great figure loomed out of the dripping evergreens in front of me. I went up to it and saw that it was a huge granite image, flat and broad like one of the monoliths of Stonehenge. Lions and horses appeared between the trees as I got nearer to the house. The lions wore agonized looks, their mouths were torn wide open and their tongues lolled out.

I felt nervous as I rang the bell. Nobody would know me; I had only been seen before as a small child. The Boy took my name and left me in the Edwardian Gothic hall while he went to find Mrs Fielding.

After some minutes she came down the stairs, arching her neck and smiling encouragingly towards me. 'Yes, who is it?' she asked gracefully, in bewilderment, as if she were speaking into a telephone.

'I'm Denton Welch,' I said doubtfully. She took both my hands and led me into the drawing-room, which looked like a vague, faded water-colour in the dying light. We passed through this into the dim conservatory. There were no flowers here and it was cold. A white blot lay on the floor in front of the wicker chairs.

They creaked as we sat down; the white blot lifted its head and I saw that it was a Persian cat. Little ripples of cold came through the glass from the blue garden. We were silent after the first exchanges, searching for things to say, but not feverishly. The stillness was broken by Mrs Fielding's youngest daughter, who was my own age, but mentally defective. She came slowly into the room, fixing me with her moony, dark, animal's eyes. She held out her hand and lifted her smooth white face.

'Ruth, this is Denton Welch,' Mrs Fielding explained.

She sat down beside me and lifted the white cat into her lap. We did not move until nearly dinner-time when I got up to go. Mrs Fielding's husband and her two other daughters had still not come in, so I was asked to lunch the following Wednesday to meet them.

As I passed the stone giant and the animals again, on my way out, I knew that I would like these new friends.

When Wednesday came I dressed carefully, putting on my grey flannel suit. It was the first time I had been asked out to lunch alone. I looked in the glass anxiously; I wanted to look nice. I had borrowed Paul's razor to make sure that my face would be smooth.

The family were in the garden when I arrived. The lunch-table had been spread under the trees and the sun shone through the damp air, making things look pearly. I was introduced to Mr Fielding, who looked up at me through dark glasses. A Panama hat perched on his head like a bird. I wondered at all these precautions against the gentle sun.

'And this is Elaine,' said Mrs Fielding, leading me towards her second daughter, who was lying on some rugs. She drew herself up until she knelt, then she held out her hand to me. She had a long white neck and red springy hair, like a bracken-mattress, but she was not dressed in russet or sage-green drapery and did not really look like a Pre-Raphaelite.

'Vesta has gone into the house to get some more rugs and cushions, but she'll be out in a minute,' said Elaine, trying to make conversation.

I saw a figure coming across the lawn. It was small and graceful, but top-heavy from the load it was carrying. I went to take some of the things from her, and saw the pale, compact face and dark curls behind the pile of rugs.

'You're just as I imagined you'd be,' she said disconcertingly. 'And Muddy tells me you're crazy about old things. Have you bought anything yet?'

'Yes,' I answered. 'I bought an old ivory gourd-shaped scent bottle at Hong Kong, and I went down the town the other day and found a small wine-cup of very good Fukien ware or blanc-de-Chine as it is called.'

My nervousness must have made me sound pompous,

for her eyes opened wide as she said maliciously, 'Oh, you do know a lot; you're quite a connoisseur.'

I felt slapped, and was resentful. Surely she could see that I had not been trying to impress her. She smiled very charmingly and the Boys in their white gowns came sailing across the lawn, bearing a huge old-fashioned tureen of soup and rolls of bread in a pretty basket.

We sat down and began to drink the soup. It was delicious; pieces of pimento swam about in it like goldfish.

Next came a shining chafing-dish and small plates heaped with raw food. I watched Mrs Fielding as they were placed before her. She lit a match and held it under the chafing-dish until a fragile mauve flame sprang up; then she melted a square of butter in the dish and sprinkled tender pink prawns over it, adding, when they began to splutter, sherry and cream.

I had seldom enjoyed food so much. I stirred the coffee in my gold-lacquer cup. I did not like it. It made me feel anxious. I thought that the gold might be dissolving below the dark surface of the boiling liquid.

Vesta took me round the garden, while the others left the table to sink back on to the rugs and cushions again.

It was very English, with a tennis-court and tall trees and a thatched, decaying summer-house where insects lived. The only foreign note was a small, round swimming-bath. It was empty and dead leaves chased each other round the sloping sides; but Vesta said that I must come and swim in a month's time when it would be filled.

We went into the house and she took me upstairs to her own sitting-room to show me her treasures.

'Some of these were wedding-presents,' she said as she put them before me. The remark startled me. I had not realized that she was married.

'Bob ought to be in any time now,' she went on. 'He had to stay down town to see some other architect.'

I heard tyres on the gravel as she spoke.

'Why, that's him,' she cried. She left me and ran down the stairs. When she came back again she had with her a tall good-looking man, quite fifteen years older than herself. His face was soft and kind and just about to crease into middle-age.

'Bob, this is Denton,' she said.

He held out a big hand and squeezed mine painfully. He clearly had nothing to say.

'I'd better go down and have my tiffin,' he got out at last. We were left alone again.

'Bob's very shy,' Vesta explained. 'But you'll like him when you know him.' I murmured something, but she was still talking in a mournful, far-off way.

'We live here because I told him that I would not marry him if I had to leave the family. I just couldn't bear it.' There was a silence, and when she spoke again her voice was even more distant. 'We were married in the garden – under the trees.'

And before I knew it I found myself stupidly saying, 'I hope the weather was fine.'

I began to go to the Fieldings' house regularly. Vesta took me with her to the Russian dressmaker's, where I watched her try on a half-finished crimson dress. I rubbed a little snippet of the cloth between my fingers.

'It is Peau d'Ange, angel's skin, Monsieur,' said the dressmaker. She had a black down on her upper lip and smelt of armpits and musk. As Vesta turned in front of the glass she crouched down and darted at her, gashing the dress with her blue chalk and pinning expertly.

I was repelled and fascinated. The room almost smelt of skill and despair and overwork. When at last we left, the air in the street had never seemed fresher.

Vesta also asked me to chaperon her when she went to her Hungarian 'cello master. She had only just begun to learn and was afraid, from his behaviour, that he had designs on her.

From the depths of the cheap, luxurious chair where I had been placed, I watched as carefully as I could.

He seemed impatient and irritated, frequently giving that quick, exasperated smile which is so insolent.

I supposed that he was trying to punish her for her prudery and caution in bringing me. He seemed puzzled by her.

When the lesson was over we ran over the pavement and jumped into the car. As it drove away we laughed and joked until we had recovered the self-respect his contempt had stolen from us.

'Never go there again,' I said. 'He's awful and his mouth's full of gold teeth.'

'I shuddered all over when he put his hairy hand on top of mine and tried to show me how to hold the bow,' Vesta added.

I suddenly had an idea. Perhaps he was giving value for money. He might think that the only reason a young woman had 'cello lessons was that she could be alone with a male for two or three hours every week.

I told Vesta, and we laughed and laughed and thought more kindly of him.

CHAPTER 17

'WOULD you like to go into the Interior?' my father asked me one night at dinner. As I was too surprised to answer he went on, 'A friend of mine is going up to Kaifeng Fu on business. He used to be a Consul and speaks Chinese well. He says he'd like to take you round. All the dealers go up there to buy bronzes and china.'

I suddenly felt very excited; I might never have this chance again.

'I should like to go very much,' I said, 'When does he want to start?'

'The day after to-morrow,' my father answered, 'so that he can get back before the hot weather begins.'

'Will I need any new clothes?' I asked.

'I shouldn't think so. You'll be back before the end of May. After dinner you'd better decide what you want to pack; then if you need anything more you can buy it to-morrow.'

When the meal was over I left the table and hurried into my bedroom. Soon the bed was covered with clothes. Before I went to sleep that night I wrote down 'socks and white shirts' on a scrap of paper.

I went into the town with my father the next morning, and we bought cotton shirts with wide collars and socks of beautiful raw silk. In case the weather grew hot before I returned, we bought khaki shorts and a soft, floppy khaki hat lined with red, against the sun.

In the afternoon I walked to the Fieldings' house and told them that I was going to Kai-feng Fu. Elaine said that I must keep a diary, and Vesta told me to buy her a Buddhist head in stone, cast-iron or bronze; if I could find one.

I felt very uncomfortable inside as we drove to the quay. I had never seen this Mr Butler before. I wondered what he would be like. My mental pictures shifted every moment from a delightful man to a horrible man and then back again; so that it was an anticlimax to be led across the deck and introduced to a mild, well-covered person, with crinkly hair and rather piggy eyes.

He was very assured and confident. He made my acquaintance lightly and then gave his attention to my father. He said that we would have to share a cabin as the boat was full. I hoped very much that he did not snore or have any peculiar tricks.

Before my father left he pushed a hundred dollars into my hand and told me to buy 'curios' with it. I felt very grateful each time the notes crackled in my pocket. I longed to buy something with them.

The ship pushed out into the middle of the river and Mr Butler said, 'Come down and see our cabin.' His Boy had already unpacked our suitcases and was spreading our pyjamas neatly on the bunks. A damp, mournful breeze blew in at the porthole.

After the evening meal, when we had a strange dish of rice and olives, I went to bed, so that I should not have to undress in front of Mr Butler.

I heard him come in later. His braces gave a squeak and slither as he unbuttoned them and threw them over his shoulders, and his false teeth tinkled as he dropped them into the tumbler of water.

He did not snore; he only breathed deeply and let the air whistle out of his nostrils as if he were terribly unhappy.

Mr Butler and I lay in our bunks, drinking early-morning tea and talking. He looked rather tousled and his eyes were more pig-like than ever, but I had been impressed when he had carried on a long conversation with the Boy in Chinese. He told me that I must learn to speak it too.

A flat, cream face poked round the door. 'Young master, baff leady.' I jumped up and went out, taking my clothes with me so that I could dress in the bathroom.

I did nothing but talk to Mr Butler and watch the other passengers for the rest of the day.

The most picturesque was a bearded priest who, I suppose, was a Catholic missionary. He smiled broadly like a bear, his crucifix bounced against him as he walked, and he seemed to be always taking snuff, although he may only have been picking his nose.

There was a young man with string-coloured hair and a large mouth who walked round the deck, trying to catch the eye of an older woman. At last he was reduced to going up to her as she leant over the side looking into the water. When he spoke she gave him a small, narrow smile out of the corner of her mouth, and after that they walked round the deck together.

Once we passed a beautiful pagoda, half seen through the mist. I ran to get my book, but only succeeded in drawing something which looked like a centipede.

In the evening I tried to read the long poem on the American Civil War which Elaine had given me, but it was boring. I let it fall and thought about Nanking.

The streets were crowded and there were no tall buildings. There was nothing grand about the city except the crawling grey wall. I wanted to walk along the top of it, so I left the house and walked towards a great closed gate.

We were staying for a few days in Nanking with a friend of Mr Butler's.

At the side of the gate I found a rough path leading up an earth ramp which reached almost to the top of the wall. Across the path was some trodden-down barbed-wire. I stepped over it and walked on until I reached the wall. I saw then that it was made of huge blue-grey bricks.

From above, the upturned corners of the roofs looked like stalagmites on the untidy grey floor of a cave. Shallow grey hills surrounded the city.

I stood looking at the scene until I heard a shout and then footsteps running along the top of the wall. It was as if a piece of the picture had detached itself, for the man's clothes were of the same slate-blue, and to help the illusion they were in rags and tatters which blew about like clouds or smoke.

I suddenly realized that the man was some sort of soldier. He waved a rifle uncertainly as he ran. I held my hands above my head and then, ashamed of the stagey gesture, dropped them to my sides again and waited.

As he came up I saw that his face was distorted by rage. For a moment I was really frightened. He seemed about to ram me in the stomach with his rifle. Short, sneering Chinese words cascaded out of his mouth. I looked as innocent and stupid as possible.

'Me no savvy,' I said, walking backwards slowly and deliberately. He followed me in fitful jerks, charging and then stopping to shake his gun at me. When we came to the trampled barbed-wire he pointed to it and seemed to be asking how I could have neglected such a sign.

At last I was on the road again. I walked away, trembling slightly with anger and the reaction from my fear, I looked back once and saw the soldier's close-cropped, naked-looking head above the parapet of the wall. He looked like a helpless baby-vulture in a lonely nest.

When I got back to the house I found it empty. Mr Butler and his friend had gone out. There was only a little grey kitten in the drawing-room. It came towards me across the dark, highly polished floor, and we played together between the legs of the black-wood furniture and over the slippery silk backs of the chairs.

It rolled with its paws in the air and I saw that they were sticky with some oil. I took it up in my arms and went into the bathroom. I turned on the taps and held its paws under the water. It struggled, so I put it in the bath and let it paddle. A thrill of power went through me as I saw it trying to climb up the slithery sides. It mewed miserably and I began to feel happy and cruel. I was washing its paws for its own good.

The more it cried, the more fierce and excited I felt, until, suddenly, something bit into me. It dug deep down, making me feel raw.

I gathered the kitten up and kissed its wet fur as it trembled against me. I asked it for forgiveness and was very maudlin.

I was still in this queer, exalted mood when the Boy came in, carrying a long object which he said had been left by a dealer for Mr Butler. It was wrapped in puce satin. I untied the tapes and saw that it was a carved ivory tusk, stained tawny with opium. When I held it to my nose I could still smell the drug.

Carved on it were a deer and an Immortal walking through a forest of bats, peaches and flowers. I had never seen such a lovely carving before. I longed to have it for my own. I was still gazing at it when Mr Butler came in.

He looked at it priggishly, dismissing the smiling Immortal, the tender deer, the charming symbols.

'I hate stained ivory, don't you? Why can't they leave it alone?' He curled his lip in the way a dog sometimes does.

I did not know what to say. I thought nobody could miss such obvious beauty.

'I must say it's very well carved. I might have it if it wasn't artificially coloured.'

He tied the tusk up in its satin case and handed it back to the Boy saying:

'You talky your friend, me no can buy.'

'O do,' I called out. 'I want to buy it.'

The Boy looked at me rather insolently. 'Young master can pay eighty dollar?' he asked.

Mr Butler broke in. 'No, Boy, young master no wantchy; too dear.'

He turned to me. 'You don't want it. You won't have enough money left if you spend most of it now.'

The Boy went to the door, taking the vivid sheath with him, and I was not strong-minded enough to say anything more.

Mr Butler's friend arrived and we all had drinks. He was a youngish man with pale moustaches and sagging, rather pink eyelids. I was surprised to see that he poured out plain lime-juice for himself. He drank it slowly, letting it linger on his tongue in the way children do when they are pretending that cold, clear tea is wine.

He told us that the Consul had asked us to lunch the next day; then he settled down to a long string of questions about Shanghai. He had clearly been waiting a long time to ask them. Mr Butler did his best to answer everything. He had to talk about business, racing, parties, games, theatres, outrages and disturbances, and lastly gossip.

'I hear Mary Worth is going to marry Jim Butts. I suppose she knows how much he drinks,' his friend said gloomily, trying to draw something more out of Mr Butler.

'I have heard that they were engaged,' was all he got for an answer. Mr Butler shut his mouth very repressively and looked into the distance; but his friend was not to be put off. Something had been loosened in him. He went on talking in his flat voice, which now began to take on a faint, whining tone.

'Why, I don't drink anything at all now! You can see for yourself that I've only had lime-juice. She won't have me, but she doesn't seem to mind marrying a man who gets blind every night!'

I began to feel uncomfortable, especially as Mr Butler

implored his friend, with fierce glances, to stop this un-English display of feeling.

The lime-juice could not have done its work better if it had been the strongest gin. Mr Butler's friend burst into tears. I jumped up and made for the door, saying loudly that I was going to get ready for dinner.

I wanted to cry in sympathy as I sat on the bed in my room. It must be terrible, I thought, to be alone in Nan-king, drinking lime-juice, when the woman you wanted to marry has chosen some other drunkard instead.

I hoped fiercely that Mr Butler would comfort and calm his friend before dinner-time.

What an emotional day yesterday was! I thought, as I leant out of the window, and looked towards the low hills. The sun shone brightly. There was a monotonous creaking from a little reed hut below my window. I looked into the dark mouth of the doorway and saw a bare chest and arm moving backwards and forwards rhythmically. The man stopped his pumping and came and stood in the doorway. He saw me staring and lifted his head, so that the sun fell on his magnificent chest and arms, making them glisten. He was like no other China-man I had seen. He had not the immature, slight look. He was more like a Roman boxer or athlete, glistening with oil.

I left the window, and soon afterwards I heard him go back to his work. I wanted to watch his loose, powerful movements. I went into the garden and leant against the doorpost of the hut. He did not stop pumping. It was like watching a superb horse. I touched the muscles as they raced across his back under the elastic skin. He did not even look up. It was like judging the points of a beautiful dog.

The Consulate was perched on a near-by hill. Mr Butler and I walked to it. We arrived rather early and had to wait in the drawing-room. Along one wall was a

Coromandel screen. It was not red or black, but a rich, deep purple-brown, like the varnished skin of a date. The incised figures were painted with pure, delicate colours which age and dirt had made subtle.

Mr Butler became almost lyrical. 'It must be K'ang Hsi or Yung Cheng,' he said. 'I shouldn't think it's later.' He seemed much nicer – forgetting himself and thinking only of the screen.

The Consul and his wife found us still peering at it. They were quiet people – like Quakers or school teachers, I thought. They moved about, helping us to sherry and smoked salmon on small squares of toast. I wondered if the smoked salmon came from Siberia. I had not seen any in China before.

We began the meal with insipid lettuce soup which left a strange wild flavour in my mouth. The bitter taste somehow appealed to my mind, but not to my stomach. We ate bread, as dark and damp as gingerbread, with it. I wondered if this could be the black-bread given to prisoners; but decided that it was too delicious to be looked on as a punishment.

Mr Butler talked solidly to the Consul and did not think of leaving until after tea, when the sky was beginning to darken. They had spoken mostly of the recent troubles. Some of the Europeans in Nanking had been killed.

After listening to the Consul I carried a confused picture away; half-naked women ran down a hillside until they were caught by brutal soldiers who raped them and then plunged bayonets into their screaming bodies. I know that he told me nothing like this. It was only a picture of horror I painted to frighten myself.

We had been in Nanking for three days. Mr Butler had at last finished all that he wanted to do. He took me to the tomb of one of the Ming emperors. The vast courtyard, the grass growing on the roof, and the stone guardian lions gave me a weary feeling of desolation. I thought how suitable tombs always were. There was this – and there was the eighteenth-century pile of marble in Westminster Abbey, where trophies, coats of arms, busts and weeping cupids heaped up a pyramid of despair. How fit they both were for their purpose!

On the day that we left the city we drove to the station in the Pan-chen Lama's sulphur-yellow car. It had been lent to us by one of Mr Butler's Chinese friends, who had himself been given it when the Lama went back to Thibet.

It was conspicuous, and we were stared at, which pleased me; but we did not receive that reverence which a pope has a right to expect. I was disappointed that nobody prostrated himself.

Mr Butler's friend, whose guests we had been, was almost reduced to tears again when we said good-bye. He seemed to have enjoyed our visit and to hate the thought of being alone once more.

He looked very miserable as he gazed up at the carriage window, blinking his pink eyelids. I hoped that he would not go mad, drinking his lime-juice all alone, watching the little kitten dance over the shiny floors.

It was strange to ride in a *wagon-lit* – just like France or Switzerland; only when I looked more carefully did I notice the Oriental differences.

There were sinister newspaper parcels left under seats, and small jelly-fish of spittle quivering on the floors in the passages and compartments.

In the dining-car the waiters seemed to be serving dirty grey rags and string out of cracked, steaming pudding basins. I suppose it must have been some sort of spaghetti. We paid no attention to it, but waited till Boy had heated some of our tinned food.

I sat looking out of the window at the eternal hills and plains and cities of dried mud. Everything was the same, tawny, earth-brown. Even the city walls were of baked gold mud which made them look imitation, like the scenery at a searchlight tattoo.

Fields of poppies raged against the universal mud-colour. They were not only the scarlet that we see in English cornfields, but pink, white, mauve, crimson, and deep, dried-blood purple. They were as large as garden flowers.

'What are these flowers for?' I asked Mr Butler.

'For opium, of course,' he answered.

'But they're not allowed to sell opium now, I'm told. How can they still grow it openly like this?' I asked again.

'The art of turning a blind eye is practised with even greater virtuosity in the East than in the West.' He smiled as if he had said something very neat and witty.

CHAPTER 18

A YOUNG student who had been Mr Butler's secretary came to the station at Kai-feng Fu to meet us. He wore European clothes and horn-rimmed glasses. The clothes looked cheap and flimsy, and the glasses tough and strong.

He led us to a waiting car and we were soon hooting our way through the crowded alleys, where babies greedily sucked the breasts of their apathetic mothers; and women with shredded bamboo brushes scoured bright red, subtly graceful commodes. We passed more than one coffin. They were carried gaily on springing poles, by chanting coolies; the coffins looked like flat-bottomed, square-nosed boats. One was black and glistening – it reminded me of the blood-pudding I had once seen in a delicatessen shop; another was red – all red from tip to toe. Nothing could be gayer than a red lacquer coffin.

We passed through the city and drew up at a European house. It was almost the only one in the place and had been built for a missionary. But the missionary and his wife had both died, and the house was now lived in by a member of Mr Butler's firm.

He came to the door to meet us, and I saw that he was fat and seemingly jolly. It was not long before I learnt that he had once been a schoolmaster. He stood talking to Mr Butler in the hall while the Boy led me upstairs to my room. I hoped that I would not be given the bed where the missionary and his wife died. Everything had been taken over just as it was, Mr Butler had told me; except, of course, the corpses, which had been buried. I tried to make myself believe that they had both died in the big double bed in Mr Butler's room.

I noticed that everything was covered with a fine, sandy dust. I thought that the coolies and Boys must be very lazy. It was only after I had been outside that I realized how dry and full of dust the air was.

Li, the student, had been told to take me out and show me the sights, as Mr Butler and Roote wanted to talk business. He took me first to his university. It was housed in squat, grey Chinese buildings. They had the air of poverty and makeshift which hangs round expensive private schools in England.

Li left me in the library while he went in search of some of his friends. The books were placed in such a way that the whole large pavilion was divided into narrow cow-stalls. The librarian led me down the middle alley until we came to what were clearly the treasures of the collection. I expected to see beautiful calligraphy which I would not be able to appreciate fully because of my ignorance; but instead the librarian pulled down a wide, silk-bound copy of photographs called 'Peking the Beautiful.'

As he turned over the artistic matt-brown pictures he said lovingly and softly, 'This lovely book, Peking Beautiful!' And I was suddenly very touched and wanted to agree with everything he said; although I knew that the book was dull and commercial.

'Yes, it's a lovely book,' I said. I wanted to admire the university. That the girls played net-ball in serge knickers did not matter. I did not mind the youths who were screaming 'I'm singing in the rain' in their strange falsetto voices. Their snobbish love for worn-out Western dance tunes did not matter. Everybody was trying to enjoy life, refusing to be ground down. 'Peking the Beautiful' had served its purpose when it had made the librarian say, 'This lovely book, Peking Beautiful!'

Li came back and asked, 'Will Mr Welch like to come and see the Iron Pagoda; very old and beautiful?'

I noticed that Li and the librarian were always using

153

the words: beautiful, pretty, lovely. They pronounced them charmingly.

'I would like to see it very much,' I answered. 'But is it really made of iron?'

'That I cannot say, Mr Welch; it is always called the Iron Pagoda. I think it is eight hundred years old.'

It stood quite near, on a piece of waste ground covered with weeds. Tufts of grass grew on the curling roofs, and some of the bells under the eaves still tinkled dryly. It was delightful and fantastic. I wanted to go up inside, but Li said that it was too ruinous.

He took me back into the town, to his parents' house, where he lived with his young wife. We left the street and entered a quiet courtyard. His rooms led off this. They were dark, the fretted windows being covered with paper instead of glass. Across one end stretched a large bed, piled high with quilts. There were tall stools and a marble-topped table. Two elegant little cups and a tea-pot stood on the table.

Li poured out some of the cold tea and began to drink, but he would not offer me any. 'Not good, not good,' he said, and he tapped his stomach and waved his hand as if to explain that it was poison.

'I make you some new, proper tea.' He disappeared into the other room.

I went up to the table and looked into his half-empty cup. The liquid was a bright tawny-red. I had expected it to be green. Li afterwards explained that green tea, left standing, goes this almost metallic colour. 'It is then not good, not good at all, Mr Welch.'

I remembered that I had read of eighteenth-century ladies in England who feared that green tea was not wholesome.

'Why do you drink it yourself if it is not good?' I asked.

'Oh, I am used! my stomach is strong.' He drummed on it as if it were a tom-tom, and grinned.

While I drank the delicate fresh tea, Li told me about his wife, who was also at the university.

'She is very clever girl, Mr Welch, but too lazy. She want to stay at home and by-and-by have some babies; but I say "Modern Chinese Girl" must be up and doing.'

She came in soon after this. She was short and very young and she had had her black hair waved, which gave a Jewish twist to her Mongolian face. She was dressed in an abbreviated gym tunic and carried a hockey-stick. She said she was tired from the game, and did not seem to mind when Li suggested taking me to a restaurant, but did not include her in the invitation.

I did not want to go, being afraid of what I might be asked to eat. I tried quickly to find an excuse, but could think of nothing.

When we reached the eating-house Li took me upstairs. He said it was quieter and more select. We sat down at a high little table and Li chose the dishes carefully. It was only to be a light repast, he explained. Four o'clock in the afternoon was not the time for anything substantial.

I anxiously watched as the little plates were brought. Each one had some different cold and pickled vegetable piled on it. I began nervously to pick at them, tasting the delicate, watery flavour on my tongue. It seemed a fresh, airy sort of meal, but being afraid of it, I hated every mouthful.

Mr Butler and Mr Roote drank their cocktails that night out of Ch'ien-Lung cups. The missionary, of course, had kept no wine-glasses.

'I've got an awful one,' Mr Butler groaned. 'Why will the Chinese, in spite of all their refinement, insist on putting yellow next to pink? Just look at these blowsy great peonies sprawling on the jaundiced sides of my cup!'

I looked, and thought the arrangement very gay and pretty. Mr Roote brought out other porcelains and showed them to us. He treasured most a lavender-grey bowl, dabbed with livid purple birth-marks. 'The Chinese call this "Chün yao",' he said. 'They prize it so much that they set broken bits of it as jewels and ornaments.'

He flicked a pale, thin bowl with his fingers, making it ring. 'This is another type of Sung porcelain called Ying-ching or "shadow blue",' he explained to me. He let me hold it in my hands. It made me think of melted aquamarines spread like butter on creamy notepaper.

His face became intent and anxious as he undid the next box and lifted the lid.

'What do you think of these, Butler?' he asked, passing over a tray of small drab-coloured objects encrusted in some red powder.

'A man came to the house with them. He told me they were Han funeral jades, still covered with the cinnabar they were buried in.'

Mr Butler took one up and frowningly examined it. I saw that it was shaped like a curved fish. A dusting of brilliant powder fell from its dull, polished sides.

'They don't look at all right to me,' he said at last brutally. Mr Roote's fat face winced.

'Do you mean they're fakes?' he asked, allowing his mouth to gape stupidly.

'Yes, I'm afraid so,' Mr Butler answered.

'Well, are these any good? I bought them from the same man.' Mr. Roote unwrapped two black bowls and held them out. Their glaze was like a dark, wet road, spotted with silver oil.

Mr Butler shook his head and handed them back.

'You ought to have been warned; knowing how rare "oil-spot temmoku" is,' he said gravely.

Roote sat glumly chewing at his pipe. 'Never buy

from people who come to the door,' said Mr Butler with a certain amount of satisfaction.

Roote only gave a grunt for answer. He resented Mr Butler's smugness and his greater knowledge.

I said good night and went to bed, to escape the tense, gloomy atmosphere.

A bugle woke me. It was so unexpected that I jumped out of bed and ran to the window. I felt the soft, silky dust grating between the soles of my feet and the polished boards.

The dried-up garden looked like a landscape on the moon. Over the mud wall at the far end stood the bugler. He was dressed in soldier's uniform, with soft grey cap pulled down to the top of his slanting eyes.

When he looked up and saw me, he began to blow fiercely so that the bugle made obscene, tearing noises. His puffed-out cheeks went red and lent him for a few moments an almost English look. Then he spat violently, raking his throat from top to bottom, and walked off across the wide expanse of trodden mud, after giving me a last evil look.

'Foreigners are not very popular here,' Mr Butler told me at breakfast. 'So I don't think you ought to go out alone.'

My heart sank. I hated to be dependent on other people. They would never want to do what I wanted to do. I began to feel imprisoned. I took up the moth-eaten balls and the old tennis-racket which were lying in the hall, and went into the garden.

I hit the balls fiercely against the stable doors until I was too hot and unhappy to go on. I sat brooding on the steps. I might have been in Sydenham for all I could see – a European villa and a line of poplars; yet outside lay a Chinese city which I was longing to explore.

After lunch I decided that I could stand it no longer. Mr Butler and Mr Roote were still deep in their morning's discussion, so I let myself quickly out of the back gate and walked along the sandy lane which led into the country. Mr Butler could not mind my walking in the country, I thought.

Everything was still and silent, in an early-afternoon torpor. The only sound came from the stunted bushes which squeaked and grated linguistically as the wind passed through them. Pillars and scarves of dust and sand rose up from the ground, eddying and swirling themselves into flat sheets which hovered in the air. Harsh spears of grass stuck up through the sand. The soles of my shoes began to burn and I looked round vainly for some shady place. I enjoyed the dream-like stillness and wanted to stay out for as long as possible. I thought that if I walked on I might find a place. The road led towards the hills. Across the sandy plain the city walls stood up like cliffs. Turrets and bastions were ruined cottages, crumbling into the sea.

I walked on, fixing my eyes on a black speck some way in front of me. I wondered if it could be a cat crouching in the middle of the road; or perhaps it was a dark boulder.

As I drew nearer, a haze of flies suddenly lifted, and I saw that the object was not black but pink. The loathsome flies hovered angrily above it, buzzing like dynamos. I bent my head down to see what it was. I stared at it stupidly until my numbed senses suddenly awoke again. Then I jumped back, my throat quite dry and my stomach churning.

The thing was a human head. The nose and eyes had been eaten away and the black hair was caked and grey with dust. Odd white teeth stood up like ninepins in its dark, gaping mouth. Its cheeks and shrivelled lips were plastered black with dried blood, and I saw long, coarse hairs growing out of its ears.

Because it was so terrible my eyes had to return to it whenever I looked away. I stared into its raw eye-sockets until waves of sickness spread over me. Then I ran. The whole plain and the bare hills had suddenly become tinged with horror.

I found myself between high banks. I would soon be coming to a village. There were signs of cultivation. When the first cur barked, I turned and ran back the way I had come. I did not know what to do. I would have to pass the head again.

I tried to avoid it by making for the city walls across the pathless sand. My feet sank in, and my shoes became full and heavy. My only idea was to get back to the house.

Tall rank grass grew in the shadow of the wall. It was dry and sharp as knives. I pushed through it, looking up at the towering cliff for a gate or steps to climb. Nothing else seemed to be alive except the insects. I could only hear their buzzing and the slap of them when they hit the wall.

There was no gate. I began to feel desperate. I ran towards a bastion, wondering if I could climb up to it in any way. I knew that I could not.

Suddenly I realized with a violent shock of relief that the house was not inside the walls at all. My feeling was too intense to be pleasant. I sank down on to the ground, feeling very tired. I lay there, gazing through the forest of grass, pulling the petals from a pale wild flower.

'Un peu, beaucoup, passionnément, pas de tout.' I murmured automatically the words someone else's French governess had taught me when I was small. I wondered if 'passionnément' was right. It sounded queer. The petals ran out at 'un peu'. The denuded flower-head in my hand suddenly reminded me of that other head covered with filthy flies. I would never know how that man died.

We went next day to an antique dealer's house. We walked through a serene, dilapidated courtyard to reach the first pavilion, where he received us. He and his assistants bowed, scraping their feet backwards and clasping their hands together in ceremonious fashion, and we returned the greeting more clumsily. Then cigars and cigarettes were brought, and tea. Each cup had a lid, and when I lifted mine I saw whole leaves swimming in the water like a school of fishes. They were pale green. Some had not yet uncurled. I watched them opening with pleasure, and I thought that we missed a lot in England by not leaving the tea-leaves in our cups. To watch them swirling and drifting is like watching the smoke from a cigarette. And what is smoking in the dark?

I was soon to learn to drink the tea through a narrow crack between cup and cover, so that the leaves were left at the bottom in a little pile like a wet autumn bonfire.

Having drunk my tea, I turned to look at the room. High black-wood stands stood against the walls, with bronze and porcelain things arranged on them. The dealer allowed us to examine them rather like a grandfather who, for peace and quiet, at last allows the children to take the best tea-set out of the cabinet.

Mr Butler chattered to him in Chinese and he answered, sometimes laughing strangely, as if he were God watching us from far away.

By the end of the morning Mr Butler was surrounded by Chou bronzes, T'ang grave figures and Sung porcelain. He had spent several thousand dollars and seemed quite flushed – like a stage-gambler. He saw me looking at a Ming blue and white artist's brush pot. It had a diaper of magical ducks hiding under lotus leaves.

'Do you want that?' he shouted rather drunkenly.

'Yes,' I answered. 'But it's ninety dollars.'

A long talk in Chinese followed. Without understanding a word, I could tell how urbane and insincere it was. The dealer turned to me and said something. Mr Butler grinned and interpreted.

'He says that, as he wants to please me, he will give it to the handsome youth; for he sees that you are a great favourite of mine!'

As he spoke, Butler underlined the words 'handsome youth' with irony, as though they were most inappropriate, and he finished his sentence with an enormous wink and leer aimed at me.

I flushed with pleasure and embarrassment as the dealer passed the brush pot to me. Before he put it in my hands he caressed it with a show of love; then he smacked his lips hungrily, as if he found it very delicious.

I held it tightly, fingering its cold, smooth sides. I wanted to concentrate on it. I left the others and stood by the ruinous carp tank in the courtyard. I heard laughter coming through the fretwork windows. They were amused that I wanted to be alone with my new possession.

On our way back I stayed too long looking at something in a shop and got separated from Mr Butler. I walked through the crowd rapidly, looking ahead to find him. I saw some Chinese students coming towards me. They were dressed in European clothes and walked with a certain swagger. As they drew nearer, one of them detached himself from the others and, crossing the road, walked straight into me, so that our heads, chests and knees buffeted together. Then he passed on swiftly while I was still too dazed to think. The next thing I heard was the guffaw of laughter from his friends when he rejoined them.

I pushed on, feeling hot and humiliated and furious.

'What's wrong with you?' Mr Butler asked when at last I found him, 'you look very queer.'

'I've been running. I thought I'd lost you,' I said. I found I could not tell him what the students had done.

CHAPTER 19

WE did not often have visitors, as there were few other white people in the city. Only once do I remember a Chinaman being asked to dine with us. He was old and venerable, with a straggling beard and weeping moustaches. His skin was very dry and withered so that he looked, in his long gown, like a valuable relic, a saint's bone, wrapped in a grey flowered satin case.

I showed him my brush pot, for he was a great connoisseur. He flicked it lightly with the long nail on his little finger and said, 'Ta Ming.' That is, Great Ming. I felt very satisfied.

It gave me a malicious pleasure too when he took one of Mr Butler's bronzes and scraped it with the same long nail. The false patina, made of wax, flaked off in little ruffles. Mr Roote could not hide his joy. His hurt pride was soothed. Someone else had bought a fake.

Mr Butler took me one hot afternoon to see the head of the missionaries, who also was a keen collector. We waited for the Bishop in a dark, lofty room where all the blinds were drawn down.

When he came in I was surprised to see that he was so small. He was like an ermine, with his white head poking from side to side and his creamy teeth showing in a smile.

'I should like to see the gold and bronze Han mirror I'm told you have, Bishop,' Mr Butler said.

The Bishop gave him a swift, rather hunted look.

'I'm afraid I've shipped it to the Metropolitan authorities and I expect they'll keep it; but even if they don't it's a very costly object, Mr Butler, very costly indeed.'

Mr Butler was ruffled by the suggestion that the mirror would be too expensive for him.

'I'm quite willing to pay for it if you have anything worth buying,' he broke out angrily.

The Bishop immediately began to soothe him. His accent became more sweet and nasal and Canadian.

'I'm sure you are, Mr Butler. I'm sure you are. I only thought I'd better warn you. The article is quite unique and has cost me a great deal of money.'

'Have you anything else to show us?' Mr Butler asked, still rather rudely. 'I'm told that all those carved reliefs from the Han tomb have also been sent to America,' he added with bitterness.

The Bishop did not look at us, but went to draw up one of the blinds.

'America is the only place that really appreciates things, so what can I do? I'd like to keep everything in China but it's impossible. Nobody wants the things,' he said.

There was an uncomfortable silence which might have lasted for some time if the Bishop's wife had not come in. She brought with her a refreshing, housekeeping flavour.

'Do you know, we've got a new food-safe that's just dandy. Some sort of chemical keeps it cold. You can't get ice here,' she explained. 'Before, we used to have to keep everything in a deep earth-well, but even then the butter turned to salad oil and the meat smelt to high heaven in no time.'

The Bishop frowned at her, and then gave her a nervous little smile to counteract the effect of the frown.

She turned to me. 'The Bishop's so taken up with his work and these Chinese antiques that he thinks it's just awful to talk about food,' she said comfortably, as if she were describing her child's hobbies.

Roote had a letter one morning from a friend of his who was coming to Kai-feng to buy bronzes for a

European museum. The friend was a famous expert on Chinese art. A room was prepared and we waited, looking forward to his visit. Two days later, just as we were sitting down to lunch, he arrived.

A grey, cadaverous man with parrot's beak nose and spiky, scarecrow fingers came into the dining-room. He was smiling, and talking rapidly with a Scandinavian accent.

'You are very good to have me. I am so pleased to be here. I must wash before I eat.'

He disappeared and came back a few minutes later, rubbing his hands together in the way that is supposed to be Jewish.

I found myself listening to everything he said and wanting to hear more. I tried to spend most of my time with him.

Every morning I would watch him as he sat in the window-seat cataloguing the things he had bought the day before. He had collected for many famous people and he would tell me stories of their meanness, greediness, and ignorance. But he would never calumniate his royal customers. They were always charming, simple and unpretentious.

He had nothing good to say about his wife.

'She is a whore, she is nothing but a whore!' he would shout. 'I have left her in Peking where she can go to the devil. I've given up bothering. All Russians are the same – no good, and full of sex. She would go to bed with her own rickshaw coolie and he'd be too good for her. Now she drinks whisky all day and you should see her face! It is dull purple, like a birth-mark, and her teeth are decaying. God preserve me from disgusting women, there's nothing worse in this world.'

As if to wash away the thought of disgusting women he would bend over the piece of bronze he was holding and murmur something extravagant about its beauty as he rubbed his dry lips over it. He would liken its surface to the most secret things, and when I turned away in embarrassment he would laugh and ask me what I knew about women. I suddenly thought of the awful time when a prostitute walked behind me in Hyde Park, saying 'Hullo darling.' I had never been able to decide whether she were serious or jeering.

Sometimes he would tell me about the shady tricks he had played on people. He never showed a trace of shame.

'I dropped the mirror on the floor. It was one of those thin Han ones – very brittle. It broke into five pieces. I took it to a man in Peking who stuck it together and covered the cracks with patina scrapings mixed with wax. When he had finished it was almost impossible to tell that it had been broken. I sold it to a French naval officer who was very delighted with it.'

He did not repress the things that most people do. He seemed to find no difficulty in talking about them.

'My hands and feet were covered with some skin disease. They were all swollen up and peeling. I had to go about covered in bandages. Even my daughter made a face when she came into the room!'

The dealers' attitude towards him was interesting to watch. They seemed to acknowledge that he was an expert, but that did not stop them from testing him.

One morning we were all puzzled by an extraordinary thing: a bronze horse standing on a column which in turn was fastened to a wide, round base. Nobody knew what it was. We all waited to see what he would say.

'It is obviously made of ancient bronze,' he began slowly. The dealer and his assistants waited quietly. I think they were hoping that he was going to say something silly. He was turning it round in his skeleton fingers. 'I do not know what it can be,' he muttered. Then his face lighted up excitedly. 'I've got it, I've got it. It's a wheel-shaft, a dish and the ornament off an incense-burner all joined together.'

A sigh went up from the dealer. There were no

outraged denials; only smiles and nods. The bronze was taken away to be kept for someone less astute.

The dealer asked us all to lunch in celebration of the morning's business.

In the courtyard of the restaurant was a tank of fishes. They were the colour of black pearls and their flesh seemed soft and plushy, like moleskin. We went into a little private room where servants dipped towels into boiling scented water and then, after wringing them out, held them to our faces. The scent was lavender, reminding me of bread-and-butter and unbecoming English shoes. When our faces dried they looked shiny and tight.

We were led into the adjoining dining-room. A round table, covered with little dishes, almost filled it. There was much shuffling and politeness, and I found myself sitting next to the dealer.

The meal began with sweet rice soup. Then came a little procession of servants bearing dishes. Nothing was left long enough to be finished. We were only supposed to pick delicately and then pass on to something else. The dealer treated me charmingly. He found titbits for me and tossed them gracefully into my bowl, making noises at the same time to stimulate my appetite. He reminded me of a woman saying, 'Swoop, swoop, sup, sup, nicey, nicey!' to her lap-dog.

The only dish I found difficult to eat was the little minnows floating in gold syrup. As the dealer poised one of the dripping fish over my bowl I looked anxiously towards Mr Butler. I knew how rude it was to refuse. 'Eat it up!' was all he said sternly. 'You'll find it very delicious.'

There was no help from him, so I smiled and swallowed the fish whole. I felt its little tail scraping on the back of my throat, and then I tasted the sweetness which wrapped it round.

The meal finished with dry rice which everyone refused. I wanted to eat mine, to take away all the other rich tastes in my mouth.

After the meal, when we passed through the courtyard again, I saw that only two of the big, soft velvet fishes were left. I suddenly knew what had happened, but I turned to Mr Butler.

'Where are the other fishes?' I asked.

'Inside you and me,' he laughed.

I began to be tired by the wrangles and arguments about antiques. When I first came I thought that I could never hear too much about them. So I was pleased when Mr Butler told me that he had to make a journey to some coal-mines.

We started one hot morning. We travelled through the dusty landscape until the railway carriage became a heated metal tube. At one of the many stations where we halted, a ragged, middle-aged soldier scraped against my window and then turned round.

'*Parlez-vous français?*' he asked me.

'*Un peu,*' I answered warily, not wanting to be put to shame.

He must have known from this that I was English, for he said, 'I also speak English. I learn French, English in the Great War. I dig trenches for Allies.'

As he spoke the train began to move. He ran beside it and started to sing in his Chinese, alto voice, '*Enfants de la Patrie, le jour de gloire est arrivé!*'

He broke off suddenly, having reached the end of the platform. He stood there waving to me and smiling broadly. Just before he disappeared I saw him jerk his fingers up in a sexual sign which he must have learnt from British soldiers.

I sat back in the corner seat and thought how pleasant it must have been for him to be able to show off his European accomplishments.

When at last we arrived I saw a quiet body of people waiting on the platform. They looked like a large family party.

As the carriage settled after the final jar of brakes, the whole scene changed. Explosion after explosion tore the air. For a moment I was terrified. I thought that we were being attacked by bandits; then, as coloured streamers flew towards us and rude paper tongues were blown out by smiling faces, I felt reassured. No bandits had ever been known to behave so heartlessly; though I remembered that Claude Duval had danced with his victims.

Mr Butler bustled up to me saying, 'Don't look so frightened. The people from the mines have come to give us a welcome.'

Rockets were still bursting, making it almost impossible to talk. A brass band struck up as we stepped on to the platform, and an enormous shout went up from the crowd.

'Surely they can't be as fond as all this of Mr Butler!' I thought. I tried to imagine an English firm greeting one of its directors in this way.

Someone called Pepper bundled me into his car and drove off. Mr Butler had to ride in state with the manager and his wife. Pepper was already dressed in khaki shorts and topee, and I soon found that it was hotter here than at Kai-feng. I could see the sweat glistening at the roots of his little moustache. It looked like water seen through close-cropped grass.

He took me to his bungalow, and after we had both washed he led me across the compound to the bigger house, where we joined Mr Butler, the manager, and his wife for lunch.

To finish the meal we had strawberries. The manager ate them greedily. His eyes glistened and he reminded me of a lucky-pig charm, the sort that have two imitation stones for eyes.

We left the table, and I went to sit with his wife on the sofa. She astonished me by saying softly and quickly, 'We have to hide the chocolates, as John, my husband, likes them so much.' Then she deftly pulled up the lid of the music-stool and hissed, 'Take one.'

I put my hand in and fumbled, hoping that her husband had not seen or heard anything. He seemed to be busy, lighting his pipe.

The chocolate had a cream centre. I was sorry that I had not been able to choose one quietly and carefully.

Mrs Murray began to talk to me confidingly. She had no woman friend and wanted to gossip to someone.

'I shall have to go away in another month,' she said. 'It gets so hot here that the men like to go about with nothing on, and they don't want to have me about then. I should like to stay myself, but I don't think it's fair to them; so I'm going to the sea.'

Then she went back to the subject of her husband's greediness.

'I do wish John wouldn't eat so many strawberries. They're not good for him; but I've given up trying to interfere. When I told Cook to send only a few to table, John disgraced himself by eating most of them. I was terribly ashamed, as we had two guests staying with us.'

It seemed indecent to be discussing her husband's greed in this way. I would rather have talked about his lust or any other vice. I was pleased when Mrs Murray suggested that we should go to the university and watch the students playing tennis.

The games were languid. The players seemed to be frightened of showing bad taste by any display of skill or energy. A racket was found for me and I reluctantly decided to play, fearing that the students would be insulted if I refused.

I hit the balls clumsily into the net, and my partner pursed his lips grimly as if he were determined to win in spite of me.

The stiff, ceremonious figures, hitting the white balls gently, made the game seem like some old, religious ritual.

CHAPTER 20

I SLEPT alone that night; in a bungalow some way from the others. Its owner, becoming very ill, had been taken to Shanghai. No one expected him to live.

Two soldiers were put to guard me, but when I saw them standing on each side of the door a tingle of fear ran through me. They looked poverty-stricken and desperate.

I shut the door behind me and stood in the long dark passage, smelling the strange, uninhabited, human smell. A lamp was burning in the sitting-room. I went in and began to look at the furniture and ornaments. Many things, when lifted up, showed typewritten labels stuck to their bases. 'Bought at X.' 'From N. tomb.' 'Given to me by Z.' The supposed date of the object would follow.

Most of them were too obvious to be called fakes. I wondered if the owner really believed his notices.

I began to explore the other rooms. A ghostly smell of liquor hung about the sideboard in the dining-room, and the dried sediment in the empty decanters reminded me of scabs on sores. I sat down in the armchair, which let out a dirty sigh of dust and tobacco-smoke.

I was fascinated by the fearful, shop-soiled feeling in the house. I was to be alone in it till morning. I went to look at the bed. From the ceiling, a grey cataract of mosquito-net fell round it, giving it an important, grim look.

The bathroom shelves and tables were ranged with medicine bottles. There was a sort of hum of colour as your eyes tried to take in all their labels at once. The bath was high and deep, with two yellow stains underneath the brass taps. In the far corner was a mahogany commode with squalid, worn steps of Axminster carpet.

I opened some of the bottles and tried the medicines;

then I undressed and stood up in the empty bath. I turned the water on and watched the brownish water splashing over my legs. When I sat down, the bath still felt cold through the warm water.

The lamp's wick burnt straight in the stillness. It elongated itself until I thought that it needed trimming. The silence was so strong that I hated the noises I made, yet I found myself splashing unnecessarily in an effort to reassure myself.

Suddenly I heard what seemed to be a deep, snorting intake of breath. I jumped up, and in desperation pulled the net curtain away from the window. There, hideously smudged and flattened against the glass, was the face of one of the soldiers. He seemed to be in a trance, for he did not move until his eyes suddenly focused on my naked body. Then he jumped back grinning, more terrified than I was.

I rubbed the cold beads and rivulets off me and ran into the bedroom, where I hid under the mosquito-net and the bed-clothes.

I had a long, troubled night, and felt ill when the Boy woke me in the morning with an unappetizing breakfast on a tray. The house seemed to have tainted the marmalade and tepid eggs and greasy coffee.

When I took off my pyjama jacket I noticed a red rash on my arms and chest, but it did not seem important after my night of suppressed and cloudy fear.

I walked up to the manager's house and found Mrs Murray sitting on the verandah. I thought that I had better tell her about the rash.

'It's the strawberries,' she said triumphantly. 'They often give people a rash. You must come to my bedroom and I shall give you some medicine.'

She clearly enjoyed having someone to nurse. She led me to her room and filled a glass with water; then she threw some powder into it which began to fizz madly.

'Drink it before it stops bubbling!' she shouted.

I swallowed the bursting, pricking bubbles and then gulped for air. 'That'll do you good,' she said. 'Now you're to take these two aspirins and you're to lie down for the rest of the morning.'

I took the two pills and felt almost grateful for her fussiness. She made me lie back in the creaking wicker chaiselongue and settled down beside me with her needlework.

'You know, you remind me of my brother when he was your age,' she said. 'He had curly hair too.'

I moved my legs uncomfortably. 'He was a medical student and very good at games. His voice was just like yours – it didn't break properly till he was twenty.'

I did not answer. If I had at first felt uneasily flattered, I now felt insulted.

'Would you like a job up here?' she asked me suddenly.

This came as a complete surprise. 'I don't know anything about business,' I answered guardedly; knowing from the seriousness of her voice that I must protect myself.

'My husband says that there's room for someone like you in the Company,' she added, looking straight at me.

I turned away, confused. I thought of her life and the life of the dying man whose bungalow I was using. As if she had read my thoughts, she said, 'It's not bad up here really, you know.'

'But I've only come up with Mr Butler to see something of China,' I broke out. 'I never meant to stay. I'm interested in old things and painting – things of that sort.' I tried to explain.

'You'd have plenty of time for your hobbies,' she said soothingly. 'The country's thick with tombs, and you could paint in the afternoons.'

Then, seeing that I still refused to think seriously of her suggestion, she stuffed her work into her bag and got up. 'I must go and order lunch,' she said coldly. 'We have a guest coming, a missionary doctor from Yi-ching.'

I felt sorry that I had offended her. I hoped that nobody would bring up the subject again, but I was disappointed; towards the end of lunch the manager turned to me and said heartily, 'Well, Denton my boy, would you like to stay up here with us?'

I looked at Mr Butler, but as usual he gave no help. He just stared back.

'I'll probably have to go back to England soon,' I said weakly. As I spoke I was surprised to see a look almost of relief come into the manager's eyes.

'We might have found something for you if you'd wanted to stay,' he mumbled with his mouth full.

The idea suddenly came into my head that his wife wanted me to stay and had told him to find me a job; then I saw how conceited it was. Does everyone feel that he must be irresistible to other people? I thought.

I had hardly spoken to the young Canadian doctor yet. He came and sat next to me on the veranda, and for some moments we drank our coffee in silence. He had a very pleasant brown face with a little golden-red moustache. Golden-red hairs glistened on his arms and bare knees also.

'If you're just having a look around China, won't you pay us a visit at Yi-ching?' he asked in a powerful, sleepy voice. 'My wife would like to have a guest and it's a real Chinese town with hardly any foreigners.'

My mind seemed willing to take suggestions from him.

'I'd love to,' I said without any hesitation.

'I'll go right now and fix it with Mr Butler then, shall I?' he asked, getting up.

I saw him leaning on the back of the cane settee, taking his weight on his arms and hunching his shoulders. Mr Butler had to twist his neck round, which annoyed him.

'I've invited Denton to come and spend a night or two with us, and he wants to know if that's all right by you,' MacEwen began.

'He can do anything he likes as long as he's back here before I leave,' Mr Butler answered testily. After a moment's thought he added, 'Who's going to come back with him? He can't travel alone,'

'That makes it more difficult. I hadn't thought of that,' MacEwen said.

'Well, Li can go with him, if you can put him up as well.'

'Sure we can – that's fine. It's settled then, Denton,' MacEwen called to me.

So late that afternoon the three of us set out for Yiching. The train was very primitive. A double seat ran down the middle of the carriage and there were seats against the walls. They were all crowded with Chinese. Some were eating, some were sleeping; some were quarrelling, some were laughing; some were giving their babies suck or making love, and others were crying and praying.

MacEwen passed up and down the carriage talking to the ones he knew. Every now and then he would come back to me and tell me things about the countryside. Li sat haughtily, looking straight in front of him. He made me understand that he was a student and that these were cattle, mere grubbing peasants.

A man came in from another carriage. His eyes were searching. Someone must have told him that MacEwen was on the train. When he saw him he pushed quickly through the crowd, and after a hurried greeting pointed urgently to his ear. It was covered with dirty blood-stained bandages. MacEwen lifted them calmly and I turned away, not wanting to see the disease or wound.

They talked for some time; then the man thanked him and disappeared. MacEwen came back to his seat.

'What is wrong with him?' I asked, one part of me not wanting to know.

'He's got syphilis,' MacEwen said simply.

The word came like a sharp smack. I had only heard it at school, never outside, and there it had been used in

174

telling jokes. It had been something disgusting to laugh over; something sent to punish lecherous, 'dirty old men'. Now I was sitting next to someone who dealt with it every day.

I began to hate the people in the carriage. I wanted to escape. As soon as the train stopped I jumped out on to the baked-mud platform. I watched the other passengers scattering in all directions. I felt glad that I should never see any of them again.

We crossed the river in a great, squat ferry-boat. The lion-coloured city walls towered higher and higher above us as we drew nearer.

We passed through the gate and walked up the main street. There was a strange mixture of bustle and languor in the town. A cart drawn by bullocks lurched round a corner, the driver swearing hysterically, while under the shade of a tree a knife-grinder delicately whetted his tools and sang softly to himself.

'I've tried, till I'm blue in the face, to get that man to grind his razors our way,' MacEwen said, 'but he won't. He says his way is better, although it takes twice as long and the result is not nearly so sharp.'

We went over to the knife-grinder and watched him bending over the blade, rubbing it slowly on the stone. When he smiled and looked up, I saw with a shock that the bridge of his nose had collapsed. The flesh was blue and red and the nostrils trembled flabbily as he breathed out.

'Has he got syphilis too?' I asked, trying to lessen the horror by talking about it.

'Yes,' MacEwen answered.

'Will he die soon?' I asked eagerly.

'No; not for years. He'll give it to half a dozen others before he passes out, the old sod!' MacEwen laughed gaily.

When we arrived, the missionary compound was quite still. The front door of MacEwen's house was open. He ran up the steps, calling 'Mary.' Li and I waited in the garden until he reappeared.

'Mary's just getting everything ready for you boys. Li will have to sleep in the boxroom if he doesn't mind,' he said.

Li made a little noise in his throat which told me that he did mind. I looked at the grey tennis-court and at the high wall with weeds growing on the top. MacEwen watched me; then said quite suddenly:

'My predecessor and his wife were murdered as they ran across that tennis-court. They were strangled by anti-foreign demonstrators.'

He saw the effect of his words on my face, for he said, 'Don't bother about all these horrors. Come in and see Mary.'

We went up the steps and were greeted in the hall by a small dark woman with big eyes. I could see that her plans had been upset by our sudden arrival, but she said, 'Come right in,' brightly, and led us to the sitting-room.

It had just the atmosphere that I was needing. The walls were hung with a tiny sprigged paper and the curtains were made of a chintz that exactly matched; so that they gave the effect of the walls falling into folds. Glistening cream paint, pink cushions and soft green carpet completed the picture. It looked like something labelled 'Colonial' in a shiny American 'homelovers'' magazine. It was so clean that it seemed to cry out at our dirty intrusion.

'We ought to go and wash,' I said involuntarily.

'I expect you're feeling kind of travel-stained,' Mrs MacEwen said. 'Jim, show your friend where the bath is,' she added, turning to her husband.

He led me upstairs and opened a door. He turned the taps on and said, 'You get in first while I have a shave.'

He pulled his limp shirt over his head and stood over the basin, lathering his chin. I undressed hurriedly and got into the bath. I lay back and watched the silky muscles running over his back as he moved his arms, scrubbing vigorously at his face. He had a fine body, smooth and hard and rounded. I admired it enviously, wondering if I could make mine like it by doing exercises every morning. The sweat and steam made his shoulders glisten and I thought he looked like a marble statue.

He began to scrape his face and I heard the bristles crackling under the razor. I wondered if he had to shave twice a day.

'Give me the loofah and I'll scrub your back, Denton,' he said when he'd finished. I bent forwards and felt him rubbing my skin roughly. He ended by ducking my head under the water and holding it there for a moment. The water got into my eyes and nose. I felt annoyed. 'Now I guess you'll be clean all over,' he laughed.

Li was surveying the boxroom when I passed him in the passage. 'It is not fit, Mr Welch. It is not fit. I am student, not Chinese coolie,' he said.

I looked into the room. Like all the rest of the house, it was extremely neat and clean, but it was filled with boxes except for the corner where a bed had been put up. I thought of the dirt and untidiness of his own home, and said, 'You ought to be comfortable in that nice bed, Li.' As I said the words I realized that they sounded smug and patronizing. Li evidently did too, for he brushed past me without a word and disappeared down the stairs.

He was in a better, if still very dignified, mood when I found him later in the sitting-room. He was reading a book and greeted me with the words, 'What dynasty does King Lear belong to in your history, Mr Welch? Is he an ancestor of your present king?'

'Oh, no, I don't think he was a real person at all,' I answered.

He looked disappointed for a moment; then his face brightened. I could see him putting my answer down to ignorance. He began again.

'Does Bernard Shaw write in English as well as Irish?'

'So far as I know, he only writes in English,' I said.

'Yes?' His voice sounded scornful and patronizing. 'It says here that he is Irish, so I think it more likely that he writes in his native language. You have no doubt read translations.'

I knew that it would be useless to argue with him. I got up and went out on to the sinister tennis-court.

At breakfast the next morning we had buffalo milk on our porridge. I tried not to imagine it squirting from tingling, leathery udders. It reminded me of the soft rich mud round a pool where cattle go to drink.

Next came a plate of waffles. I was told to spread mine with butter and then to pour maple syrup over it from the tin shaped like a little log cabin. Just as I was finishing it, another plate of cakes, hot from the waffle-iron, was brought in. This happened four times. I put down my fork, beaten hopelessly.

'You don't eat much, Denton,' MacEwen said solemnly.

He went upstairs to put on his shoes and stockings before starting his work in the hospital. I watched his bare legs flashing as he ran up. I envied them as I had envied his arms and shoulders when he was shaving in the bathroom.

I was to go with him to the hospital for he wanted to show it to me. It was very near – just across the compound. It looked like a playful, rather sordid little villa, with its balconies of leafy and flowery cast-iron.

It was quite different inside. All was cool and stark. A few old people lay in the skeleton beds. Strange-shaped instruments and kidney-dishes stood in lines on rubber-wheeled trolleys.

I left him there with his two Chinese assistants. I wondered how they would ever deal with the crowd in the dispensary.

Mrs MacEwen was moving about the sitting-room with

a duster. She seemed pleased to see me again. She went out of the room and came back with two cups of coffee on a tray. She sat down beside me and began to talk.

'Jim's just crazy about his work out here,' she said. 'It's all right by me so long as he's happy, but I just sometimes wish that I could say "good-bye" to China and the Chinese.' She was silent for a moment, then I heard her say, almost to herself, 'The dirt; you've no idea what it's like, fighting the dirt!'

I pictured her in a trim Canadian suburb with smooth lawns sloping to the road and no garden walls. I was sorry that she could not have what she wanted.

Li and I left that night. It was better to travel then than in the heat of the next morning. To have to exchange MacEwen's company for Mr Butler's was depressing. I felt a sharp pang as the ferry-boat pulled out into the river. All I could see in the dusk was the glowing end of MacEwen's pipe. He had crossed his eyes and stuck out his chin as he lit it. I did not want to remember him looking mad with crossed eyes and clenched teeth.

Li began as soon as the train pulled out of the station.

'I do not think Dr MacEwen understood my position. I am private secretary to Mr Butler, not schoolboy coolie!'

I tried to soothe him, but he was determined to be hurt. He opened another attack.

'You do not take your Chinese lessons very seriously, Mr Welch. You have done nothing for two weeks.'

'So much has been happening, Li,' I said guiltily. 'Also I do not think I will be in China long enough to make it worth while. It is so difficult.'

'If you are content to be ignorant, I can do nothing.'

He lapsed into silence and crossed his hands; then he tried to thrust them up his narrow Western sleeves in the ancient Chinese way.

CHAPTER 21

Mrs Murray hoped that I had enjoyed myself. 'What a nice man Dr MacEwen is!' she said, 'so manly and dependable.' I thought how sorry she must be that her own husband was not manly, but only greedy, so that she had to hide the chocolates in the music-stool and then, without saying anything, had to watch him as he rooted about, looking for them behind cushions and bookcases.

Mr Butler had some cynical remarks to make about missionaries. He asked me if I had had to sing hymns or say prayers.

'We had grace before meals, but it was only "For what we are about to receive",' I answered.

He laughed as if I had made a joke. 'What a nice mind you have for gauging things!' he said. 'Anything longer, or in Latin, would be very archaic, but the hackneyed "For what we are about to receive" is still quite permissible in a religious household.'

This long explanation of my remark annoyed me. I left the others and walked across the compound to my bungalow. The soiled, nasty atmosphere still hung about it. I saw its tired, sick owner coming home after his day's work and sinking into one of the dirty chairs. I imagined him drinking his whisky-and-soda, with only the faked antiques for audience, then I heard him running down the hollow-sounding passage and throwing himself at last on the creaking bed.

'How very silly!' I said aloud to destroy the picture. But I'm glad we're going to-morrow, I thought. I'm glad I've only got one more night here.

The train which was to have taken us back to Kai-feng Fu was suddenly commandeered by some war lord to carry his troops in quite a different direction. We found ourselves sitting on our suitcases, watching the sun go down behind the squalid station. There was very little hope of catching another train that night. Li and the Boy were questioning everyone, but the answers were so varied that they added to our confusion. They went in search of the station-master and came back running.

'Mr Butler, Mr Butler,' Li panted. 'We must get into the cattle-truck of the waiting train. At once, at once, before it goes. Otherwise we will be here all to-night, and all to-morrow too, maybe.' He gave Mr Butler a sharp look and added even more rapidly: 'You must give me fifty dollars for the station-master.'

'What!' Mr Butler exploded. 'Fifty dollars for the privilege of travelling in a cattle-truck when we already have *wagons-lits* tickets! It's ridiculous, Li.'

'He will not take less, Mr Butler.' Li became hysterical. 'If you do not give it we will be left here and perhaps bandits will capture us; then you will have to answer for the ears of the innocent boy.' Weeping with excitement and eloquence, he pointed to me.

Mr Butler took out his pocket-book heavily and flicked five ten-dollar bills into his outstretched hand. Li was through the crowd and away in a flash. The Boy took up as much as he could and shouted at us, 'Master, young master, carry something. Train he go chop chop.'

We jostled through the crowd and threw the suitcases into the stinking cattle-truck; then we climbed into it ourselves. Two bags were still left on the platform. We saw Li ploughing towards us and shouted at him to bring them. He looked up, startled and terrified; then he caught them up and ran on with the bags banging clumsily against his legs.

We took his arms and dragged him up into the truck just as it began to move. He lay across the luggage for a few moments, gasping for breath; then he sat up and smiled very comfortably. As I saw this smile dawning, the idea jumped into my head that most of Mr Butler's fifty dollars was in Li's breast-pocket. I went very close to him and bent my head, but I could not hear them crackling.

I began to take in my surroundings. The truck had a corrugated-iron roof and wooden walls. There were no windows, but the fading light came in through the door-less opening. From it I looked down at the track, watching the earth and pebbles running dizzily together. The smell of manure and animals was so overpowering that it drove me to the air. Gradually I began to get used to it. The excitement had improved Mr Butler. His eyes sparkled and he began to chant dirty limericks. I laughed and suddenly felt very gay.

The Boy was unpacking some provisions. He put the camp-table up between us and stood two candles on it; then he lurched towards us, bearing the open tins cere-moniously from the sideboard which he had improvised out of luggage.

We ate the asparagus and then tried to catch the cold, slippery peaches between our fingers. They often escaped, plopping back richly into the slimy syrup. Li sat beside us watching. He hated foreign food. Every now and then he would say, 'It very lucky we caught this train.'

Mr Butler pulled a silver flask out of his dressing-case and poured some liquid from it into the peach tin. 'Drink it,' he said, pointing to the tin while he held the flask to his own lips. I felt the hot, sickly brandy trickling down inside me. I did not like it at all and hoped that he would drink the rest himself. 'There must be many bugs in this truck,' he said between gulps. I began to feel drugged and soothed by the food and the jogging of the train. I leant against the dung-coated side of the truck and fell asleep.

The scream and hiss of steam and the insane clashing

of the couplings woke me. The truck was jarring to a standstill.

'What's happened?' I asked anxiously.

I was still half asleep, and thought that there had been an accident.

'Nothing has happened,' Mr Butler said irritably. 'We've only come to a station. Boy's putting up the camp-beds so that we can lie down. This journey is going to take hours.'

Two neat beds were being unfolded at the other end of the truck. When they were ready I lay down gratefully and waited for the train to start again. I was enjoying the unexpectedness of the journey and was thankful that we were so well provided with food and bedding.

Suddenly short, sharp voices sounded outside, and then two soldiers pushed their heads in at the opening. They climbed into the truck and began to look at all our things. They held the empty tins upside down, letting the juice trickle on to our luggage. They kicked the rolled-up bedding, and finally one came up and pulled and patted my hair. His fingers were so filthy that my face went quite stiff with disgust. He grinned broadly at my fixed expression.

'Ask them what they want, Boy,' Mr Butler ordered nervously. He evidently thought that the Boy would make a better ambassador than Li. There was a long harangue. Then the Boy turned to Mr Butler and said:

'He say he b'long only poor soldier; master b'long rich foreign man. Maybe you can pay he some litty cumshaw.' He bent down and added in a quiet, more urgent voice, 'Master, pay he some cigarettes, some American canned chow.'

'I'm damned if I will,' Mr Butler muttered furiously; then he seemed to relent a little. Pushing forward a packet of cigarettes and a tin of celery soup, he said, 'Now tell the devils to go away.' He refused to speak to them himself. I had never known him to be so tactless.

I wondered if he could be drunk, but decided that the flask had been too small.

The soldiers backed away, looking surly and unsatisfied. I knew that something was going to happen. There was a most unpleasant silence and then we heard voices again. This time the soldiers brought four others with them. They began methodically to throw all our things on to the platform. The Boy saved as much as he could by snatching it up first, but more than one splinter and crash, by its painful noise, made me more frightened and tense.

Not wanting to be thrown out myself, I jumped down on to the platform and waited. The Boy was still our unnecessary interpreter: 'Soldier say he must have more room. No room for foreign man.'

'That means we'll have to spend the night in this bloody hole, which we can't do, there's nowhere to go. Tell them I've paid fifty dollars to travel in that filthy truck!' Mr Butler was almost screaming at the end of his speech. The Boy shouted something, but by this time the train was moving. The soldiers gathered in the opening and jeered at us, pointing and grinning like devils in a medieval picture. One put his thumbs in the corners of his mouth and stretched it terribly; at the same time rolling his eyes until only the whites showed. Another danced like a monkey on a chain and ended his performance by spitting richly at us. I watched them until the train disappeared. Their revenge seemed to satisfy them and I felt that we had escaped lightly.

When I turned from staring, Li had already disappeared on one of his missions. He came back looking smooth and confident. 'There is good hotel in the town, Mr Butler; I have discovered,' he said.

'Come on, then,' groaned Mr Butler. 'Get the luggage together and hurry, for God's sake.' He seemed to be trying to patch up his self-respect by bullying.

We pushed our way down smelling, dark streets. Once

or twice we passed casual, lurid torches burning wildly against the navy-blue sky. Li led us to a peeling stucco gateway. I could just read the cut-out metal letters which arched it. 'European and American style Hotel,' they said. The door was open, so we walked into a wide passage where naked electric-light bulbs swung in the draught. Benches stood against the walls, punctuated by powder-blue spittoons. The spittoons were decorated with white bows and wreaths of pink roses. Nobody seemed to use them, for the floor was starred all over with mounds of glittering, trembling spittle.

A wasted-looking servant came out of one of the rooms and led us up the brass-bound stairs to another wide passage. Here the reek of opium was quite unmistakable. It hung, heavy and sickly, in air which was already loaded with smells of garlic and sweat. The most disgusting smell of all was the breath of scent which floated corruptly on the backs of the others, like a top-dressing.

Sleeping people lay on the benches. One had just woken up and been sick. His vomit lay in a pile beside him. A door opened and two Chinese youths ran out. They were dressed only in European shirts. As they darted past I saw with a shock that one of them wore a little ebony and ivory crucifix which bobbed stupidly up and down on his chest. The weary servant took no notice. He led us to the end of the passage, where he threw open two doors; then he left us.

'They're both equally horrible,' said Mr Butler, looking into the rooms. Callous lights glared from the middle of each. I went into the one nearest to me and shut the door. I walked up and down wondering how I was going to be able to sleep in such a place. Against one wall stood a huge Chinese bed hooded grimly in dark blue cotton. There was a modern wash-basin with shining taps, and I saw with relief and fear that the windows were barred.

Before I was able to look at anything else the door flew open and Mr Butler burst in. 'Don't wash in the basin,' he said excitedly. 'People have probably been pissing in it for years, and for God's sake don't drink any of the water unless it's boiled.'

At that moment the servant, coughing gruesomely, came in bearing tea and hot towels. We steamed our faces in the towels and drank the clear, fresh tea. I left a little in the bottom of my cup, so that I could clean my teeth.

The Boy came in and unrolled my bedding, arranging it under the dark cotton canopy. The mixed flavour in my mouth of toothpaste and green tea made me feel sick. I went to the door to turn the glaring light out, but could find no switch, so I wrapped my blazer round the bulb. A ghostly blob of light shone through the dark blue flannel.

I lay down on the bed and stared at the horrible hangings. Noises came in through the barred windows and from the passage. I thought that I would never fall asleep.

I must have done, for I was woken by my own choking. I sat up wide awake, but still dazed; with no memory. The room seemed to be full of acrid smoke. It stung my eyes and nose and I could see it eddying in thick waves round the shrouded light. I ran to the windows, but realized that I could never get between the bars. I opened the door into the passage, expecting to see it all in flames, but it was unchanged. The sleeping bodies and the wreathed spittoons were still there.

The smoke was getting thicker. I decided to go at once to Mr Butler's room. As I turned to do so, I heard a faint thud behind me and the room blazed with light. The sudden change terrified me; I could not understand it. Then I remembered my blazer. I stooped down and was just able to see it through the smoke. The charred remains of it lay on the floor underneath the light. I picked it up, and half a heraldic bird stared at me from the pocket. The smell of the burnt flannel was disgusting. I wanted to laugh. To be burnt while serving as a lampshade in a

Chinese opium den and brothel was such an extraordinary end for a school blazer. It seemed to make the evening amusing instead of vile and frightening.

I threw the stinking remains into the street. I wondered what the beggars would do with them when they found them in the morning. The smoke gradually floated out of the windows. I lay down on the bed again and waited for the dawn.

It came in a little thread, like an inflamed eyelid against a grey face. The morning seemed dead and old and tired before it had begun. The life in the passage revived. There was vomiting and retching and the noise of servants quarrelling.

We heated our last tin of soup and, with our spoons, dived into the thick pease pudding. We had not dared to dilute it with water. Then we packed our bags and fled from the evil house, preferring to wait hours at the station.

CHAPTER 22

MR BUTLER wanted to leave Kai-feng as soon as possible. Each day the sun grew hotter and the dust more maddening. As before, I was left alone in the mornings, while he and Roote were closeted with typists and secretaries. I used to take my painting things into the garden, where I sat under a crazy old umbrella which reminded me of some disreputable tea-shop. There was nothing to paint – only the straggling poplars and the sandy road winding into the hills. I did not like the poplars; they looked as if they had been planted by a careful householder who wanted to shut out a view of trains at the bottom of his garden.

I had not been out alone since the afternoon when I saw the flies feasting on the dead man's head. I wanted to paint the city wall and the pagoda, but I dared not venture out with my easel and paint-box and umbrella. I felt that I looked peculiar and would attract unwelcome attention. In the afternoons I would sometimes go with Mr Butler to one or other of the dealers, but Li never took me anywhere now. His pride had been hurt at MacEwen's and he seemed to hold me responsible for it. I was sorry, for although he was pompous and silly, I had enjoyed the first few days in his company. He was the first Chinaman I had known, and that in itself was interesting enough. Now he confined himself strictly to business. I only saw him as he glided in and out of Mr Butler's room, carrying papers importantly.

Once again the sense of confinement grew too strong for me. I wanted to wander down the squalid streets and stare at everything, alone.

I remembered a gilt bronze Buddhist god, half monster

and half man. I thought that I would like to see it again. I set out for the dealer's house, and this time nothing happened to me.

The dealer seemed amused to see me alone. He and his partners laughed and offered me a big cigar with my tea. I was now quite expert at drinking the tea and leaving the charming unrolled leaves at the bottom of the cup. I refused the cigar and asked to be shown the god. It was brought, and my interest evaporated. Like so many things, it was fantastic and yet seemed to be ordinary. I tried to think of a good way of leaving without buying anything.

'I must think about it,' I said. None of them understood English, but they knew exactly what I meant. They bowed politely and indifferently, and I felt insulted.

I got up quickly and went out into the courtyard. The carp in the ruinous tank seemed enormous. They looked almost as old as they were supposed to be. Although some of them were diseased, they were still mournfully beautiful, as they appeared and disappeared in the dark water with their gills working and their mouths drooping sadly.

'When you go out alone you might at least tell someone where you're going,' were Mr Butler's first words on my return. 'We've been looking high and low for you.' He annoyed me by stressing this last sentence as if he did not really think me worth the trouble.

'There is no need to fuss,' I said rudely. 'I can look after myself.'

Something must have told Mr Butler that it was silly to quarrel, for he suddenly changed the subject.

'We shall be leaving at the end of the week, so you'd better begin packing your things,' he said mildly.

I was pleased to hear that we were going back to Shanghai. I went upstairs feeling quite friendly towards him. The door of his room was open, and as I passed I saw the Boy, surrounded by round tins and cotton-wool, bending over a packing-case. He was putting each piece of bronze and porcelain in a separate tin.

No tins had been provided for my own few things, so I wrapped them lovingly in my clothes and put them in the bottom of my trunk. I enjoyed the work of fitting all my possessions into the trunk. It seemed to draw me together; to make me more concentrated inside myself.

The day of our departure was very hot. The sun, shining on the dust motes, cast a filmy, disintegrating glitter over everything.

Roote came down to the station with us. As the train moved out we left him there like a stranded jelly-fish. Li stood, waving his hat in a severe, well-bred gesture. He seemed to be trying to make up for the shapeless, flabby thing at his side by his own very correct behaviour.

I was glad to see the last of the tawny-yellow walls. I thought again of the day when I had run from bastion to bastion; when I had heard nothing but the dry grass creaking and the insects banging their wings against the bricks.

Towards evening we made our way down the rocking corridors to the dining-car. As we waited for Boy to bring us our heated provisions, I looked at the other passengers. The first one to catch my eye was a European woman in a Chinese man's gown. Her full cheeks and brown wavy hair came as a shock after its plain, severe cut. She spoke, and I heard an American voice. Mr Butler had noticed her, too. He turned to me. 'She's an authoress from Chicago,' he said. 'Or a missionary trying to get inside the Chinese mind.'

I wondered if she was as surprising to the Chinese as an Eastern woman dressed in shirt and trousers would be to us.

The next thing I saw was the startling whiteness of a man's hair as he leant his head back against the dirty upholstery. His nose and lips were smooth, well shaped and plump. It was altogether a striking appearance.

When the food arrived I noticed that there was dirt on my plate.

'This plate is dirty,' I said to Mr Butler.

'Don't be fussy,' he retorted. 'Everything is dirty. If you're fastidious at your age, what will you be like when you're mine?'

'Perhaps it will have worn off by then,' I wanted to answer pertly.

The white-haired man smiled sweetly and then joined in our conversation. It was done very gracefully.

'How I agree about everything in China being dirty,' he said. 'It certainly isn't wise to look at anything too closely.'

Mr Butler darted a shrewd glance at him; then I saw his face change.

'Is this your first experience of China?' he asked affably.

'Yes,' was all the man replied.

There was a little silence.

'Oh, I've been out here for years,' Mr Butler said. 'In the Consular Service,' he added casually.

'Have you?' The face surrounded by the white hair smiled almost condescendingly. 'You must know a lot about the country then. The thing that has impressed me most during my short stay is the wonderful Art of the Chinese. I've managed to get hold of some lovely things; also some extremely interesting relics of the Nestorian Christians.'

'Really!' said Mr Butler, politely raising his eyebrows. 'We are just returning from Kai-feng Fu. I've brought back quite a good collection of early bronzes and Sung porcelain.'

'I wish I could see them,' the man said with a collector's greediness.

'I'm afraid they're all in packing-cases, but, if you are

going to Shanghai, perhaps we will meet there some time and I could show them to you then,' Mr Butler suggested.

'Unfortunately I go back to England in a few days' time,' the other replied.

As he was speaking, a group of people approached him from behind. One of them leant forward and, shaking him heartily by the hand, said, 'How do you do, Dean? I surely am pleased to meet you. I've brought along a map that I'd like you to look at.'

He spread out the map on an empty table and the others gathered round, bending their heads and hunching their shoulders like a rugger scrum.

'Who do you think he is?' I whispered to Mr Butler.

'He must be the Dean of Canterbury. I'm sure I've seen pictures of that face. I expect he's out here on the Flood Relief Committee. Strange to meet an English Dean in the wilds of China. It's like meeting a bull in a china-shop, or rather a china-shop in a bull!' He laughed. He liked turning popular phrases inside out.

I saw the Dean disappearing through the door, followed by the train of missionaries. We came across him again on the way back to our own compartment. Still surrounded, he stood in the doorway of a second-class carriage. We said good night and passed on.

As soon as we were out of earshot Mr Butler boiled over. 'Why is he travelling second-class?' he spluttered. 'No Englishman travels second-class. Why, even first-class is like a pigsty, and often the *wagons-lits* are not much better. It's disgusting affectation, and I for one don't think any the better of him for it.'

'Perhaps he didn't realize the difference between England and China,' I suggested. 'As most people always travel third in England, he may have thought that second would be quite possible in China.'

'I don't expect he thought anything of the sort,' Mr Butler rapped out. 'It's just repulsive, mawkish sentiment. It's his way of demonstrating what a good Christian he is. I'm afraid it's far too theatrical for me.'

Mr Butler seemed to be taking it personally – as if the Dean were travelling second-class especially to outrage him.

Farther along the corridor, the American woman in the Chinese gown was also standing in her doorway. A Chinese man was with her, but she seemed very forlorn. She looked out of the window, away from him, and then at us. Her face wore the yearning, almost lecherous expression that exhibitionists have. I felt very sorry for her, because she had no audience.

We said good-bye to the Dean at Nanking. He was catching the first boat to Shanghai, while we were waiting until the next day, as Mr Butler had to interview some people. I must have shown some disappointment at this delay, for, some minutes after the Dean had left, Mr Butler said, 'What a pity I didn't ask him to take you back to Shanghai; then you needn't have kicked your heels here until to-morrow.'

I wished that he had thought of this earlier. I would like to have heard more about the K'ang-Hsi blue and white which the Dean was buying for his grey-walled room at home. The stories about the Nestorian Christians intrigued me. I did not know that such people had existed.

From the deck I looked down into the cleft of my father's hat. I could see where his head just touched the crown.

'Well, has he behaved himself?' he asked as we set foot on shore.

'Oh, Denton and I have got on quite well together, haven't we?' Mr Butler turned to me.

'Yes, I've enjoyed my trip awfully,' I answered. I did not want to say that I had got on well; I wanted to escape now that there was no longer any reason for being with him.

It was a relief to drive home and to be left alone to un-pack and gloat over my new treasures. I rang Mrs Field-ing up to say that I had come back. She told me to jump into a taxi and to bring my things with me. I packed them into a suitcase and set off.

We discussed them and passed them round while we drank tea and ate slices of Italian cream cake. The cake looked like a glistening porcupine, because it was stuck all over with almonds, angelica, and cherries.

Instead of a beautiful Buddhist head I had only been able to find a little iron god for Vesta. It was lacquered and old but not exciting; and I did not want to show it to her. I knew that she would buy it and feel dissatisfied. At last she asked me:

'Were you able to get a head?'

'I'm afraid this is all I could find.' I pulled the god out and showed it to her.

Her face did not change, unless the same expression held in place can be called a change. 'I thought you'd rather have it than nothing,' I said hurriedly. I felt ashamed of it.

'I'll have it; I asked you to buy me something.' She took it silently between her hands.

I was angry with her for martyring herself. I could do nothing about it, so I left early. I put the things back into the suitcase and started to walk home. The suitcase banged rhythmically against my leg. 'I'll never buy any-thing for a friend again,' I said in time to it.

CHAPTER 23

To be able to go into the country without a thought of danger was wonderful. In the morning, after my father and brother had left, I would tell Cook to get me a picnic lunch – sandwiches, biscuits, an orange and some chocolate – then I would set off down the wide, new road which lost itself in the fields.

I usually sat at the foot of a grave-mound to eat my meal; there would be a glint of gold and silver in the long grass. This was the symbolical paper money, offered for the dead man. Sometimes a little fire was still smoking. I thought how nice it would be to have burnt sacrifices offered to me when I was dead.

Peasants passed and stared at me. At first I wondered if they thought that I was sacrilegious; but when I saw them dropping their trousers and squatting on the graves, I felt that they could not mind my eating there.

Once I came across a mound which had been levelled on one side. A corner of the lacquered coffin jutted out. Jagged pieces of it had broken away. The love of horror made me go up and look between the cracks. A dry smell, like mildewed books, breathed out of the coffin. And then I saw the dull shine of dead hair. It seemed to be amber-red, which made it more horrifying. No Chinaman has red hair. I ran away, not understanding it, making up a story for myself, that a foreigner had been killed and buried there.

The fields were covered with death. You could not escape it anywhere. The unfinished road cut through like a dried-up river. Deep, impassable trenches had been dug across it. The peasants had done this at night to stop the road from ever being used. They did not want to be disturbed.

Only the villages gave any signs of life. All the dogs would come rushing out, to show their teeth hideously and snarl at me; but if I was not afraid, they soon began fighting and playing erotic games amongst themselves.

One day, as I walked through one of these mournful villages, I saw a strange creature steadying himself against the counter of an open shop. He was in rags, and his chin was covered with stubble, but he was young, and against the background of jeering Chinese faces his skin looked almost startlingly white.

He was evidently begging from the shopkeeper and the crowd was taunting him for being drunk. I guessed that he was Russian.

He lurched and caught hold of the doorpost just in time. He thrust his other hand out for alms and the shopkeeper spat neatly into it. Everyone laughed. The young man jerked and flicked his hand, trying to shake off the phlegm; then he made a grimace which was meant to be a smile, and I felt terribly ashamed.

I watched him trying hopelessly to push through the crowd. He was swaying dangerously and a vicious kick brought him down. He lay still, with his face in the gutter. People spat on his back where the white skin showed through the rents in his paper-thin shirt. Others aimed playful kicks at his hard, trembling buttocks. A little boy jumped on his shoulders and straddled his neck with small fat legs and dimpled knees. He grabbed two tufts of the man's hair and jigged up and down on his neck, riding him as if he were a horse.

I waited until the crowd melted away; then I went up to the man. He lay breathing into the dust, making a frightening, grating sound in his nose and throat. I was about to try to turn him over when he groaned and muttered something angrily. I stepped back and watched him staggering to his feet. He began to sway very slowly out of the village. I walked behind, keeping my eyes off him for fear of seeing him fall again.

196

Suddenly he began to sing, throwing his head from side to side, and waving his arms wildly. He shouted the words and rolled along as if he were happy; then, as suddenly as he had begun, he stopped. His hands dropped, his head fluttered weakly and he fell. But this time it was soft grass that received him. We were all alone in the country. I looked down at his face lying sideways amongst the blades of grass. A little trickle of saliva ran out of the corner of his mouth and lost itself in his young beard. He looked like Jesus.

His whole face twitched as though a bee had stung him. Little gurgling sounds floated up from his stomach and burst in his mouth. The palms of his hands were seamed with black lines like the roads on a map.

I felt in my pocket. I had one dollar and fifty cents. I put both the coins in his hand and kneaded his fingers round them; then I got up to go. I could do nothing else.

As I walked away, I wondered what it would be like to have no pocket-money till the end of the week. I could not ask for any more until then. I stopped walking and stared down at the ground; I did not know what to do.

I decided to turn round and go back to the man. He was lying just as I had left him. I looked furtively around me; then I knelt down, opened his fingers, and took out the dollar. The fifty-cent piece looked very small, alone on his big palm. I shut his fingers on it to hide it.

I put the dollar in my pocket and started to run. I wanted to get away.

When I looked back I saw a tiny figure moving among the grave-mounds. I felt the dollar, warm against my thigh.

Sometimes, when the country grew stale, I walked into the heart of the city. I had a passion for walking. I would ride nowhere when I was alone. If I walked, I could stop when anything interested me.

Trams clanged by and people spat all over the dusty pavements. Terrible beggars waited at the temple doors, and the food in the food-shops looked too fantastic and nightmarish for anyone but a demon to eat. But I enjoyed the squalor half-fearfully. I told myself that I could leave it and go back to the penthouse or the empty country at any moment.

There was a whole street of second-hand shops, called Peking Road. I never tired of exploring it. The things were mostly European – the remains from auctioned houses.

One day I saw the little head of George the Third winking up at me from the hall-marks on the back of a silver ladle. After that, I started to search more thoroughly. I went from shop to shop, trying to look into every corner. I think the shopkeepers mistook me for some new kind of detective, on the look-out for stolen property. But in spite of their suspiciousness I found two old finger-bowls with lips, they had shallow cutting round the base and stood very high; three more late Georgian spoons and a most beautiful lustre jug. It was quite large, and oyster-coloured, with a fine, bluish glaze. It was fluted and shaped like a classical urn. A thick silver band of interwoven leaves and birds and flowers circled its middle.

'How much?' I asked rather coldly. I had not yet realized that this is a silly trick.

'One dollar twenty-five,' said the thin shopkeeper. 'But no talky any man I sell broken goods.' He turned the jug upside down and showed me a curious little crack on the base, as if someone had shot at it with a catapult.

'I won't tell anyone,' I said fervently. He handed it to me.

I started to walk home at once. I wanted to wash my jug and could think of nothing else – until I came to a street which was half in shadow because of its tall buildings. There, I felt a peculiar air of tension which I could not understand. Then I realized that the crowd was not moving but standing still, waiting for something to happen.

The eyes of the people were on a little band of men. Talking had sunk to a whisper as the crowd watched the group going from house to house. There was something grim and alarming about the men.

Catching a message from the people nearest to me, I turned to look at a food-shop which had not yet been searched. Through the open front I could see a man in grey, crouching over a bowl of rice at the counter. He had his back to the road and was hunching his shoulders, so that nothing of his face could be seen.

The band of searchers drew nearer. Now they were only a shop away. Still the man did not move; he seemed to be talking in undertones to the shopkeeper.

When they were on the threshold he reached up and helped himself to another dish. He held his bowl up and arched his arms round his head.

One of the searchers came silently up behind him; grabbing him suddenly by one shoulder he spun him round. The bowl fell from the man's hands and crashed on to the floor, where the china splinters stuck through the mess of steaming rice.

A tremor passed through the crowd. There was a queer sound, stifled almost as soon as it was made.

The man looked up self-consciously and smiled. His captor drew a truncheon and hit him across the face. His hands flew up and he rocked his head in pain, but when he took his hands away, his face was still grinning, only this time there was a purple-red mark across it and blood ran out of his mouth.

The other plain-clothes men began to hit him too. He knelt down and they dragged him along under a shower of blows. He gave a hoarse scream and they all began to kick him, hopping, to take aim, as they walked. The crowd suddenly grew materialistic and bustling, like a theatre-audience after 'God save the King.' They had no more time to stand and stare.

At the end of May the city prepared itself for summer. The houses that I visited all looked different. Carpets had been taken away and cool matting put down instead. Soft, thick curtains had given way to stiff, fresh ones, and fans as big as aeroplane-propellers hung from the ceilings of some rooms.

It was the time for swimming; and for this reason I at last decided to go to the Country Club. My father had had me elected as a junior member when I first arrived, but I had not been in yet. I did not play squash, or even tennis, except on the uneven lawns of friends who also only played for fun. I did not drink, and although I loved it, I hardly ever dared to dance, for fear of looking foolish. But I did swim; so I took up my bathing-suit and set off.

What I saw under the fat *porte cochère* pleased me very much. I was in a dark lofty hall which seemed to be an almost perfect relic of the middle years of Queen Victoria's reign. There was the Queen herself in a rich gold frame which suspended a plaster crown above her head. She was dressed in all her robes, with the Garter pinned across her bosom. The artist, by emphasizing the droop of her mouth, had made her look like the Frog Footman. The walls were covered with a flocked damask paper which had faded from the colour of fresh to the colour of dried blood, and there were console tables charmingly patinated with dust and furniture polish.

The Chinese page did not let me admire these things for long. He hurried me down a passage and left me outside the door to another world. Cries and splashes came from inside. I opened the door and saw a lot of pink bodies in bright blue water. People sat at little tables round the edge, sipping drinks and talking. I had to pass in front of them to get to the dressing-rooms. As I did so, I heard one woman whisper piercingly to another, 'My dear, sandals!'

Looking down at my feet, I realized what she was talking about. How silly, to go to a Country Club in sandals! I turned bright red. I wanted to humiliate the woman. I wanted to push her into the bath so that her skirts would float up and we should all see her suspenders pressing against her waxy, hairy, blue-veined thighs. I almost ran into the changing-rooms.

Boys bustled to and fro, carrying clothes and towels to their masters. Behind a glass partition I heard shower-baths hissing and spitting. Most of the bodies were very ugly, with swollen stomachs and hanks of hair in the most improbable places. One man had a grey down all over his back.

As I stood near the door, wondering what to do next, I heard a voice say, 'Hullo, you've not been here before, have you?' I looked at the speaker and recognized him as a friend of my brother's. Now, with his dripping hair plastered into a fringe on his forehead, he looked rather like a Mexican Indian. His skin was swarthy and very smooth. In his clothes he had been quite ordinary.

'Can you tell me where to leave my things?' I asked him.

'Bung them in here.' He lifted the lid of the locker next to his own.

I undressed and wriggled into my bathing suit; then he led me to the shower-baths and waited. We went into the swimming bath together. I was pleased to have someone with me. The whispering woman had made me self-conscious. Crowther dived into the bath very superbly. When his head bobbed up he turned and looked in my direction. I felt that something was expected of me. I climbed on to the highest board that I could contemplate without feeling sick. I dived into the blue water and hit my head on the bottom of the bath. I rose to the surface dazed and sore, hoping that my legs had not spread apart grotesquely and indecently as I had seen some people's do.

Crowther was swinging towards me on the metal rings which hung over the bath. Hanging by his arms he looked very strong and lusty, and more primitive than ever. He dropped into the water beside me and said, 'Come and meet my sister.'

We swam towards a girl in a green bathing-cap. She was well covered; freckles ran together at the base of her nose and spread over her masculine brick-red cheeks.

'Oh, you're Paul's brother, are you?' she said in an uninterested voice and began to scramble out of the bath. We followed behind, and as she pulled herself up, I noticed how full and tight her thighs and buttocks were. I thought they looked like full wine-skins; although I had never seen a wine-skin.

We sat on the edge, swinging our feet in the water. Crowther called to the waiter and ordered drinks. I asked for lime-juice.

'With nothing in it?' Crowther's sister seemed unable to believe her ears.

'I think I'll just have it with water,' I said nervously.

'Have whatever you like with it.' She turned away grandly and started to drum on the tiles with her fingers. We sat in silence, until her Dalmatian sneaked in furtively from the terrace and tried to sniff between my legs.

'Go away, Simpson!' she cried. 'You know you're not allowed in here!'

I put out my hand to stroke its spotted, fish-like head; but it started back and lifted its lips off its teeth, not fiercely but fearfully.

Crowther's sister smiled. 'He hates children,' she said.

I wondered why she disliked me so much. Perhaps she realized that I thought her buttocks were like full wine-skins.

I got up, thanked them stiltedly, and walked away. I decided to leave the Country Club, where I had received nothing but insults.

As I combed my wet hair I noticed two huge bottles

standing on each side of the looking-glass. One, filled with what seemed to be cold tea, was labelled 'Bay Rhum'; the other colourless, gin-like fluid was called 'Hydrogen Peroxide'.

Surely, I thought, after the first shock of seeing these names together, the members of the Country Club don't peroxide their hair! I looked round, trying to discover signs of bleaching, but every head seemed to be the same mousy colour.

As I turned to leave the glass another man approached and took my place. I waited to see if he would use either of the bottles. He began by pouring on Bay Rhum. When he combed his hair forward the glass became spattered with cloudy brown rain. I was disappointed. I still did not know why the peroxide was there. The next moment I saw him move towards it. He tilted the bottle, and after soaking a piece of cotton-wool, applied it to his ears, screwing it round and round into a spiral; then he rubbed between his toes and threw the cotton away. Although he was being hygienic, his actions were rather revolting to watch. I went down the long passage and found myself in the hall again. Someone was sitting on the sofa. In the dimness I could not see who it was. 'Hullo,' the person said. 'I don't suppose you know who I am.'

I peered down at the sofa and saw a woman of about forty or fifty. Her dress was grey and very pleated. She wore large crystal beads round her neck and a thin gold chain round her ankle. She was the first 'aesthetic' woman I had seen in Shanghai.

'I know your father well,' she said. 'And I've often seen you about with him. He told me the other day that you've been into the Interior. I wish I'd known before you'd started, I'd have asked you to get some things for me. Of course, I would have given you a commission,' she added, smiling archly as only middle-aged women can. I had the probably quite wrong impression that she would expect all sorts of services for her money.

'I wouldn't have wanted any commission,' I said hastily.

'What a thing to say!' she laughed merrily. 'You won't get on in this world if you talk like that!' She became even more arch and I moved my weight from foot to foot uneasily.

'Sit down and tell me all about your trip,' she said, patting the sofa.

I lowered myself rather gingerly and was about to say something about my journey when she jumped up. 'Oh lord, there's my husband – he's just disappearing into the bar and I've been waiting all this time to catch him. We want a fourth for bridge and there isn't anyone else. He hates the drawing-room, the woman's part,' she explained, 'and so I have to drag him there by force. Do run after him and catch him. I'm not allowed in the bar – it's reserved for you males.' She gave me a roguish look.

'What's he like?' I asked, getting to my feet.

'Oh, exactly like all the others,' she said contemptuously. 'You'd never be able to pick him out. I'd better send a Boy after all. Will you ring the bell?'

I made my escape when the Boy appeared. 'Well, good-bye,' she said. 'You must come and see me one day and tell me all about your interesting experiences.'

The air felt cold on my hand after her rather warm grasp; but I was glad that I had met her. She had washed away some of the effects of the whispering woman and Crowther's sister.

CHAPTER 24

BRITISH soldiers were quartered in one part of the public park. I could see their huts through the tightly-woven fence. As I walked between the bamboo groves I stopped to watch a soldier who was carrying a bright red blanket. First he shook it, then he threw it over a clothes-line and began to beat it with a stick. He must have seen me through the fence, for, dropping the stick and lighting a cigarette, he ambled over to me and said, 'Hullo, mate.'

'Hullo!' I gulped, rather taken aback.

'Oh, you are English! That's good. There are so many foreigners here, you can't be sure what's what.' He puffed at his cigarette in silence; then he said, 'I've been sick – malaria – but I'm all right now – just taking it easy for a day or two.'

'What's it like, having malaria?' I asked.

'It's not so bad when they get it under – they give you this quinine; – makes your teeth and hair fall out,' he added gloomily.

I looked at his hair and teeth; they both looked bright and glossy.

'It doesn't seem to have done them any harm yet,' I said politely.

'No, but you can't tell. They might go any day.' He spoke with sombre relish. There was another silence.

'Do you live here?' he asked.

'Yes, at the moment, but I haven't been here long.'

'Makes a difference when you've got a home. There's nothing for us fellers to do when we're off duty; except mess about down town.'

I thought for a moment; then I found myself saying

rather primly, 'Would you like to come to tea this afternoon? If you're at a loose end. I live quite near.' After the first plunge the words came one on top of the other in a hurried string.

He looked at me soberly through the separating fence. 'What would your Mum and Dad say to a stranger?' he asked.

'I've only got a father, and he won't be there,' I answered.

'Well, if you think it's all right – it would be a nice change for me. How am I going to find the way, though?' he added doubtfully.

'I'll meet you at the park gates at half-past three, then you can't get lost,' I said.

'All right, mate, and thank you. I'll be there.'

He went back to his blanket and I walked on through the bamboos. At the end of the path I turned to wave, but he was too busy beating his blanket to see me.

As soon as lunch was over and my father had left, I rang the bell for the Number One.

'One master for tea, Boy,' I said. 'What thing have got?' We must have a good tea for him, I thought. He will be hungry.

'Have got angel food, litty cakes, some chocolate biscuits. Plenty 'nough I think so, young master,' he answered.

'Good, Boy. Make some sandwiches, some toast.'

I fussed about, putting cigarettes and small tables in convenient places. I had never had a guest of my own before.

I set out for the park in good time and had to wait at the gates, where the stone horses stood. When at last I saw him approaching, he looked quite different. Instead of his old shirt and trousers he had on his fresh, summer uniform. His belt sparkled and twinkled with pipeclay and polished brass. A few paces from me he stopped, lifted his hand, banged his legs together and gave me the most extravagant salute, grinning all the while.

For a moment I said nothing, only smiled at him. The salute had given me an intense pleasure and I felt rather ashamed, thinking that other people would say it was childish of me. I knew that as long as I lived I was never likely to get another, either in earnest or in fun.

'How punctual you are!' I said, although, because I had been waiting, I really felt that he was late.

We started to walk back to the flat.

'That's where we live,' I said, pointing to the tall building. 'Right at the top.'

He eyed it doubtfully. 'Looks a bit posh to me – Hope there aren't any officers knocking about.'

'Why?' I could not understand what he meant and felt rather alarmed.

'They might wonder what I was up to in there,' he explained.

'Couldn't you just say that you'd been asked out to tea?'

'They might think it a bit queer.'

'Oh, well, I don't expect we'll meet any officers.' I turned quickly into the drive. I was determined to have him to tea.

The lift rushed us up. The Number One must have been watching out of the window, for he had opened the front door and was standing by it. Although, as always, he wore his actress's smile, I could see the shrewd look in his eyes as he summed up the rank of the soldier. He took his cap and cane and opened the drawing-room door for us. I asked the soldier to sit down, and waited for Boy to bring in the tea, the hot water and the buttered toast.

'Is it China tea?' the soldier asked anxiously when it was brought.

'Yes, don't you like it?' I stopped pouring, but still kept the pot above his cup.

'I'm afraid I can't stick it,' he said.

'I'll ask Boy if we have any Indian.' I rang the bell.

'Only have got China tea, young master.'

'I'm sorry. What else would you like? You must drink something.' My eyes looked helplessly round the room until they lighted on the decanter on my father's desk.

'Will you have a whisky-and-soda? You must drink something,' I repeated.

'All right,' he said submissively.

I was about to ring again, for soda-water, when Boy appeared with two bottles fresh from the ice-box. It was as if he had realized that the outcome of the search for Indian tea would be whisky-and-soda. I poured some of the whisky into a glass and passed it to the soldier, together with one of the bottles of soda-water; then we settled down to eat the toast and sandwiches.

'Nice place you've got here,' he said at last.

'I'll show you round after tea if you like,' I replied. 'It'll be cooler in the hot weather as it's high up, and there won't be so many mosquitoes; they only rise to about the fourth floor, but of course some come up in the lift.'

'Artful little beggars, aren't they?' he said seriously, and I found myself wanting to laugh at the idea of a family of mosquitoes deciding thoughtfully to take the lift to the top floor.

He had nearly emptied his glass, so I leant forward, stretching for it. 'Let me give you some more,' I said.

He held it back politely and reluctantly. 'What'll your Dad say if he comes back and finds I've drunk all his whisky?' he asked.

'I can fill the decanter up from another bottle before he turns up.' I wanted to appear cool and daring.

'Coo, you'll cop it one of these days – playing about with your old man's drink! Still, if you don't mind, I don't mind.' He held out the goblet. I began to pour from the decanter.

'Whao,' he shouted. 'Is this whisky-and-soda or soda-

and-whisky?' He was grinning and his face had begun to look rather hot.

'I thought it wasn't any good unless it was strong,' I said.

'Don't you ever touch it yourself?' he asked.

'I drank some of my grandfather's once and it made me feel very sick, so I hate it now.'

'That'll learn you,' he said jovially.

We had nearly finished the food. I was sipping my last cup of tea; the second whisky was disappearing rapidly. I waited; then filled up his tumbler before he could protest. I wanted to be as hospitable as possible.

'I'll be tight if you go on like this,' he protested weakly.

I passed him a cigarette and took one myself.

'You smoke like as if you thought it was going to blow up,' he said after watching me for some moments.

'I don't smoke often,' I admitted, turning red.

'You come over here and I'll show you how to smoke.'

I went and sat on the arm of the sofa and looked down over his shoulder.

'First you put it in the side of your mouth, not in the middle; then you breathe in deep.' He demonstrated. 'Now you take it right down inside you till it gets to your belly.' He grabbed my hand, and scraping it down the buttons on his tunic, banged it at last on his stomach, which he had made tight as a drum. I imagined the smoke churning about inside.

'Next you breathe out; but you've eaten most of it by then, as you can see.'

Only a little puff came out of each nostril.

'Now you try,' he said. He handed me his cigarette. My own had gone out while I watched. His was wet at the end and I did not want to put it in my mouth.

'Put it in the corner,' he ordered. 'Don't have it sticking out like a bloody maypole. Now breathe in.'

I filled my lungs. The smoke began to choke me. I spluttered.

209

'Go on sucking it in,' he shouted wildly.

My eyes filled with water. I gave two tearing gasps and all the smoke belched out.

'Oh, you're no good,' he said scornfully.

I lay back, recovering my breath, while the soldier poured some more whisky into his glass and offered it to me. He held it under my nose, so that I had to breathe through my mouth to avoid the sickly smell.

'Take it away,' I groaned.

He looked at his glass thoughtfully. 'Seems a pity to waste it.' He tipped the contents down his throat and gazed contentedly into the distance.

There was a delicate rattle, like a mouse scraping. A key was being fitted into a lock. I looked wildly at the clock. It was nearly six. We should have left the flat at half-past five. I waited in fear for my father to open the door. I wondered what he would think when he saw the soldier and the half-empty decanter.

I decided desperately to try to bundle my guest through the dining-room into the kitchen and so down the back stairs; but it was too late, the door-handle was turning, and the next moment my brother stood gazing at us in astonishment.

'Oh, I thought you were Daddy!' I flopped into a chair, limp with relief.

The soldier had jumped up, expecting some sort of encounter. He stood with careful steadiness, staring solemnly at Paul.

'We've just been having some tea,' I said gaily, trying to ease the situation.

'It doesn't smell like tea,' Paul muttered; then he said in a louder voice, 'You'd better clear the mess up before Daddy comes in. He'll be back almost any minute now.'

I pushed the bell feverishly.

'Have finish tea, Boy, can take away.' I deprived the soldier of his glass and put it firmly on the tray, together with the soda-water bottles, their metal tops and the bottle-opener.

'Paul,' I said imploringly, 'will you open another bottle of whisky and fill up the decanter while I show my friend the way out?' I thought how silly and school-girlish the word 'friend' always sounded. One part of my mind began to wonder if people would soon stop using it, and if so, what other word would do instead.

My brother said, 'Damned if I will!', which brought me down to earth. I grabbed the soldier's arm and led him through the kitchen into the servants' quarters. I thought that the back stairs would be safer than the lift, where we might meet my father. I wondered if the soldier was drunk or not. He had seemed quite all right in the drawing-room, but now he was lurching rather queerly. I should have given him more soda-water, I thought. We reached the ground floor.

'Will you be able to find your way back to the park?' I asked anxiously.

'Yes, mate, don't you worry about me,' he answered.

I felt guilty as I watched his stately progress down the drive.

'See you soon again,' I shouted out. He waved his cane.

I hurried upstairs to fill the decanter.

Paul had already drawn the cork from a bottle. He tilted the spirit into the decanter savagely, so that it plopped and gurgled. He was furious.

CHAPTER 25

I COULD not sleep for the squeaking of the crickets in the penthouse. The summer had come. I sat on my brother's shoulders and searched above the door.

'What are you doing?' my father asked suspiciously.

'Looking for a cricket which is hiding up here. It makes so much noise I can't go to sleep,' I answered.

'Leave it alone. You're not to kill it. It doesn't worry me,' he said, and he stressed the 'me'.

'I wasn't going to kill it.' How insulting the suggestion was! 'I was going to put it out.'

'Stop fussing and go to bed.'

I climbed down from my brother's shoulders and went back to my room. I lay there, watching the mauve glow on the ceiling. It came from the lights of the city. I felt unbearably hot. I wished that I was in England, in a damp meadow by a stream. I wished that I was lying in the stream, with big black fish near me. I thought of the fish holding themselves taut against the current, not moving an inch; only working their gills and sometimes twitching their tails in order to keep perfectly in line.

I turned over, but no cool part of my pillow was left. I tried to think of the next day. Mrs Barbour had asked me to go on the river with her daughters. We were to sit on the decks of the house-boat and paint junks and other water traffic.

'It will be cooler in midstream,' I thought; and fell asleep at last.

I woke late and found the tea and orange-juice waiting for me on the table. I gulped the freezing cold and then the hot. The two sensations chased each other down my throat.

Except for my tie, all my clothes will be white, I thought as I pulled on my Palm Beach trousers. And because I imagined that the others would probably be looking artistic, I dragged my school tie from the back of the drawer and put it on. It looked bright and gay and old-fashioned.

I started to walk to the Barbours' house. To keep cool I walked very slowly, and so I was late. The party had already collected in the hall. Nervously I began to wipe the sweat off my face with my paint-rag.

'Stop it, Denton, stop it!' the girls cried. 'You're smothering your face with paint!'

Then we bundled into two cars; the food and painting gear was piled on top of us and we set off for the Bund.

The boat was very trim and shining. It had tiny little brass-rimmed portholes. I started to explore as soon as we had pushed out into the river. There was a galley, a saloon, two cabins and a bathroom. All the fittings were mahogany and there were green baize curtains with little pompoms round the edge. It fascinated me.

Mrs Barbour began to unpack the provisions and the chafing-dish. The Yugoslavian painter was gallantly setting up the girls' easels on the deck. He looked at me and showed his gold teeth in a reproachful smile, because I was not helping. His nose was pitted and his cheeks were rather purple. I turned away. Margot had been most misleading when she had talked about her drawing-master.

I did not want to paint. I wanted to hide in a corner of the boat. I shut myself in one of the empty cabins and climbed up into the top bunk. The counterpane smelt stale and aromatic. I put my ear close to the ship's side and heard the waves slapping and sucking. They were even as corrugated iron. There was a little watery tinkle, as if a glass bell were sounding. A greenish jelly-fish of light shook and trembled on the ceiling.

'Denton, where are you?' I heard Margot scream. I hurriedly climbed down and ran into the saloon; then I went up on deck, feeling rather dizzy.

They were all painting busily. I settled in a corner and started to put down the huge, glaucous eye of a junk. It stared accusingly back at me from the white sheet of paper. I liked it, floating there alone. I did not want to add the confused mass of rigging, but felt that it was expected of me. I had not the courage or the conceit to paint the eye and nothing else.

The Yugoslav was scrubbing vigorously with stiff hog's-hair brushes. I wished for my own oil-paints; I had brought my dirty water-colour box because it was so much lighter. I regretted it now; I wanted to wriggle rich worms out of fat tubes.

Margot dropped her hands into her lap and said, 'I'm the biggest messer on earth!'

The Yugoslav bent over her like an anxious hawk.

'Miss Margot is not to say so,' he ordered masterfully. 'Look how young! How much experience she will have time to gain!'

Margot and I both left our work and went up to his canvas. A mass of brilliant junks already sprawled across it. The sun caught it, taking away the colour and turning the thick glistening paint into a silvery relief map.

'It's like a Van Gogh,' Margot murmured hopelessly.

'But look how many years' start I have had! You will both be good painters if you work hard. Why, I was painting when you were still being fed at your mothers' breasts.' He smiled benignly at us and I found myself turning red; but Margot took no notice, she just stared silently at his picture.

'Lunch is ready, children,' Mrs Barbour chanted from the foot of the companion-way. We filed down ceremoniously; Margot first, her younger sisters next, the Yugoslav, and then myself. We had caught some of his punctiliousness.

The white cloth was dotted with blue dishes bearing chicken-joints, big Japanese prawns, tomatoes, pale yellow lettuce hearts and decorative rings of hard-boiled egg. Home-made lemonade stood in already frosted glasses. The food looked charming, and we began to eat it hungrily, spoiling the patterns of the dishes. The Yugoslav seemed to distrust his lemonade.

'Would you rather have had lager or whisky, Mr Mantovic?' Mrs Barbour asked anxiously. She never remembered his name quite correctly. 'I'm so sorry; I never thought of bringing any.'

He held up his glass. 'This is better than any wine, Madame,' he answered solemnly.

After the peaches and cold creamed rice, we leant back against the buttoned upholstery and sipped our coffee contentedly. We were peaceful and silent, and I could not understand why the Yugoslav suddenly jumped up and threw himself against the mahogany door. I decided that, probably, he felt sick and there was no time to spare. We all politely pretended not to have noticed anything.

The next moment he was screaming down to us from the deck. 'Come up, come up,' he yelled frantically. 'We are going to be rammed.'

The words meant nothing at all to me. They sounded like gibberish. But Mrs Barbour awoke immediately. 'Go up on deck at once, children,' she ordered, grabbing the two younger girls by the hand and signalling to Margot and myself.

The Yugoslav thundered through the saloon, shouting, 'I am going to unmoor us!'

We heard him wrestling with the rope in the stern.

Once on deck, I saw what threatened. A tramp-steamer, seemingly out of control, was lurching across the river, heading straight for us. A heavily laden coal-barge rowed by two coolies was trying to pass through the ever-narrowing channel between the steamer and our house-boat.

One of the tramp's crew stood in the great, towering bows, looking down cynically.

We all stood together, watching the terrifying sight. Margot kept saying, over and over again, 'I've left my sun-glasses in the saloon! I've left my sun-glasses in the saloon!' Her two sisters were apathetic, like animals, and Mrs Barbour told everyone to keep calm. I prayed. I remembered what I had been told about the river – how the current sucked you under, so that no man could swim in it. The Chinese said that the dead men caught you by the feet and pulled you down. The black slime and mud were too horrible to think of. I knew that I must save myself, whatever happened. I wondered if I could jump and catch hold of the rope that dangled over the side of the junk to which we had been moored.

'Try to get on to the junk,' I shouted. Even at this moment I wanted the others to approve. I did not want to jump for the rope if they thought it stupid or cowardly.

Nobody paid any attention. All eyes were fixed on the bows of the tramp-steamer. The Yugoslav was the only one who seemed to have the power of movement. He ran up and down the deck, shouting threats and filthy words at the figure in the oily white boiler-suit.

The coolies on the coal-barge were rowing madly, shouting and screaming as they rocked their paddles to and fro. Just as they got between us, the steamer closed up and rammed the barge full in the side. It in turn crashed against our stern.

There was the squeaking, splintering sound of wood being crushed, and the next thing I saw was the broken barge, its bows and stern pointing to the sky, disappearing into the water.

In a few seconds it was gone and only two heads were left above the surface. The coolies were still screaming, but the noise was turned into gurgles by the water which they swallowed. They beat the water with their arms, and were borne away swiftly by the current.

The steamer's progress had been stopped. Five yards away it rose above us like a huge, pointed wedge. The oily figure still looked down at us calmly.

'Don't you know how to steer a ship yet?' the Yugoslav shouted. He was hoarse with rage.

'What's the matter? You ain't hurt,' the man in the bows yelled back. He leant forward lazily, taking his weight on his elbows.

'You have probably caused the death of two men. We are going to report that, and also the damage you have done to our boat.' The Yugoslav snatched my sketch-book and began to write in it.

I left him and ran to the stern. There was a large crack above the water-level. I called Margot and we stuffed it with our paint-rags and spare clothes; then we flopped down on the plush seats in the saloon. Fear had exhausted us. We no longer wanted to paint. When Mrs Barbour joined us we told her that we felt hungry. She hurriedly made tea and we all sat round, eating biscuits and cakes out of the tins. We talked of nothing but the accident. In spite of the heat it was very cosy.

Soon the boat was chugging back to the quay. We all felt anxious and stood about, holding saucepans and bowls. But we did not have to do any baling; the boat arrived safely.

'What would we have done without Mr Vantomic?' Mrs Barbour asked as she set foot on shore. 'He undoubtedly saved the situation by unmooring the boat. Without him we might all have been drowned!'

The Yugoslav only scowled at her tribute; because she had mangled his name.

My brother and father were not impressed by my escape from death. 'You'll be late if you don't hurry, we're going out to dinner,' was all my father said.

I ran into my bedroom and threw on black trousers and short white mess-jacket. I liked myself in the mess-jacket, although I sometimes wondered if it made me look like a steward on board ship.

Nobody spoke in the car, and when we arrived, there was an even greater air of depression.

The house was airless. Every window was screened with mosquito-netting. The lamps were so shrouded that they illuminated only the ceilings. The rooms were ghostly, flood-lit aquariums. Our host's thick cigar-smoke floated about in them like trails of seaweed.

He was old. His neck was more wrinkled and cracked than his face. An eye-glass dangled against his waistcoat, but he never seemed to put it in his eye. It reminded me of one of those little windows that vivisectionists let into the stomachs of animals.

'So these are your sons,' he said to my father. He looked us up and down as if we were horses and he was trying to decide which one to buy.

'Are you the one who ran away from school?' he asked me at last.

Nobody else had been quite so crude about it. He knocked down my barricades. I could only answer 'Yes.'

'When I was at Marlborough we had a chap who ran away – funny little beggar – '

A flood of reminiscences began to flow out of his mouth. I listened, because I wanted to read between the lines and despise him.

The Boy announced dinner and we trooped downstairs. I was amazed when the dining-room door opened. Most of the room was drab enough, but over the service-hatch and almost covering one wall stood an extraordinary little erection, the façade of a Tudor cottage. There was a section of roof, thatched with real straw; a pattern of dummy beams; diamond-paned windows with paper roses dangling round them; and under the eaves, in big Gothic capitals, the words 'Ye Tucke Inne'.

I gaped. I had never before seen anything quite so pointless and silly.

'Ah, I see you're admiring my inn,' the old man said. 'I told the decorators that I wanted something rather novel, not a cocktail-bar or anything like that; so they thought this out for me. It looks just as if the food were being passed out of the window of an old Tudor cottage, doesn't it?'

We all agreed, and said what a clever idea it was. The food began to appear. It was very tired and quite tasteless. The ginger-ale, which I had not asked for, was lukewarm. I hated the old man for giving me such nasty food and drink.

We went back to the drawing-room and listened to more stories while we drank good coffee. The buzzing of the useless little fan maddened me. Suddenly I said something rude and insulting. It could have been passed off as mere clumsiness, but Mr Quinn knew exactly what I meant.

'What right have you to say a thing like that to me?' he shrilled. Anger made his voice much clearer and younger.

I jumped up, frightened, but enjoying the scene because I felt alive again. My father rose slowly to his feet and said, 'I think we ought to be going, Quinn, these two mustn't stay up too late.' In the stress of the moment he was treating us like small children.

Mr Quinn, still deeply resentful, followed us into the hall. 'You at least are a good listener,' were his last words to my father.

My eyes filled up with water. I felt tired. I suddenly had a picture of the tramp-steamer coming towards us as we stood on the deck in the hot sun.

CHAPTER 26

THE next morning I woke up late. I remembered what had happened and decided to go on with my painting; but when I looked at it I was so discouraged that I took up my easel and paint-box and set out for the near-by Chinese village. I sat down under some willows, beside a green pond. The duckweed was so thick that no water could be seen. It looked like a layer of rough shagreen. Puffy, English clouds floated in the blue sky, making the curling roofs seem exotic.

I squeezed out my paints and set to work. I started on the stone steps which led down to the pond. They were a silvery-blue and I loved painting them. It was cool under the willows. I could feel contentment spreading over me. It started in the middle and welled up to my head. I was afraid that I might think of something which would break the spell. I tried to concentrate only on my picture.

A dusty black dog sidled up to me. It sniffed my paint-box, then lay down at my feet, flattening its head to the ground and staring up at me, pretending to be my dog.

Two peasants, carrying hoes on their shoulders, stopped to look. They did not beg, but seemed to be saying polite things about the picture. I felt very friendly towards them and wished I had something to give. My sun-glasses seemed to be the most suitable present, but I could not spare them – besides, I persuaded myself, to be fair I would have to give two pairs of glasses.

I packed up my paints and went back to the flat. I was so pleased with my picture that I wanted to show it to Vesta. After lunch I took it carefully by a corner and started to walk across the fields. The soft wind caught it and blew it about, and my finger and thumb ached from the effort of keeping it rigid.

As I passed some grave-mounds I heard laughter and the noise of spades ringing on stones; then there was a whimper, tender and shrill. I climbed up the mound to see what was happening. A shower of stones and earth fell at my feet; but they were not aimed at me, they were aimed at a tiny puppy. It cried out again piercingly from under the stones and mud, and the three men who were digging laughed. I knelt down and scraped the earth from the puppy. It was sweet and pig-like, with black and white spots.

I was about to pick it up when another shower descended. A sharp stone hit my hand and I swore furiously at the coolies. This made them laugh even more than the whimpers of the puppy. One of them jerked open the slit of his buttonless trousers and started to make water all over the puppy.

I snatched it up and tucked it under my arm. My wet painting dangled dangerously from the other hand. I walked away shouting filthy words at the men. They laughed gleefully and danced about. Stones whistled past my head, but the men were not throwing to hit. 'Damn-fooloo, damn-fooloo,' they cried after me. It was the only English swear-word they knew.

When we were out of view I put the puppy down and wiped it with bunches of long grass. It still whined gently, but it was not hurt. It settled down comfortably when I tucked it under my arm once more. I wondered what I was going to do with it. I knew that my father wouldn't want it in the penthouse. I was hoping that the Fieldings would adopt it.

They were in the garden, playing tennis, when I arrived.

'What have you got there?' Mr Fielding asked as he saw me approaching clumsily with the puppy and the picture.

'I've brought a picture to show Vesta, and on the way I found this little puppy. It was being ill-treated by three grave-diggers. I couldn't leave it, they would have killed it,' I said.

'It can't stay here, it might develop hydrophobia.' He seemed very uneasy.

'Don't be silly, Roland,' said Mrs Fielding, who was a Christian Scientist. 'At least it can play on the lawn for the moment.' And she went into the house to find some food for it.

I sat down to watch the game, and the puppy roamed into the bushes. Vesta and her husband were playing against Elaine and a Norwegian girl. The Norwegian girl said she was tired, so I was asked to take her place. We played for some time, and I quite forgot about the puppy until tea was brought.

'He must be here somewhere,' I said as I searched through the bushes, but no puppy could be found.

We scattered, looking in every corner of the garden; then I went out into the road.

At the corner, near the creek, stood a tough little French policeman in his military-looking helmet.

'Have you seen a little dog?' I asked.

'What colour little dog?' He spoke so quickly that his toothbrush moustache jumped up and down, as if it lived a life of its own.

'White with black spots,' I said. I hoped he would understand. I did not know the French word for spots.

He nodded his head. 'Small dog run out, motor car catch him here.' The policeman put his brown hands on his flat stomach and let out screams and groans. 'I pick him up and there is much blood. He is no good, so I break his neck.' He made a clicking in the back of his throat to imitate the sound. 'After, I throw him in the creek.'

He gave me a shrewd cheerful look, as if he had killed the puppy very neatly and would be willing to kill

another, if necessary. His efficiency made me feel squeam-
ish. I thanked him and went back into the garden.

I wondered why none of us had heard the noise of the
car or the screams of the puppy. I had seen no marks on
the road either; but I had to admit that I had kept my
eyes half closed for fear of noticing any revolting signs of
the accident.

'The French policeman says that the puppy has been
run over,' I told the others.

They made sympathetic noises. The Norwegian girl
said something in her own language and then was silent.
She evidently did not like to go on talking about German
baroque churches.

'Well, perhaps it's for the best,' Mr Fielding sighed.
'This is no country for dogs.' He was relieved and felt
quite friendly towards me again.

'Poor little thing,' said Elaine, and waited until the
'time limit' was up before reviving the conversation. 'To
tell you the truth, I think baroque is rather vulgar,' she
admitted.

'Ah, that's because you're a Puritan. All Americans
are Puritans,' came the answer.

Much better to have left the puppy with the coolies, I
thought. Even if it hasn't been run over, that little Gipsy-
ish policeman has sold it to someone to cook for dinner.

Vesta came across the lawn to me.

'Don't worry about the poor puppy,' she said. 'You
did all you could for it. I think your painting is so promising. It's much better than I thought it would be.'

The vinegar in this last remark set me tingling. It did
not quite make up for the honey. Arguing about painting, we went into the house together.

As I was leaving, Mrs Fielding ran across the hall and
stopped me.

'Would you like to do something kind?' she asked.

I felt embarrassed and said, 'Yes, what is it?'

'Would you take the lustre jug you found and show it

to a friend of mine who's been very ill? I told her about it, as she collects, and now she's very keen to see it.'

'Wouldn't you rather take it yourself? I could bring it here next time I come.'

'Oh, no,' Mrs Fielding said. 'I've told her all about you and how interested you are in old things, so she wants to see you too. Could you manage to-morrow afternoon? I know that's a good time for her.'

'Yes, I'll go to-morrow if you tell me where she lives.'

There was no escape. The address was written down and I was given full instructions on how to get there.

I felt hot and had an uncomfortable thickness inside me as I walked towards Mrs Abercrombie's house. I dreaded the new meeting.

The Boy kept me waiting for some time while he went to tell his mistress. My gaze wandered round the hall. Lances and spears hung on the walls. Lumpy bronzes held frothy, cascading ferns. There was a little pagoda of bells to call the household to meals.

'My wife will be ready to see you in a few minutes,' a voice said.

I looked up and saw a tall man with a wispy, stained moustache standing on the stairs.

He led me into the drawing-room. 'Effective things, aren't they?' he said while I stared at the water-colours. 'My daughter does them.'

Sloppy, liquid flowers stuck up into a blue sky where pieces of white-of-egg floated.

'They are all corners in the garden,' he explained. 'I think I like the one of the summer-house best.'

Underneath his social manner a deep black bog of melancholy seemed to float.

'They are very pretty,' I said. 'The flowers are done beautifully. Your daughter must be very clever.'

'Oh, she is, is she,' he said. 'But what comes of it all? That's what I should like to know.'

The Boy came in to say that Mrs Abercrombie was ready.

Nervously I followed her husband up the stairs. I tried to imagine what she looked like.

Against the banisters at the top of the stairs stood a full-sized but movable bath. The enamel up to a certain level was discoloured, and immediately I had a picture of cattle drinking out of just such a bath, as it stood derelict in a field.

'My wife looks very different now. You mustn't be surprised.'

I felt warned and horrified. I had expected someone in bed with wasted grey-coloured face, but instead she was in a wheel-chair by the open window and her face was blotched yellow and blue and red. I could not look straight at her, but I made myself go forward with a smile all over my face.

'I've brought the jug,' I said gaily. I unwrapped it and put it on the table in front of her.

Her eyes puckered at the corners and her mouth curved upwards, but I could not quite tell if she were smiling, as the shape of her lips had disappeared in the general ruin of her face.

I found that although I could not look straight I had to keep glancing at her.

She did not try to touch the jug, she only read every detail of it with her eyes. When she spoke, it was not to mention the jug at all.

'Henry, would you open the other window a little, it's so hot.'

Her husband pulled the top sash down, and immediately her papers and letters blew off the table and scattered themselves all over the floor. I bent down and began to collect them.

'Oh, it's no good,' she wailed. 'Everything blows about. I think we'd better have it shut again, Henry dear.'

Coming from that mouth, her voice seemed startlingly normal. It was just like any other woman's.

Her husband pushed up the sash again and, after looking at us mournfully, left the room before he could be asked to do anything else.

I was left alone with her.

'I've been looking at your daughter's water-colours,' I began desperately.

'Aren't they frightful?' was her reply.

I was too surprised to say anything but 'Yes.'

'Well, can you do any better?' She shot the words at me venomously.

'I don't know, perhaps not.' I felt bewildered and snubbed, and longed to escape. I stood up.

'I think I ought to be going. I have a long way to walk.'

She stared at me as if she had only just seen me, and wondered what I was doing there. Then she waved her hand jerkily.

'Good-bye,' she said. 'Thank you so much for bringing the lustre jug.'

I picked it up and knew at once that she expected me to leave it with her.

'Oh, I see you've decided to take it away after all!'

Her terrible face crumpled up and I thought she was going to cry.

'Good-bye,' I said, hurriedly making for the door. I shut it noisily and hummed to myself as I clattered down the stairs. I did not want to hear any sounds from her bedroom.

CHAPTER 27

Now that the nights were so hot I went to bed late. If we had no guests I would slip out quietly after dinner and go for long walks.

The plane trees were heavy now with dust. Their leaves hung in grey sprays across the pools of light from the street lamps. Underneath moved a throng made up of all nations. There were many uniforms. Brass and dark leather suddenly caught the light and glittered.

Chinese and Russian girls walked with the soldiers and sailors. The Chinese were dressed in long flowered gowns, split to the knee, and the Russians in short-skirted, musk-scented black *crêpe-de-Chine*.

These were their uniforms, as rigid as the soldiers' or sailors'.

If I caught fragments of their talk it was always staid and old-fashioned.

'The night is very hot.'

'Will you be staying in our city long?'

'No, thank you, I do not smoke in the street.'

One night I found myself on the edge of French Town. I was in a long, unhappy street where European refugees lived. The trams clanged up and down. Between the grim buildings were squalid pieces of waste ground. Although it was late, lights still gleamed in some of the small shops.

I stopped to watch a young man moving furniture. He held the ungainly pieces with great skill and strength, carrying them across the pavement and depositing them on a barrow.

Two Chinese watched his feat of strength respectfully,

but did not help; then, when the barrow was loaded, with much argument and talk they trundled it away.

The young man went back into the shop and started to pick up the newspaper and sweep the floor where the furniture had stood. When he had finished he disappeared into the back of the shop.

I walked on. I wondered if he was Austrian, as the place was called 'The Vienna Furnishing Store.'

I had only gone a few paces when I heard steps behind me, and the next moment he hurried past, carrying two swinging objects which looked like money-bags. Intent and springing, he moved in front of me until he turned a corner. I was just in time to see him enter a stadium where boxing and that Basque game, which is played with a basket on the hand, took place.

I decided to go in too, but when I came to the doors I found that they were locked. There was no fixture for that night. Quickly I made a mystery for myself. I wondered what he was doing in the empty building and how he had got in.

I ran down a little alley which led to the back of the stadium. The only light was from an open window on the first floor. I pulled myself on to the top of the enclosing wall. A cat was already there. It spat and arched its back and then subsided, deciding that I was not terrifying enough. I stood up carefully and looked, across a gulf of blackness, into the upper part of the room.

At first I thought it was a bathroom; all I could see was the naked back of a man, looking very pink and glossy under the bright light. Then he turned and I recognized him as the furniture-lifter, and at the same moment I had the explanation of the money-bags, for he raised his hands and they were encased in boxing-gloves.

He began to spar with someone else and I watched quite fascinated. Their bodies darted in and out of the frame of the lighted window. It was like some wonderful, exasperating picture which disappeared and came again.

Watching their fierce, darting punches and listening to the shouts and laughter, I forgot about the narrowness of the wall, and so kept my balance perfectly.

At last there was a break, and before I could move, the furniture-lifter came to the window and stood there, letting the air fan his chest. My impulse was to jump into the alley, but in that moment when the body gathers itself together I heard a burring half-European, half American voice drawl softly, 'And what might you be doing, may I ask?'

It was horribly startling. I stood quite still.

'I've been watching you,' was all I could say.

'Oh, a sportsman, I see. Would you like to come up and have a go yourself?'

He was making fun of me.

'I don't know anything about it,' I said coldly. 'I've never done any boxing.' I turned and jumped off the wall.

'Not so fast,' he shouted. 'If you'll wait a minute I'll come down and let you in.' He disappeared from the window.

I started to run. Although a part of me asked eagerly to stay, escape seemed simpler. But I was glad when I saw him standing at the end of the lane, cutting off my further retreat. I knew at once that if he had not been there I would have run home and regretted it always.

Wrapped in a dirty old bathrobe, and with the street-lamp shining on the glistening spikes of his disordered hair, he looked strange and rather magnificent.

'Come right on up, Son,' he said, ushering me before him.

We went into the dust-smelling passage and climbed a flight of stairs to the first floor. There was no light. I felt my way along the wall and followed his directions.

At the end of a long corridor we stopped. A crack of light shone along the boards. He held open the door for me, saying, 'Kindly step inside, please,' with American politeness.

The sudden light was uncomfortable. All I could see for a moment was a roped-off ring and a heap of old bolsters. Then I noticed a fair, sunless-looking man lying on the bolsters. The grey towel over his shoulders, the newspaper he was reading, the cigarette stub in his mouth, all matched his pale hair and skin, and the striped bolsters.

He looked up at us, and the furniture-lifter said to me, 'That's Mik. He don't speak much English; he's Russian.' He paused. 'My name's Ernst. What might yours be, may I ask?'

'Denton,' I said, making it sound rather flat and silly.

'That's kind of hard. Ain't you got no other name?'

'Will Maurice do? It's my first name, but nobody calls me by it.'

'Maurice will do fine!' He drawled it sleepily, as though it were spelt More-is.

'Well, let's get going,' he said, taking down a pair of gloves and bringing them to me. He looked at my feet. 'You got rubbers on?' he asked.

'Yes, but do you want me to take my shoes off, because I will if you like.'

'No, they'll do. Hold out your wrists and I'll fix these gloves.'

The gloves felt sticky inside. There were ridges where sweat had dried, hardening the leather.

'Gee, you're thin!' he said as he laced them.

'Oh, I eat plenty.' In the hurry to defend the size of my body I caught some of his Americanism. He unbuttoned my shirt and turned the collar in; then he got Mik to tie his own gloves.

He stood squarely in front, and showed me how to guard my face and body and how to distribute my weight. Then, in slow motion, he started to fight, shouting directions and warnings before he patted me with his smooth gloves. He did not punch, but ordered me to do so. I hung back and he became angry, so I hit him as hard as I could on the chest. But it made no impression; my feeble punch seemed to bounce off him.

We threw ourselves down on the bolsters to rest. I was panting for breath and the sweat trickled into my eyes and stung them. I felt very happy. Mik just looked at me and then went on reading his paper.

'One more go before bed,' Ernst said. 'This time I won't tell you what to do.'

He dragged me to my feet and we shook hands like dogs who have been taught to 'beg'.

For a moment we circled on our toes; then Ernst flashed forward and hit me. One blow struck my ribs, and the other my face.

'Why don't you look after them?' he asked patiently.

Hot blood ran out of my nose and trickled into the corner of my mouth. I felt sick and dizzy.

'Lie down flat until that stops,' Ernst said. He went to the tap and brought back a damp face-towel. I lay on the bolsters, trying to define to myself the flavour of the blood, while he wiped my face and neck. The coolness was delicious. I hoped that my nose would not stop bleeding. The towel and my handkerchief were soaked to a wonderful red. What a pity it doesn't last! I thought. My lip was beginning to feel inflated and leathery.

I lay quite still for a few minutes, then I sat up. There was an upsurge of warmth in my nose, but only a trickle of blood came out.

'It's stopped at last,' I said. 'What do we do now?'

'Guess we'd better be going home. It's getting late.' Ernst turned to me. 'If you'll come round again to-day week, I'll teach you some more.'

I jumped up to thank him, and my nose started to drip again. Round blobs sunk into the soft wood floor. I held my face over the sink while Ernst untied my gloves. Then he and Mik pulled on their shirts and trousers, and we left the room, locking the door behind us.

Mik said good-bye at the main entrance. I walked with Ernst towards his shop. I warmed towards him because he asked no questions. All he said was, 'Meet me outside here about 8.30 next week.' I nodded.

'That's fine. You can't get into the stadium without me,' he explained. He fitted his key into the lock. 'Good night, More-is,' he said, and disappeared.

'What have you done to your face?' my father asked at breakfast the next morning.

'I banged my lip on the corner of the gatepost as I turned into the drive last night. It was so dark; I couldn't see anything.' I felt ashamed of the commonplace lie. My father looked at me, and my face grew hot. He dropped his eyes.

'You'll be kidnapped one of these nights if you insist on prowling about alone. God knows where you go.'

'Oh, I only go out for a little air before bed.'

'You weren't in till after twelve last night; I heard you.'

Rustling the paper, he got up, and soon afterwards the front door slammed.

I wondered what to do. I decided to look in the library for books on boxing; then I would be more prepared for Ernst's next lesson.

An empty silver inkstand and a bedraggled quill pen stood on the desk between the tall windows. Below, the blue roofs of the city trembled in the heat.

I sat on the cool, slippery floor and wondered why I hadn't used the room more often. I could even make it my room, I thought, as no one else seems to come in here.

I began to search the shelves. The heaviest books had sunk to the bottom. On a level with my face were two photograph albums and a fat book of exquisite flower-paintings done by my great-grandmother. The name of the flower, her own name, and the date sprawled across the corner of each ivory-smooth card. The painting was bright and luminous as enamel. Tiny veins and blemishes patterned the leaves and flowers.

I forgot about boxing. I started to read the *Ballad of Reading Gaol* and dropped it after the first page. On one shelf I found a little collection of elaborately stamped and embossed bindings. They were old American literary souvenirs and collections of verse: the *Magnolia* of 1837 in rich morocco and gold; and *Friendship's Offering*, 1840, dark and shiny as wine-jelly, with an all-over pattern of raised acanthus leaves and honeysuckle. They, too, had my great-grandmother's name in them. I imagined them lying on her drawing-room table, or perhaps beside her bed, with her lorgnons and double scent bottle.

I asked Boy for some furniture cream and began to polish them carefully. As I put them back, a drab little book in modern binding fell off the shelf. It lay open at my feet and I could see that its pages were stained and yellow. I picked it up. It was a cookery book. I turned to the front page and read, 'Directions for Cookery, Philadelphia, 1828.' I realized then that it had been rebound. The pages had been trimmed and the print reached to the very edge.

I began to read the recipes for A-La-Mode Beef, Meg Merrilies Soup, A Pyramid of Tarts, Sweet Basil Vinegar, Federal Cakes, Seevets, Lead Water, A Squash Pudding, Mince-Meat for Lent, Apees, Kisses, An Antidote for Laudanum, Hungary Water, Green Ointment and Sweet Jars.

For Sweet Jars it said, 'Take a china jar and put into it three handfuls of fresh damask rose-leaves; three of sweet pinks, three of wall-flowers, and stock gilly-flowers, and equal proportions of any other fragrant flowers that you can procure. Place them in layers; strewing fine salt thickly between each layer, and mixing with them an ounce of sliced orris root.'

I discovered from the dictionary that orris root was the dried root of certain types of iris.

I decided to go to the park and collect as many of the flowers as possible. I could have gone to the Fieldings' or some other friends' garden, but the park was much nearer, and probably better stocked, I thought.

I set out with a little covered basket. It had rained during the night and all the bushes and flowers steamed in the sun. First, I went down the winding path to the rose garden. Nobody was about. I shook the heavy, bloated heads into my basket and snapped down the lid; then I went in search of the other flowers. The search for the orris root would be the most difficult, so I left it till the last.

The Japanese garden was the most popular; I had to wait for the people to go back to their lunch. I ran to the water's edge when I was alone, and plunging my arm into the tepid water, I felt in the mud and slime for the roots of the iris. I pulled up a great dripping handful. The cool mud smelt rich and clean, but through it I caught whiffs of something strong and perfumed. I was delighted. I felt sure that I had found the orris root. After rinsing it hurriedly in the water, I thrust it into my basket. A thick wave of scent floated up when I lifted the lid.

I went back to the penthouse and spread the flowers on a tray in the sun.

'What are these things?' my father asked when he came home.

'I'm making sweet jars,' I said. 'These are the ingredients – they have to be dried.'

'Where did you find them?'

'In the public park.'

I left before he could ask any more questions. I went on to the veranda to look at the rose-leaves. I saw that they were withering in the hot sun and that I would need some more.

I decided to go back to the park in the evening. I climbed up the little iron ladder to the roof of the penthouse and prepared to sunbathe.

Perhaps it's dangerous and I will get sunstroke, I thought.

I took my shirt and trousers off and spread them on the baking concrete. Then I lay down naked, with my topee, like a candle-snuffer, over my face.

From under it, I looked slantingly down my chest, through a forest of beads of sweat which formed round each tiny hair on my body. Large, velvety smuts came to rest on me. They blew down from the chimney of the hot-water system. If I brushed them off, they left long smears of black on my skin.

The glorious, fierce sun was burning into me. I turned over, and little rivulets of sweat ran off me and trickled on to the concrete, where they made dark patches.

I lay quite still until I felt my back coated with heat; then I got up rather dizzily and climbed down the ladder. I rang the bell for tea and went to soak in cold water until it was ready. Afterwards, to cool my flesh, I rubbed myself with my father's eau-de-Cologne, but it stung me so fiercely that I had to plunge back into the bath. When the pain wore off, my skin settled down to a pleasant simmering and tingling.

At dusk, I went out again with my basket. The park looked lovelier than ever. The leathery, polished lotus leaves spread out in perfect stillness on the water.

It was almost dark when I reached the rose-garden. I did not notice the dark form on the bench. Swiftly I began to pull off the over-blown heads.

'Hey, what are you doing?' a voice suddenly asked.

'Oh, just picking off some old heads,' I said as casually as possible.

'I thought you was a Chink, pinching things,' the voice answered placidly. Something white was thrust towards me. 'Have a cigarette?' he asked. As he leaned forward I saw the outline of a peaked cap, and I wondered if he was a policeman; but when he lit a match I discovered that he was a soldier. For a moment I thought he might be the one I had asked to tea.

I sat down beside him on the bench and took in his smell. It was a mixture of Blue-Bell polish, tobacco, hair-oil and onions.

'I know what you've been eating,' I said archly and stupidly, to make conversation.

He grunted. 'What do you think of these Russian girls?' he asked.

'I'm afraid I don't know anything about them,' I answered awkwardly.

'Ain't you started yet, then? I had my first when I was fifteen.'

'That was early,' I said, beginning to feel rather desperate.

'I wish you was a nice bit of skirt,' he went on earnestly.

'Yes-it's-a-pity-I'm-not-from-your-point-of-view.' In my embarrassment, all my words ran together.

'You got any sisters?' he asked in a yearning voice.

'No.'

'What's your Ma like?'

'My mother's dead,' I said severely and repressively.

I got up and threw away my cigarette.

'You going, boy?'

'Yes.'

'If you see anything, send it my way.'

'All right, good night.'

I walked over the misty grass. At the gates, two women were waiting. They might, or might not, have been prostitutes. As I passed them, something prompted me to shout, 'Go into the rose-garden.' Then, horrified by my peculiar behaviour, I started to run. I wondered if they would follow my advice. I imagined them chasing the soldier over the rose-beds.

As the Number One opened the front door I heard voices and laughter. I had forgotten that the woman who wore the gold chain round her ankle was coming to dinner.

CHAPTER 28

I WAS already waiting outside Ernst's shop at eight o'clock on the right day of the next week. I had been too impatient to stay at home any longer. I told my father that the Fieldings had asked me to dinner.

As before, the shop was lighted but empty. I stood opposite it, on the other side of the road, and looked at the upper windows in the hope of seeing Ernst preparing to come out.

A light went on and I saw the outline of a woman against the window. She seemed to have Edwardianly dressed hair and a bottle-waist. She stood so still that I moved about nervously, thinking that she had seen me. I was relieved when she disappeared as suddenly as she had come. I looked at my watch; it was nearly half-past eight. I crossed the road, expecting to see Ernst at any moment. Now that the light had been turned out, the lace curtains at the windows above the shop hung in milky loops like pouring water.

I walked up and down impatiently. No one came out of the empty shop. I looked up at the first-floor windows again. Something was happening. One of the curtains was trembling. The next moment it was pulled aside and a face pressed against the glass; not the front of the face, but the side, so that I saw a flattened section of cheek and an eye peering out of an apple-ring of greenish-white flesh.

The ugliness of it was startling. Now I knew for certain that I was being watched. I took refuge in a doorway farther down the street. I supposed that they were refugees with an obsession about secret agents.

I returned once more to the shop in the hope of finding

Ernst, but the face was still at the window. I began to feel afraid. I decided that I could stay there no longer, so I went and sat on the dirty steps in the dark entrance of the stadium.

At nine o'clock I walked down the side alley to see if there were lights in the boxing-room, but there were none. The whole building seemed dead. I waited without any particular hope until half-past nine, and then decided to go home. I dared not pass the shop again, so I returned another way, over some waste ground.

As I walked I realized that I ought not to be back too early if I was supposed to be out to dinner. I began to dawdle, dragging out the walk as much as possible.

I was near Bubbling Well. I stopped to look at the extravagant, wild temple with its rich, curling roofs. It was beautiful without the trams and the cigarette-posters. I went into the middle of the road and looked over the carved balustrade of the great square well. The moonlight just caught the treacly surface far below, and showed up the evil bubbles bursting and winking. There was music from St George's Cabaret. Mood Indigo floated out, mixed up with the shuffle and knock of dancing feet.

An American marine went by. He looked at me, and must have thought that I needed cheering up, for he stopped and shouted out gaily, 'Come on in and get tight!' I did not move or say anything, so he grasped me boisterously by the arm and pulled me forward. It was clear that he was more or less drunk already. I hung back, protesting that I did not want to go to the Cabaret; but he took no notice; he just dragged me along as if he were taking a sulky child for a walk. I was not nervous for some reason. I suppose I realized that he was essentially good-natured.

I had given up resisting by the time we arrived at the entrance, and only protested half-heartedly when he threw down two dollars for our tickets.

'This is my do, buddy,' he chanted in a sing-song voice. 'Didn't I drag you here by main force?'

238

The smell inside the glaring dance-hall was exciting. Scent and sweat and tobacco and dust, and a special uniform smell was all mixed together. The iridescent halos round the lights seemed to be an embodiment of the smell.

The marine pushed his way towards the prim row of dancing partners. I wanted to escape, but I followed in his wake, not knowing what else to do.

'Choose your pick, Son,' he said grandly.

'I don't think I'll dance,' I stammered. 'I'd rather sit and watch.' It was a horrible moment of confusion and embarrassment, but he noticed nothing.

''Course you must dance,' he said. 'If you won't choose, I'll choose for you.'

He leant forward and asked two of the demure Chinese girls to dance with us. They stood up obediently. They seemed as thin as candles in their long gowns, with only their white arms and faces showing. They were heavily and skilfully made up. I wondered if their arms left white marks on the backs of their partners. They wore no rouge, only deep lipstick and a thick, creamy foundation-paste over the rest of the face. Their hair was varnished and oiled until it looked like black treacle running snugly over their heads.

I began to dance with the one who stood in front of me. We said nothing but danced easily, like two pliable bolsters.

We sat down to rest and I grew still more uncomfortable. I suddenly realized that in such a place one was expected to buy drinks, and I had no money on me. But the marine came boisterously to my rescue. He and his partner flopped down in chairs beside us, and the next moment four whiskies had been ordered. He was wonderfully generous and impulsive and quite self-centred. We must all be gay and drunk because he was, and we must all like whisky because he did.

We were a depressed little class in the charge of an

exuberant schoolmaster. He made us drink and smoke at regular intervals, and I soon found myself melting; but the Chinese girls were as remote as ever. The only change in them was the tiny beads of sweat which, having pushed through their make-up, began to lie in clusters round their eyes and nostrils.

The music broke out again. We exchanged partners and swirled away in different directions. I say swirled because the music had taken on a Viennese flavour. People, with confused ideas in their heads, tried to follow late Victorian steps. There was a muddle of partners flying apart and coming together again not quite happily. A sort of dissolution seemed to be taking place.

Suddenly we were swept forward by a whip of laughing men and girls. They had cleared the floor behind them. Battered dancers were retiring behind the tables. My partner gave me one swift look and disappeared. I made haste to join the whip.

Being the last on the line, I flew through the air when the whip cracked. I heard glasses and a chair falling. My arm felt as if it might be wrenched off. It was thrilling. I started to yell and shout with the others.

One poor couple, lying in a corner, had covered themselves with newspaper for greater privacy. It was rudely torn off them and chewed into confetti. Soon the air was filled with floating bits of paper, and the big American sailor, who was the pivot of the whip, looked like Edinburgh Castle seen through a snowstorm.

In one way and another his appearance had suffered. A crowd of smaller people, infuriated perhaps by his size and strength, had set on him and ripped his jacket up the back. Next they turned their attention to his trousers, but outraged modesty and strong thread and buttons defeated them here.

Hairy and childish, he stood looking down with a bemused expression, rather like a baby gorilla watching the antics of the people at the Zoo.

When the air cleared, I went in search of the marine, but he was nowhere to be found. I supposed that he had gone off with one of the girls. I decided to go home.

As I made for the door I saw a soldier raise his swagger-stick and bring it down with a crack on the shoulders of another. A crowd surged round them, and they were lifted up bodily and pushed outside before they had time to fight. I followed to see what would happen.

They both lay on the ground without moving; then one got up and began to water the bushes. The other turned over and composed himself for sleep. I left them peacefully together.

On the way home my head began to ache and buzz. I wanted to taste something very cool.

The Number One came to the door, dressed in his curious night-clothes. 'Young master very late!' he said censoriously. I did not answer, but went straight into the kitchen and opened the door of the refrigerator. I found some chocolate ice-cream frozen hard, and a grape-fruit. I took them into my room and ate them greedily.

I got up late and, still in my pyjamas, began to paint a fat bunch of carnations. They were all colours of puce and salmon-pink, and they stood in a mustard-yellow jar. The surface of my board was rough. I enjoyed filling it with rich paint. I treated the paint like putty, shaping it with my palette-knife. I stood back and looked at my picture. It was most disappointing. I put down my brushes and went on to the veranda.

There was smoke in the air, as if someone had lit a bonfire. I leaned over the balustrade. Then I heard Boy calling excitedly. He came running through the french window.

'Young master, have got fire some place, I think so. Dining-room plenty smoke!'

I looked into the drawing-room. Blue clouds were belching into it. They seemed to be coming from cracks in the woodwork. We ran into the bedrooms, where the built-in cupboards were so filled with smoke that it escaped in sinister little puffs through the keyholes. Every nook and cranny was smoking mysteriously, although nothing was alight.

I ran down to the flat below and met the woman who lived there, just as she came out. My father knew her, and she often passed me in the hall, looking smart and glossy and American. She was about to be married and had asked us that night to a cocktail-party in celebration.

She looked curious now, standing on her doorstep in what I must describe as a boudoir-cap. Her figure seemed to be draped in the loose-cover off an armchair, and her face was in rather an unfinished state, which added to her blank stare of surprise.

'Come on, Sakes Alive!' she screamed, grabbing my hand. 'The place must be on fire! We'd better get somewhere out of this!'

Hand in hand we raced down the stairs, like a pair of badly matched carriage-horses. A door was open on the third floor and we ran in to ask about the fire. A placid, grey-haired woman stood by a sofa. She was gazing absently out of the window, and when she heard us, she turned round and looked at us with dislike.

'I don't know what all the fuss is about,' she said wearily. 'I only decided to burn some old letters in the grate, and now everybody has been rushing in to tell me that the place is on fire. How was I to know that all the fireplaces are dummies except the ones on the top floor? They say that in winter you don't need fires because of the steam-heat. The mantelpiece is only for ornament, it seems. But if this so-called luxury-flat hasn't even got a real fireplace, give me a slum any day!'

After this speech, she sat down in disgust and began to brood. We tiptoed out and burst into laughter as soon as we had shut the door.

'Sakes, what a scare!' my companion cried. 'The

smoke from the old dame's love-letters fairly terrified me. My, but she must have had a pile!'

Still hand in hand, but walking sedately instead of running, we climbed up to our flats again. I left her at her door.

'Don't forget my party to-night!' she called out childishly and gaily.

Her flat buzzed and sang with the noise of voices blended together. Cool and pearly now, she moved about amongst her guests, offering them drinks, and oysters wrapped in wisps of bacon. It was only just September.

The man who was going to marry her came up to my father and said:

'I can't get out of it now. She's telling everyone we're engaged!' He laughed richly, as though he were soft, almost rotten, inside. He was a big man, with a big stomach.

She came up softly behind him and, taking his hand, slipped the signet-ring off his little finger. 'I adore Charles's ring,' she cooed, holding it close to her mouth. 'I'm crazy about it, and yet he won't give it to me.'

'My good woman,' he began, 'I've given you a perfectly respectable engagement ring, so why should you hanker after a man's signet-ring which would be far too large for you even if you did have it?'

He spoke in an exaggerated, level-headed way. She looked down at her own ring and said nothing more. She liked being treated as a silly woman.

She must have got her wish in the end; for soon after they were married he died in the night.

CHAPTER 29

VESTA and her husband went to Peking in September, and Mrs Fielding asked me to stay while they were gone. I arrived one heavy afternoon and found bowls of zinnias in my room. Ruth, the youngest daughter, had arranged them with great care. She came up to me, breathing rather heavily through her Mongolian nose.

'Do you like your flowers, Denton?' she asked, pouting earnestly.

'Very much, Ruth,' I answered. 'They're such wonderful colours, and you've arranged them so beautifully.'

I really meant what I said. Many 'normal' people would not have made the flowers look half so lovely.

'I'm so glad you like them, because I went out to pick them although I didn't feel well.'

'That was very good of you, but do you feel all right again now, Ruth?'

She sighed dramatically. 'No, Denton, I don't.'

'What's wrong?' I asked, frowning at her in what I hoped was a sympathetic way.

'Well, you see, Denton, this happens regularly – –'

Her face became solemn. She was about to go into details. I jumped up in confusion.

'I do hope you'll be all right again soon, Ruth,' I said, and began hurriedly to pull clothes out of my suitcase.

She left the room, looking disappointed. I had cut her story short.

A noise of splashing came up from the garden. I put on my bathing-suit and went down to the pool under the trees. Elaine was there alone. She had been swimming under water and her eyelids were a little inflamed. They clashed with the two loops of red hair which had not been pushed under her bathing-cap. She sat on the bank, sunning herself and watching me as I approached.

'I want to try diving between someone's legs,' she said. 'Get into the water and open your legs, will you?'

I waded into the pool and waited uncomfortably, hoping that she would not make a shallow dive. Her body flashed between my legs. I had the impulse to jump, but stood still. I turned round and saw her come up smiling.

'Now you try,' she ordered.

As soon as I had dived I opened my eyes. I saw two white pillars on either side of me. Her legs looked thicker through the water. They were flecked with green filtered sunlight. I had a terror of being caught between them. I propelled myself downwards and swam under water to the other side of the bath.

'I thought you were never coming up,' she said. 'Let's try again.'

But I saw with relief that the Boy was coming towards us with a table and a white tea-cloth. So we sat on the grass, drying our hair and waiting for Mrs Fielding.

As I undressed that night in Vesta's room I looked at all her things; at her lipsticks and rouges and nail-polishes of several different reds. The bathroom cupboard held pots of face-cream and bottles of sweet-coloured bath salts. Of course there were no medicines. She was, like her mother, a good Christian Scientist.

I threw some handfuls of salts into the bath and turned on the taps. The room obediently filled with the smell of pine-needles. I soaked in the water until my fingers were like shrivelled apples.

I dried myself and went into Vesta's sitting-room. The clumsy armchairs were covered in grass-green satin. The cushions were pink and yellow. Being naked, I did not enjoy sitting on the slimy stuff. I got up and wandered round the room, looking at Vesta's treasures: at the little eighteenth-century enamelled dish: the ivory seals of some long-dead official: the rather dull Sheffield-plate candlesticks: and at her tiny, pearl-set, beflowered French watch, with its hands stuck permanently at midnight or noon.

The only sign that she had a husband was a pompous walnut trouser-press. Everything else seemed to be hers. The top drawer of the lacquer dressing-table was filled with a heap of Chinese jewellery; silver hair-pins inlaid with kingfisher's feathers: rose quartz, bell-shaped drops with caps of gilt filigree: rings carved out of pieces of jade and agate: two thick little tassels of seed-pearls, to be worn as earrings.

It was while I looked at these things that the temptation to dress up came to me. I had a sudden picture of myself locked in the lavatory of the Salisbury train, twisting my trilby hat this way and that, wondering if I could disguise myself as a woman, to escape being caught and sent back to school.

I had everything I could want now for the experiment. With rising excitement I opened the wardrobe to look at Vesta's clothes. How many there were! I did not know what to choose. At last I decided on a thin woollen dress with a wide scarlet leather belt. I slipped it over my head and it tickled my skin, as I had nothing on underneath. It fitted very well, except of course for the fact that I had no breasts. I buckled the belt and then stuffed two bunched-up handkerchiefs into my bosom, but they looked so outrageous that, laughing quite hysterically, I pulled them out again.

I found a pair of snub-nosed, high-heeled shoes and tried them on. I was glad that I had small feet. My short hair worried me. I ruffled it and pulled pieces over my face, then I quickly pressed down a tight little felt hat and I looked at the result in the glass. It was passable; indeed I was quite changed, but I felt that something was lacking. I looked rather mousy and respectable. I realized that what I needed was some paint.

I sat down at the dressing-table and began to work on my face. It was as absorbing as redecorating a room. I was not at all restrained. I used everything I could find. I sunk my eyes in wells of blue eye-shadow and arched thin black eyebrows above them. I covered my cheeks with brick-dust rouge and my lips with scarlet lipstick.

By the time I had finished, the profession to which I belonged was quite unmistakable. I felt an urgent need to go out in my new disguise. It was too good to be wasted. I knew that all the doors downstairs would be locked by this time. Besides, to get to them I would have to pass Mrs Fielding's room, and she would hear me, as she always left her door open. I went to the window, which looked on to the drive. Below me a strip of shallow roof sloped to the wooden brackets and pillars of the hall-porch. It looked easy.

I stuffed Vesta's high-heeled shoes into the bosom of my dress and climbed on to the window-sill; then I let myself down gently on to the tiles. Immediately there was a clatter; some loose piece went tobogganing down the roof. I held my breath, to hear every noise from the house. Mrs Fielding's voice at once called out anxiously: 'Is everything all right, Denton?'

'Yes, Mrs Fielding,' I answered hurriedly. 'I think the noise was only a loose piece of tile sliding down the roof.'

I was terrified that she would come into my room. I waited, still clinging to the sill, wondering what to do. At last I groped towards the pillar of the porch. I swung my other hand across and hung like a monkey up a pole then I stepped easily from bracket to bracket until I felt the cold tiles of the porch under my bare feet.

I blessed the Edwardian architect for his profusion of white woodwork. Walking along the narrow grass border, still carrying Vesta's shoes, I reached the gates. I slipped on the shoes and minced off down the pavement. It was quite involuntary. I found that I had to bend my knees and lean backwards, the heels were so high.

Gradually I gained confidence. Nobody was about. I felt brave enough to leer at the French policeman on the corner, but he either did not see or was too uninterested to return it. His indifference gave me more courage. 'I must look exactly like a woman,' I thought.

Turning down a side street, I found myself in a lonely part where untidy plots of land sprawled between new buildings. A rickshaw passed me, its oil-lamp swinging and flickering recklessly. The person riding in it was singing. Suddenly the singing broke off and I heard the shafts of the rickshaw grate on the ground. It had not stopped outside any house. As I came up with it a man leant out. 'Would this be the right way to Avenue Roi Albert?' he asked with strong Scottish accent; and as he spoke he thrust his face close to mine and for a moment was able to look straight into my eyes.

I stepped back, and for some reason he jumped down from the rickshaw. He stood on the pavement looking at me, waiting for me to answer. I suddenly took fright. 'I'm afraid I don't know,' I shouted, and then I started to run.

I fell almost at once, tripped by Vesta's high heels. Looking back desperately, I expected to see the man standing over me, but he was still by the rickshaw, just as I had left him. This did not reassure me. Tearing off the shoes, I jumped up and ran in my bare feet. I felt the soft islands of spittle and the velvety crunch of dust under my soles. Lamp-posts flashed past me. My mind caught superstitiously at them. 'I must not stop running until I've passed seven of them,' I said over and over to myself. But the seventh lamp-post, when I reached it, seemed much too near. I ran on until I was exhausted. I lay down on the grass verge, and remembering what I had once read, put my ear to the ground. I felt sure that I was being chased, although I could hear nothing. I wondered what he would do if he discovered that I wasn't a woman. I could not rest. I got up and hurried on.

The stone man stood in a trance against the dark trees, and the carved lions and horses seemed to be asleep under the bushes. I tiptoed up to the porch and began to climb. A little swing brought me across to the window-sill, and for one moment I had to stand on the tiles. None broke. Pulling myself up by my arms, I looked into the depths of Vesta's room. The green chairs floated on the darkness, and their half-hidden cushions were like ghosts crouching in them. Seen from outside, from a thief's view-point, the room was serene and frightening.

I dropped in, head first, and groped on the floor with my hands as if I were playing 'wheelbarrows.' The cool polish was lovely after the filthy pavements. I went into the bedroom and switched on the dressing-table light. The reflection in the mirror horrified me. All my make-up had slipped and sagged, because I had sweated so much. I began to laugh, and saw that even my teeth were pink.

I took Vesta's dress off and put it away gently. I polished her shoes with my handkerchief. Then I went into the bathroom to wash. When at last I lay down on the bed, the first morning sounds were beginning.

'I hope you slept well, Denton,' Mrs Fielding said at breakfast. She was looking straight at me.

'Fairly well, thank you, Mrs Fielding,' I answered. And, in an attempt to explain any noises, I added, 'I was rather restless, as it's hotter on the ground than up in the penthouse.'

She smiled very sweetly and said no more. Wanting to be alone, I took up my painting-things after breakfast and settled in a corner of the vegetable garden, where I began a picture of the browning Indian corn and the ruined toolshed.

I was still there when Elaine found me, later in the morning.

'I've been looking for you everywhere,' she said.

'Would you like to come riding this afternoon? Someone has lent me a pony and I thought you could hire one and come with me.'

I had not ridden since I was ten years old, when my horrible little black pony had at last been given away. How I had hated it! Once it had broken out of the stable and had galloped through the roses and over the lawns, showing its awful yellow teeth.

All this passed through my mind as she asked the question.

'But I haven't got any clothes,' I said.

'Oh, you could easily borrow a pair of breeches. Hasn't Paul got any? I'm sure he has.'

'But they'd be too large for me.'

'You can reef them in with a belt.' Elaine seemed to know everything. She became brisk and managing. 'We'll go back to your place now and fetch them.'

We swayed along, perched high up in the old-fashioned car. Elaine came up to the flat and helped me rummage in Paul's room. We found a pair of jodhpurs and a pair of breeches. I decided on the jodhpurs, and also took one of his silk squares to wear round my neck.

'He'll be annoyed that I've taken them,' I said.

'That won't matter; he can wear the breeches,' she replied decisively.

After lunch, I ran upstairs to change my clothes. I felt quite different in the winged breeches and the black and yellow scarf. Dressing up again in someone else's clothes reminded me violently of the night before.

We drove to the riding-school and waited in the huge, draughty covered-ring. It was roofed with straw-matting supported on bamboo poles. Ponies trotted round on the soft loam. A Cossack and his son stood in the middle of the ring, telling the pupils what to do.

Our ponies were brought. Elaine had explained in French that I wanted something quiet, as I was out of practice. The Russian smiled rather queerly, and I wondered if he were going to give me the most devilish animal for his own private fun.

It looked docile enough as it walked into the hall. The Chinese mafoo called it Hamlet, or Omelette; it was difficult to tell which he meant. For the rest of the afternoon I wavered between these two names, now calling it Hamlet proudly, when I was in command, and descending to Omelette as a pet-name, to soften its heart and mouth when it was in command.

Walking with slow dignity, we set off down the road in bright sunlight. We started to trot on reaching the fields, where the paths were still untarred. Elaine's pony led the way and Hamlet followed. I began to love him for behaving so well. I felt very happy as I rose and fell in the saddle. I remembered and exaggerated what I had been taught as a child. I could not follow quite so well when Elaine's pony broke into a canter. I was relieved when we pulled up to go over a narrow bridge. Unknown to us, a little yellow dog was waiting behind the parapet on the other side. It rushed out and started snarling and yapping at our ponies' legs. Omelette shied, and for a moment there was a frightening gap between me and the saddle.

'You all right, Denton?' Elaine asked encouragingly, looking over her shoulder.

I smiled an empty smile. Hamlet settled down again to a comfortable jog-trot. I was able to enjoy the fields and the curved roofs half hidden in bamboo groves. But not for long. The trot turned into a canter, and the canter into a gallop. Both our ponies were running away with us.

I found myself leaning back, pulling on the reins, while Hamlet's hooves drummed madly on the hard earth. Elaine was in front of me, half hidden in dust. My pony edged nearer and nearer to the high bank. I knew that I was going to be scraped against it. In my terror I jutted my legs out, so that I was almost standing in my stirrups.

251

I pulled at his mouth with all my might. The wind whipped my face, making my eyes water. Horrible thrills of fear and exaltation ran through me. I seemed to be flying in the air above the horse. I could not go on balancing fantastically like this. I was going to be trampled to death, or perhaps dragged for miles upside-down. I was gaining on Elaine. She was only a few feet in front of me and we were coming to a village. We thundered down the main street. A child and a baby sat placidly on the ground. The child scrambled to its feet in terror and left the baby weakly kicking. I shut my eyes. The baby was going to be hammered into pulp. But suddenly we swerved, and this effort of my pony made me in some way stronger and more desperate. It was as if I had said, 'My pony has been clever enough to avoid the baby, I must avoid being killed myself.'

I cannot tell exactly what I did, but it seemed that I gradually began to wind the reins round my arm. The pony's head turned and I caught a glimpse of his flickering lips and domino-shaped teeth. His speed began to slacken. The reins were now twisted round my arm up to the shoulder, so that I was pulled forward. Suddenly he stopped and I nearly shot over his head. The next thing I knew was that Elaine held my bridle. She was laughing and gasping.

I got off and sank down on the bank. I was quite weak from relief. If I had been alone I would have walked home. But even while I thought this, I remembered the horrible joy of being in the horse's power.

We mounted again and set off for the riding-school. Our ponies were sobered now and did not need the careful attention we gave them.

The mafoos came out softly over the dark brown earth and led them away to the stables. We got into the car and each lay back in a corner, not speaking until Elaine said, 'I'd never be allowed to ride again if Mother knew what had happened.'

CHAPTER 30

ON Hallowe'en the Fieldings gave a party. I spent most of the day making my clothes. I tacked two blue curtains together, making a long robe; then I stuck autumn leaves all over it with glue. I chose the biggest and brightest that I could find in the garden – lime-green and rose from the Virginia creeper, and ochre and burning brown from the plane trees.

I made a head-dress of berries and more leaves, stuck on to a tall lampshade.

An hour before the guests were expected, I began to draw black lines on my face and bare arms. I outlined all the veins, so that I was covered with a network, like a skeleton leaf. I put on the robe and the head-dress and looked at myself in the glass. I thought that I looked romantically terrifying; a cross between a magician and a personification of Autumn. The black lines on my face made me look evil and hungry. I felt satisfied, but I hoped that nobody would ask me what I was, for I wouldn't know what to answer.

I went downstairs rather nervously. Ruth, dressed as a Chinese boy, was alone in the hall. She was dancing with closed eyes to Beethoven's Fifth Symphony. The last record scraped and grated to an end. She came out of her trance and looked at me. Her eyes widened in a terrified stare. To reassure her, I said quickly, 'Do you like my get-up, Ruth? Did I scare you? I made it all myself.'

'Oh, Denton,' she said, holding her hands over her eyes, 'you frightened me so. Why, you look awful; so wicked! Come right down and we'll do a dance to Handel's Water Music.'

She went to the gramophone and changed the records. I waited on the stairs, hoping that no one would arrive while we were doing our dance. Ruth walked into the middle of the room with her head up and her hands thrust forward. Her dumpy little body was trembling. I revolved and slid round her, making shapes and patterns on the floor. She was the central pivot. She stood like a Polynesian totem which was slowly coming to life. She waved her fat little arms.

The front-door bell rang. I ran to the gramophone and switched it off. Ruth looked at me reproachfully. I waited uncomfortably for the guests. Neither Mrs Fielding nor Elaine was down yet. The Boy ushered in a young American and his wife. I had met them once before. He was a Rhodes scholar, out in China for six months to study the language. They were in evening clothes, and for a moment they did not recognize me.

'My, you do look sinister!' Mrs Firbank said. 'What are you supposed to be?'

It was the question that I had dreaded.

'I don't know,' I answered. 'I just made it up.'

There was a silence.

'Mrs Fielding will be down in a minute,' I blurted out, to fill it up. With relief I heard her footsteps, then her voice saying, 'Hullo, May; hullo, Firbank; it's just lovely of you to come!'

The Number One and Number Two came in bearing glasses of orange and tomato juice, for Mrs Fielding was strongly teetotal.

Other guests began to arrive, and soon the room was full. Then we trooped out through the dark conservatory into the garden. I saw the outline of the huge bonfire which had been stacked near the swimming-pool. I longed for it to be lighted.

Elaine, dressed like a circus-rider in salmon-pink tights, trimmed with silver spangles and white velvet, ran forward with a burning branch and thrust it into the heart of the pile. Belches of white smoke began to belly out; then a sly lick of flame crept through the boughs until the whole was blazing.

The strong man of the party held branches like a weight-lifter before he tossed them lightly on to the flames, when a gold rain of sparks would fly out. In the glow, everyone's face grew fresh. They were changed; more beautiful and less civilized.

Two white shadows crossed the lawn. The first one carried a great tureen; the second, plates and spoons and napkins. Rugs were spread out round the fire and we sat down to drink the soup.

Ruth had brought out the gramophone, and she now put on Bach's Italian Concerto. She got up between spoonfuls to continue her stately dance.

The soup was cleared away and we were each given a neatly peeled stick on which a chop had been skewered. We stood up in a circle and held our chops to the flames. The smell and sizzle of the flesh made me think of the Bible. I remembered the burnt sacrifices. With our sticks all pointing to its heart, we seemed to be giving some sort of ceremonial salute to the fire.

Round the edge, in the crumbling embers, lay potatoes in their jackets. I thought they looked like turtles' eggs, although I had never seen such things. When the skin burst, they seemed about to hatch.

The Boys moved about, serving other vegetables from silver dishes. The meal was an exciting mixture of picnic and dinner-party. It was difficult to know what to expect next. Although my chop was burnt and charred, it was very delicious; better than any chop I had ever tasted before. My potato had a little core of uncooked hardness. I took careful aim and threw it at Ruth, who was executing an elaborate arabesque. Unfortunately and unexpectedly it hit her. At the touch of the soapy thing she burst into tears. I was overcome with shame. Everyone wanted to know what had happened, but I would say nothing and all Ruth could get out between sobs was, 'Something awful hit me.' To try to make up for my cruelty, I went and sat next to her. When she had recovered, she suggested that we should do a dance; and not liking to refuse, I stood up and began to sway about with her. I thought that the others would make fun, but instead they imitated us. Soon we were all holding hands and dancing round the fire like children. I was wedged between a plump Christian Science Practitioner and a prosperous-looking business man who played the violin. He had brought it with him, and when we were tired Mrs Fielding asked him to play to us. We sat down again on the rugs and composed our faces, to show that we were really ready to listen.

He began to play Mozart's Rondo in D. I watched his silhouette against the fire. He looked like a Beardsley drawing, with his pendulous stomach; his trousers narrowing at the bottom; and with the tiny, baroque shape of the violin tucked into the folds of his bull-neck.

I was lulled and charmed by the music, so that I hated the sudden interruption of a loud splash and many genteel but manly swear-words. I strongly suspected that the person had fallen into the pool to gain a little publicity and to create a diversion. Everyone flocked to the water's brink and the poor violinist was looking rather helpless, with his hands hanging down and the instrument still clutched under his chin.

Helping hands were stretched out, but the man ignored them and swam round in the middle of the pool, like a complacent seal, refusing to be caught. His wet clothes had just the glitter of sealskin.

Seeing him in the water, others wanted to swim. I was sent into the house to fetch as many bathing-suits as possible.

Careful people went into the house to change, but the more romantic shed their clothes in the dark corners of the garden and then came running across the lawn. In the blackness, only the white skin showed, so that arms and legs seemed to be moving without a body.

I dived into the bath, but immediately turned my arms up to come to the surface again. The water was horrible by night. Somebody tried to duck me and I almost screamed. I hit out and struck the American, Firbank, on the mouth. Blinking his eyes, he wiped his lean face with his hand. I think he expected to find blood there.

'What did you want to do that for, Son?' he said mildly. 'You ought to be able to take a ducking without getting mad.'

And with these words he stretched out, and catching me by the shoulders, forced me under the water. I kicked madly against his hard body; feeling my hand pass over a cold, contracted nipple, I tweaked it viciously, and tore at the flesh and hair on his chest. But he took no notice. He held me down until he thought that I had had enough.

I came up coughing and gasping. I could not look at him. I turned round, floundering out of the bath, and ran into the house, dripping pools of water on the rugs and polished floors. I locked the door and fell on my bed.

In a few moments the pillow was quite wet from my hair and my tears. I gnawed a corner of it and tasted the soap.

Downstairs there was still the noise of laughing and shouting and the fiddle. Then there was silence, and someone breaking into it and singing:

> I love him the best.
> And if my love leaves me,
> I'll know no rest.

The sound swam up to my windows and died there.

Vesta came back at the end of that week. I was sitting by the window and heard the wheels crunching the gravel. I ran into the hall to meet her. She was wearing a Russian man's astrakhan hat, and the wind had made her cheeks red. She looked charming.

'Where did you get that hat?' I asked.

'In Peking, of course. Do you like it? It's really a man's.'

'I know it is.' I didn't want to tell her how well it suited her, so I asked if she had had a good time.

'Oh, perfect, just perfect,' she said. 'You've no idea how different Peking is to Shanghai.'

'Did you see my uncle and aunt?' I asked.

'No. We went to their house but they were out, thank God.'

I felt rather hurt.

'My aunt's a very nice woman. We used to love her when we were small; whenever we went to see her, she used to give us hot chocolate with an iceberg of cream on the top.'

'Oh, I expect she's all right, but I find those diplomats in Peking are just torture; and the British are the worst.'

The luggage was brought in. There were several exciting packing-cases.

'Do show me what you've brought back, Vesta!' I cried impatiently. There and then we began to wrench the tops off the boxes.

Vesta had bought doll's furniture for a little friend. There was a black-wood table with a marble top, and little stools to match. To put on the table, there was a pewter dinner-set with bowls and covered serving-dishes; and there was imitation food to fit into the dishes: tiny pyramids of brightly painted fruit arranged on green leaves, mysterious dressed dishes, and whole fish looking like important corpses.

One case held a flat painted stone. Three faded figures smiled at us from the red-veined marble.

'How lovely it is!'

Others had collected by now, and we all sighed in front of the stone picture. Poor Ruth nestled up to Vesta in a passion of affection. She loved her because she had been away and had come back. Vesta tried to restrain her, and we all went in to tea.

I waved forlornly out of the car window as I was driven away that night. I would probably see them all again to-morrow, but I felt sentimental, as though I were going on a long journey.

I found Paul reading by the fire.

'Hullo,' he said.

My father came in and we sat down to dinner in silence. I remembered that the next day was Paul's birthday.

'Are we going to have a party?' I asked.

'Some people are coming to dinner, and then we're going on somewhere to dance,' my father answered sombrely.

After the meal, the old cook came and stood by my father's chair. He blinked his little, kitten's eyes as he memorized my father's words. Paul chose roast duck with orange salad for his birthday party, but he could think of nothing else, so I and my father and Cook argued about the other courses.

The party was a dreary one for me. I did not exist for my brother's friends; they talked to each other across me. One of them I disliked more than the others. It may have been because all his hair had been burnt off in a Trans-Siberian railway accident. His coach had left the rails and caught fire. The hair had never grown again properly, so that, although he was young, his head was covered only with shiny skin and chicken's fluff. I tried not to look at him as I drank my soup.

The night club was strangely quiet, with little crimson lamps on each table. It reminded me of the chapel set apart for meditation in some huge cathedral. The band was not playing. The musicians dandled their instruments on their knees, as though they were amateurs, not quite daring enough to play before an audience. Couples leaned on the little tables and spoke to each other in undertones. Sitting alone was a middle-aged woman dressed all in green. On the table in front of her stood a glass of crême de menthe and she held a green cigarette between her lips. Fascinated by the bizarre effect, I watched her until she turned two dark searchlights on me in a rigid stare.

Our arrival seemed to bring with it a little gaiety. The band suddenly plucked up courage and began to play with great slickness and precision. Soon everyone was dancing except my father, myself, and a powerfully built girl called Belle. She sat stiffly beside me. I knew that I ought to ask her to dance, but could not. In her turquoise chiffon dress, she looked like a prefect dressed up for the end of term play. She was beefy.

I began to feel very uncomfortable. 'Come on,' she said lazily. 'I knew I'd have to ask you in the end.'

We stood up together. She grasped me firmly round the waist and whirled me off. We might have changed places; it would have made no difference. She was completely in command.

When the music stopped she led me back to my father. 'You don't dance badly,' she said. 'But you haven't got any initiative.'

I sat down, vowing never to be left with her again. As soon as the music began again, I got up hurriedly and approached the least frightening looking girl. She had brown hair and was pleasantly small. We started to dance rather jerkily.

'Do you come here often?' I asked.

'Quite often. The last time I was here was in the summer. It was very hot and all the windows were open. One man must have been a bit tight, because he leant back against nothing and disappeared. We all rushed to the window expecting to see an awful sight, but instead, we found him lying happily on his back, as if he were in a hammock. He'd been saved by the awning. Wasn't it lucky? The commissionaire got a ladder and fished him out.'

'What happened then? Did he go home?' I asked.

'Oh no. He came up, sat on the window-sill and nearly fell out again.'

We danced on in silence until I steered clumsily and knocked against another couple. An angry gaze was turned on me and I recognized the all-green woman. I apologized and danced away quickly, but not before I heard her say, 'That kid's been ogling me all evening.' She pronounced 'ogle' 'oggle,' and seemed to be laughing at me and at herself while she spoke.

'Don't bustle so,' my partner said.

'I wanted to get away from that woman. She's angry because we bumped into her,' I explained.

'Isn't she killing! I've seen her here in red velvet, sipping cherry brandy and smoking a rose-coloured cigarette. To-night she's all green. She always has everything to match.'

'What does she drink when she wants to go blue?' I asked.

'I don't know, unless it's methylated spirits!'

We both laughed, then stopped rather uncertainly, as if the joke hadn't been worth the trouble.

'But even that isn't blue, it's mauve,' I said, to stop the gap of silence.

'You are literal!' My partner turned her head away, saying that she was tired and wanted to sit down.

I left her and went to the cloak-room. The attendant began to brush me, and hand me towels which I did not want. I went downstairs to smell the cold air in the street. I walked up and down the pavement, enjoying the freedom. Suddenly I decided not to go in again. I asked the commissionaire to tell my father, if he should ask for me; then I started to walk home. My feet, in silk socks and patent-leather shoes, felt hot and tight. The contrast reminded me of running barefoot over the filthy pavements when I had dressed up in Vesta's clothes. It was good to be alone.

Passing Bubbling Well and the Cabaret, I thought of that other, quite different dance, when I had been the tip on the human whip and had scattered bottles and glasses. I thought of the marine who had paid for my drinks and my dancing partner. I heard footsteps behind me, and I turned round expecting unreasonably to see him. A voice said, 'Hi, mate!' I stopped, not knowing who the man was; then I recognized the soldier I had asked to tea in the summer. He had just come out of the Cabaret. He was dressed in his winter uniform, and I made this an excuse for not knowing him immediately.

'Well, how do you think I picked you out, then, all toffed up in your evening-suit?' he asked.

I looked down at my clothes apologetically. 'It's my brother's birthday and we went out dancing,' I explained.

'What have you done with him – lost him?'

And with these words the soldier sat down suddenly on the pavement. I pretended not to think it queer.

'I didn't like the women, so I came away,' I said.

Bending down, I gave him my two hands. He dragged on me with all his weight and laughed when I nearly fell on him. I felt annoyed and embarrassed. It was not the time or place for horse-play. My evening-clothes made it even more grotesque.

'Do be good and get up,' I said primly. 'You won't get into barracks in time if you don't.'

'What the bloody hell has it got to do with you?' he asked.

He rose to his feet fairly steadily and lighted a cigarette. I was satisfied, in spite of having made him angry. I took his arm, and almost at once he started to lean on me. I saved him the trouble of steering.

'What part do you come from?' he asked after a pause.

'What part of what?' I felt bewildered.

262

'What part of England of course.'

'I come from Sussex,' I said.

'Well, I come from Derbyshire!' He flung the words at me rudely.

'I was at school in Derbyshire,' I answered peaceably. 'I know some of it quite well.'

'Do you know it round Haddon Hall?' he asked. 'My home's near there.' The sound of the word 'home' made him sentimental.

'We could have some lovely times in Derbyshire,' he mused. 'I used to do a lot of singing when I was a lad.'

'Sing something for me now,' I said. And very softly he began to hum Brahms' Cradle Song; then, remembering it better, he opened his lips. The notes, dropping into darkness, were lonely. I found myself singing, too, to keep them company. How lovely it sounded! I felt wonderfully happy, but I knew that it would only last for a moment.

A policeman came up and told us not to make so much noise. We took no notice and he just stared after us hopelessly. I left the soldier at the barrack gates.

'Good-bye, mate, good-bye for ever!' he said. Singing and drink had made him quite tragic. 'We're going away to-morrow.'

'For Christ's sake keep quiet!' the sentry hissed and growled. 'You'll have the Guard out.'

The soldier wrung my hand and I ran away, hoping to be in before my father and brother.

CHAPTER 31

VESTA and I sat wedged between slim Chinese women at the opera. They used their programmes as fans to blow away the smoke from cigarettes, which they put to their lips nervously, taking them away again almost at once.

The theatre was shabby and decayed and so were some of the singers; but for nearly a week we enjoyed going to two operas a day.

We saw Paul's bald friend at one of the evening performances. He came and talked to us. He was furious because an old Italian countess had wanted him to kiss her hand. I wondered why. She was sitting on the other side of the theatre, but even from that distance her face glowed. She always wore a sunburnt, angry make-up. I knew that if I got close enough I would see two pools of hotter, brighter colour on either side of her nose, while the tip would be almost naked. I suppose the grease-paint melted and trickled down to the base of her nostrils.

The German Consul was sitting near us. He was smiling and screwing his eyeglass round, until his lids gaped painfully and turned red. He had one of those bird-like, delicate Jewish faces which always seem to be asking for confidences.

I had first met him in an antique-shop, where I came upon him praising a little gilt pagoda from Indo-China. Hung with bells, it was extremely pretty and gay.

'This was never made here, but in a hot country, a hot, steaming country.' He spoke in English so that I should understand. 'A country with jungles and bright birds.' As he said these words he fixed me with his monocle, and the effect was silly and frightening.

I turned away quickly, but he would not let me escape.

'I see you are interested in beauty, young man,' he said.

Not knowing what to answer, I nodded my head.

'Then you must come and see my own things one day.'

The piece of glass glittered so unpleasantly in his eye that it made his words seem almost like a threat.

Now he was sitting almost next to us, and I was afraid that he would speak to me again, but instead he only gave a sharp smile and turned his head away. And I suddenly felt mortified because he had not taken any notice of me.

Twice the programme-seller passed in front of us, bumping against us clumsily. When he tried to pass a third time, Vesta suddenly shot out her coral-velvet shoe and kicked his ankles. The kick gave me a shock; it made me see all the people in the audience without their clothes. I thought of the hair under their arms, the teeth in their mouths and their long pointed nails. Everything seemed wild and animal; and the coral-velvet shoe made it depraved.

The programme-seller nursed his ankle and swore in a high falsetto, as if Vesta's kick had castrated him. The ridiculous idea made me laugh, and Vesta's shamefaced, dignified expression slowly melted.

'What a sordid evening!' she said to me as we threaded our way through the crowd.

I made my way to the Jesuits' school in French Town. I was going to ask them to give me some French lessons. I waited in an ante-room while someone took my message. On the wall was a picture of Jesus surrounded by children – one pale, fair-haired sitting on His knee and one blackest quite on the outskirts of the group. I kept asking myself the question, 'Are Jesuits priests or monks or neither?'

When I turned round a powerful man in a black cassock was standing in the doorway.

'I understand you want to have French lessons,' he said in a hard, throaty voice.

'Yes, can I?' I asked.

'Not private lessons, only lessons with our Chinese pupils. I could not take you if you did not know as much as they did. It would not do to have an ignorant white person in the class.'

I was rattled by his harshness; even his smile was tough and elastic.

'I know very little,' I said hurriedly. 'I don't think it would be any good unless I could have private lessons.'

'I'm afraid we're too busy for that.' He led me to the door, sweeping along grandly, as though he were dressed all in red.

The air outside was very clear. The leaves had just fallen off the trees, leaving them fine and sharp. I walked to the grey, lumpy cathedral and went in. This stucco Gothic seemed strange beside a Chinese creek! There was no stained glass in the windows, and the white light showed up the cracks and damp patches and the dust on the lace altar-cloths. I climbed a little spiral staircase and found myself in the arched clerestory. I looked down and saw a Chinese woman praying. The trim bun of hair at the nape of her neck seemed to be offering itself to me as a horrible little black loaf of bread.

The cathedral made me think of Christmas. My aunt in Peking had asked us to go there, but both my father and brother had other engagements in Shanghai. I wondered if I would be allowed to go alone, and whether my aunt would be pleased with that arrangement.

'May I go to Peking alone if you and Paul don't want to come?' I asked my father at lunch-time.

'I should think so,' he said; and afterwards he sat down to write to my aunt.

The answer came a few days later. My aunt said that

she would be delighted to see me. I felt very happy; I was glad that I was going alone.

'You must have a fur lining to your coat,' my father said. 'It will be very cold.'

We took an old moleskin carriage rug to the tailors and had it shaped to fit into my coat.

I wore it for the first time when we went carol-singing, a few days before I left. The Barbours had asked me to go with them – to collect money for the Red Cross.

We rehearsed one afternoon, then started out by star-light, carrying lanterns.

We went first to the Argyll and Sutherland High-landers. We thought that the officers would be homesick and rich. We sang for some minutes to a large mahogany door. We felt pleased with ourselves and wondered why no one came out to us. It was so rare to hear carols in Shanghai. At last we descended to knocking on the door. The lock clicked and a young officer looked out. No one knew him. He fumbled in his pocket, brought out a dollar, handed it to us with a mechanical grin, and then hastily shut the door.

After this insult we decided to go to a house which would take the nasty taste away. An old bachelor lived there who was so fond of young people that his whole drawing-room was lined with photographs of them. There were pictures of young men, young women, children and babies.

He seemed rather bewildered at netting so many real ones unexpectedly, and he gave us so much to eat and drink that we had to leave in self-defence, but not before he had rustled something very satisfying into our box.

We went on to sing outside an unknown house. The door flew open and a tall, thin woman ran down the steps.

'Come in, come in,' she said excitedly. 'You must all drink with us. We have not heard such lovely singing since we left Germany.'

Her pleasant-looking, fleshy husband was already pouring out glasses of port when we came into the hall. We sat about on chairs and stools and ate strange German biscuits as we sipped. We stood round the fire and had to sing for her again and again before she would let us leave.

My head was singing by the time we got back to the Barbours' house. It was nearly midnight, and we sat down to supper and counted our money by the light of red candles.

I went the next day to say good-bye to the Fieldings. They took me with them to the Chinese city. We left the car on the edge of French Town and pushed our way down the streets. The smell from the crowd was weird, almost unearthly. Mrs Fielding wanted more blue and white breakfast china, so we stood in an open shop, bargaining. Against the walls bowl upon bowl nested in straw. The straw smelt dry and healthy. In the doorway a little green bird was tied by its foot to a perch.

It fluttered and screamed so horribly that Vesta insisted on buying it. We carried it off with us and found it a bright scarlet cage and some seed.

We walked over the crooked bridges until we were under the fantastic, curling roofs of the Willow Pattern Tea House. It was like 'Marriage à la Mode' inside. People gambled; others sat back vacantly, their stools tilted against the walls. Mah-jongg tiles clattered on the marble-topped tables and the players shouted in excitement and anger. Whiffs of opium floated on the steam from tea and scented towels.

We left the scene of rather greasy dissipation and went to look at the booths along the other side of the creek. There we found a little French watch, like Vesta's. How the Chinese must have loved them when they first saw them! This one was of blue enamel, set with pearls, and although it did not go, it still had its little key.

Elaine won it after much haggling, and we started to

walk back to the car. On the edge of the Concession we saw a bookshop. The Russian who kept it told us to look round. An old book on one of the dark shelves caught my attention. It had a most whimsical binding of glistening purple-brown leather embossed with scallop shells and weeping-willow trees. I opened it and found my great-grandmother's name in purple ink on the flyleaf. Above, in pencil, was written, 'First edition, rare, ten dollars.' The book was Aikin's *British Poets*. Excitedly I showed it to Vesta.

'But how could it have got there?' she asked.

'I don't know; someone might have borrowed it and kept it so that it got sold up with their things; or perhaps it was stolen,' I said.

Vesta and I between us found the money for it; then we took it home, cleaned it, polished it and began to read passages to each other. There was an autobiographical note on each author. James Beattie was 'an admired poet and a moralist'; Thomas Parnell, an 'agreeable' one. We thought that modern poets would not like these adjectives.

CHAPTER 32

M y aunt was there, on the freezing platform, to meet me. A miserable eddy of dust swirled round as we kissed. I smelt her violet scent again and remembered the bottle on her cluttered dressing-table, and how I used to spell the rococo words to myself, 'Violettes de Parme.'

When I was a child my aunt would let me play with anything. I loved the high dog-collar of little pearls which she had worn as a young woman. I used to put it on and rush round the room barking and growling and gnashing my teeth as though I had hydrophobia.

Then when I was tired my aunt would tell her maid Clutterbuck to make hot chocolate over the little spirit-lamp. I could never understand why Clutterbuck was nicknamed Clara Butt. I thought Clutterbuck much funnier and more grotesque.

At last something happened which shook our confidence in each other. We were on board ship and my aunt had come to see us off. As we waited for the siren to blow I asked my aunt if she would let me play with her ring. It was a strange scarab – most fascinating. I think I really imagined that it was alive. She took it off, gave it to me, and went on talking to my mother. Leaning out of the cabin window to get more light, I held the ring above my head and gazed at it.

Then something happened. The next moment I heard the ring rattling down the slit into which the window-frame fitted.

Too horrified to speak, I just looked at my aunt. I saw the realization of what had happened dawn on her face. The whole partition would have to be taken down before the ring could be found.

My aunt picked up the box of little wooden toys she had given me. Each one was a perfect little teapot, coffee-pot, or cup and saucer. I loved them. She held them by her shoulder for a moment, then she threw them far out into the sea.

I saw them sailing lightly on the water. I cried out for someone to save them, and when no one moved I started to scream uncontrollably. I knew that my aunt was the wickedest woman in the world.

But now this seemed many years ago; it was nearly forgotten. I put my arm through my aunt's and she led me to the waiting car. When I heard her talk to the chauffeur in Chinese instead of pidgin-English, I realized the difference between Shanghai and Peking.

I looked out on to the wide streets which had open trenches down the middle. Little clouds of freezing dust flew about, and the low grey-roofed houses seemed like large crouching mice.

The sentries smacked their rifles and we were inside the Legation. Smooth lawns flowed round clumps of spiky fir trees which half concealed the stout Victorian houses. A wing showed here, an arched veranda there.

My aunt led me into the dark hall. She had not lived in the house long – workmen were still altering it – but already it had begun to look like all her other houses.

She had a taste for richness which expressed itself in elaborate Tibetan brass and copper vessels, in prayer-wheels and sword-scabbards studded with coral and turquoise. On the drawing-room mantelpiece stood a row of those Chinese flowering trees which have been made from rather bad pieces of jade and amethyst and agate wired together.

My aunt pressed the stone petals into better position as she talked. I lay back on the dark blue damask sofa, flattening the heap of mustard and plum-coloured velvet cushions. From the corner of my eye I could see the distressing full-length portrait of my aunt in a trailing tea-gown.

After I had admired everything, I was taken up to my room. It was vast, and except for a sinister mahogany bed on a dais, seemed to be almost empty. Sand-bags lay along the sills of the double windows and hot air shimmered up from a cast-iron grating in the floor. An unforgiving electric light bore down from the ceiling.

My aunt seemed to think that some explanation was needed.

'I'm afraid your room's not really finished yet, Denton; I've only just had time to get my own more or less straight.'

She led me down the passage to it. I saw the rough gold walls hung with ikons; the French cane-work bed, covered with gold bows; the Spanish altar candlesticks, turned into reading-lamps; and the chestnut-pink velvet curtains.

I left my aunt and went back to change my clothes. It was early yet, but I wanted to be alone. There were some books on the Victorian chamber-cupboard. I chose *Tales of Mystery and Imagination* and took it into the bathroom. I took off my clothes and let the water play over my feet as I lay in the half-filled bath. Propping the book against the soap-tray, I started to read about the guest at the party in the lunatic asylum. The hot water rose round me and beads of sweat trickled down my forehead into my eyes.

Suddenly the Chinese Boy appeared in the doorway. He wanted the keys of my bags. I felt ashamed that he should see me with no clothes on, when he was so gorgeously dressed in old-fashioned silk robes. I told him gruffly to look through my pockets, and then slid farther under the water.

When I went downstairs I found my uncle alone, drinking whisky and soda. He was a little man with broad shoulders and large stomach. As a child I had been afraid of him because he had such large whites to his eyes, and because he seemed harsh and pompous. I was still a little

272

nervous. To give myself courage I thought of the story I had once overheard. My uncle, it seems, had been rather rude and supercilious to someone at a club; whereupon the offended man had picked up my uncle and thrown him over the bar, into the astonished barman's lap.

All he said now, as I walked towards him, was, 'I don't suppose you're old enough for this.' He waved his whisky-glass at me and then rang the bell for orange-juice.

The next day my aunt took me to the skating-rink. As we drove through the freezing city, little thrills of plea-sure ran through me. I loved the coldness and brightness and the feeling that my aunt wanted to enjoy herself almost as much as I did.

Like the riding-school in Shanghai, the rink was covered with matting on bamboo poles. I felt defenceless as I sat having my boots laced, while the faces of my aunt's friends loomed above me. Sometimes they smiled, show-ing horse-long teeth.

At last my boots were laced and I was able to stand up. I felt the skates biting lightly into the ice. I pushed off, leaving long, curved strokes behind me. How thankful I was that I knew how to skate! I sped round until my aunt beckoned to me. She wanted to introduce me to a mourn-ful boy and girl whose parents had the next house in the Legation. After the first few words she left us. We looked at each other very cynically. We were all about the same age. They seemed relieved when I said that I had to go back to my aunt. I found her already preparing to leave. I was disappointed, I wanted to skate all day, but my aunt said that we had to go back to lunch.

I knew that she always rested in the afternoon. When I heard her go up to her room I quietly let myself out and walked into the city. Charcoal braziers stood in front of the shops. Freezing dust blew up and stung my face. A line of camels passed me, carrying coal. Great lumps of their coats had come off, leaving bald patches. I saw a matted piece hang by a hair and then fall on to the road.

I went up to an open side gate in a wall. A rifle was leaning against a stool, but there seemed to be no sentry. On the other side of a wide, paved court stood a pavilion roofed with treacle-yellow tiles. Weeds sprouted between the paving-stones and the tiles. A snake of crimson wall encircled everything. It was dreamlike and utterly still, like a *surréaliste* picture.

I stepped over the rifle and looked to right and left. There was the sentry, against the farther wall, pulling up his trousers. He had his back to me, so for one moment I was able to fill my eyes with the scene; then I slipped out just as he turned round.

On Christmas Day my aunt gave a lunch-party. Everything was blue on the table. Lacy crackers, decorated with dyed feathers, were bunched round a central basket of spun sugar filled with spun-sugar fruits. The fact that this ornament, so like a Victorian wax group, could be eaten, seemed almost unpleasant.

Blue napkins, blue china and deep blue glass made me half expect blue food. But the caviare, from Siberia, was as black and glistening and as like oiled ball-bearings as ever.

I sat half-way down the table, wedged between the British and foreign guests. I wondered what they thought of me. The women seemed to treat me even more heartily than the men.

All the thick curtains were drawn before the plum pudding was brought in. It seemed to float like a blue fireball through the brandy-smelling darkness. Then the daylight flooded in again and I saw the gorgeous Boy carrying the plate round.

Soon everyone was digging in the dark sticky pudding for charms. I saw an exciting gleam and uncovered a fragile button. I wondered what it was made of. I sucked it until I could see the mark. It was nine carat gold. I thought how like my aunt it was to have gold bachelor's buttons, thimbles and donkeys. It combined her love of hygiene and richness.

I looked to see what other people had found in their pudding. My aunt noticed; and embarrassed me terribly by turning to a pale moustached young man and saying, 'Tony, give Denton your donkey, I know he'd like it,' as if I were still a child.

He looked at me malignantly and said, 'I'd rather keep it myself, unless he really wants it.'

His face had gone obstinate and red, and the accent he put on 'really' bit into me.

'I don't want it. I don't want it at all,' I said. 'I've got a button.'

After the meal I found myself left in a corner of the drawing-room with a woman who wore a sort of turban, and earrings made of rugged lumps of yellow stone. I thought that they were amber until she said, 'Ah, I see you are looking at my earrings; they are yellow jade.'

She stressed her words in unusual places, making them interesting and quite new-sounding. I could not guess her nationality.

'If you like pretty things,' she said, 'you must come to my house. It is an old Chinese palace, and some of the doors and windows are shaped like big leaves.'

We sat for a little longer, playing with our coffee-cups; then the yellow-earringed woman went over to my aunt and said, 'My dear, I'd like to show your nephew my house. May I take him off with me now? I'll bring him back.' As she spoke she linked arms with me, and I saw that my aunt was not pleased.

'All right,' she said rather coldly. 'But don't bring him back too late, will you?'

The woman called out to her fat husband, 'Come, Harry, I am going to show this young man the house.'

But Harry did not want to come, so we went out alone.

The chauffeur had shut himself in their white car and was filling it with tobacco smoke. He jumped out when he saw us and stood, grumbling and swearing under his breath, while she abused him. She must have been saying terrible things in Chinese.

All the windows were thrown open and the fur rugs waved about, to get rid of the smoke. Then we got in. Although the car was so long, it was narrow, and I felt her fat side pressed against me. There was a little cut-glass vase between the windows, to hold flowers. When the engine started, the carnations bounced about, like cocks shaking their combs.

The car drew up outside a scarlet door with great brass handles.

'We are in the Tartar City now,' the woman said. She led me through the door into a courtyard where marble statues stood on either side of a carp-pool. Then I saw the doors she had described. The openings in the wall were shaped like long, curving, fretted leaves. They led to an inner courtyard. There was something beautiful in their exaggerated size. We went through one, and then down a long covered passage. The windows were made in elaborate fret patterns, filled with translucent squares of oyster shell. The light, piercing through, seemed diffused and pearly, as if reflected off snow.

At the end of the corridor was a little room, very richly carpeted and furnished. I saw gleams of gold thread in the rugs. The black-wood furniture glistened like a new bar of chocolate.

'This is where the last mandarin to live here hung himself,' said my hostess, reaching up and slapping a red lacquered beam.

It was easy to imagine a pair of old-fashioned satin boots eddying to and fro, just above the ground; a crooked neck and a black tongue hanging out.

'This room is haunted by him,' she added proudly.

But instead of making the place more interesting to me,

her announcement made the room seem contaminated in some way. Trying not to think of the mandarin, I stood looking at a water-buffalo carved out of a huge piece of sage-green jade.

'That was looted from the Summer Palace by the English,' I was told. I think she said it to see if I would be annoyed by the emphasis she put on the word 'English'.

I wondered if the buffalo had really come from the Summer Palace. So many things were supposed to have come from there. It was rather like Strawberry Hill, which, apparently, at one time held all the 'Gothic' furniture in the junk-shops – even the varnished pine chairs from the parson's study.

A Boy came in, bearing absurdly graceful Empire cups, and the little dishes of hors-d'œuvres which Scandinavians serve with tea. There were star-shaped pieces of toast spread with red caviare and little circles of hard-boiled egg and gherkin. I could not eat after so much lunch, but I drank the tea from the top-heavy little urn (for that was all my cup was). The sides were engraved with a wicked-looking cupid being let out of a rabbit-hutch by the Empress Josephine, or someone very like her. Because they were so different, I began to prefer the Empire cups to everything else in the room.

After tea my hostess took me to her store-room. We crossed another courtyard and approached a small pavilion which crouched under two bare willows. Inside there was a cold, aromatic smell, something like human hair. It came from the silk wrappings and the wooden boxes. Each one contained a lovely bowl or piece of bronze.

There were ugly things too: lumps of semi-precious stone carved very unfeelingly and coarsely, and cloisonné-enamelled incense-burners, that nobody would want. Not looking at these, but only at the lovely bowls in their silk-lined cases, I said, 'What beautiful things you have!'

There was a silence and the air seemed electric. I felt

277

for a moment that she was going to give me one of the bowls; but she must have thought better of it, for all she said at last was:

'Do you like them? I'm so glad. What shall we do now?'

She jumped up and walked about restlessly. I could see that she was not going to take me back to my aunt yet.

'Have you seen any of the sights?' she asked.

'Not really,' I answered. 'I've only looked through a door when a sentry wasn't there.'

'Well, then, let's drive out to the Temple of Heaven.'

I was swept into the white car again, but this time we were closer together than ever, as she had taken my arm. I did not mind. I think I rather liked her for doing it. I watched the flowers doing their dance in the cut-glass vase, and felt peaceful.

Soon we were in the park and the dry grasses were scraping our legs as we stood looking at the three marble tiers of the great altar. The wind, blowing over the grass, broke the dream of stillness and emptiness. The dead blades hissed and talked. They were waiting for the spring to bring their children; until at last they would be so strong that even the marble balustrades would have to give way.

We walked together down the long causeway from the altar to the three-roofed temple. Marble dragons and clouds writhed between the two flights of steps. My companion said that over this part the Emperor had to pass; but I could not tell whether she meant that he was carried, or that he had to walk up this difficult sloping ramp.

Under the three glistening ocean-blue roofs the round temple was quite empty. It was stripped and puritanical; there was no pretence about it.

Looking at the woman in the yellow earrings, as she stood there, I suddenly saw how tired she was of me, of the Temple of Heaven, and indeed of almost everything.

I watched the white car swing out of the Legation as I waited for the front door to be opened. The Number One wore a serious, dramatic expression. He said something to me in Chinese, but realizing by my blank face that I could not understand, he tapped his head and then rolled it about frighteningly.

I ran past him into the hall and was about to look for my aunt when Clutterbuck appeared at the head of the stairs. I had always wondered why my aunt needed Clutterbuck when there were so many Chinese servants in the house; but I was pleased to see her at that moment. She made her lips into a straight, stiff line and said through them, 'Madam wants you to get ready to go out to dinner. Mr Randall's expecting you. It's the next house to this, you can't mistake it.'

'What's happened, Clara Butt?' I asked impatiently. I hated being bundled out of the house without knowing.

'Your uncle's very ill. We think he's had a sort of stroke; but run along like a good boy and don't ask any more questions now.'

I began to tiptoe up to my room. I stopped for a moment outside my uncle's door and heard people moving about and voices. I wondered if the room was full of doctors and nurses.

A feeling of happiness and excitement spread over me as I washed and changed. I put on my fur-lined coat and let myself out into the darkness. Ice crunched under my feet. I could feel the shapes of stones through my thin patent-leather shoes. The cold made my eyes water and my nose drip. I wiped them carefully before I rang the bell of the Randalls' house. Waiting there, I felt empty and anxious. My happiness had disappeared at the thought of the strangers I was to meet.

The Boy led me across the hall and opened a door. The gloomy brother and sister of the skating-rink were sitting on each side of the fire, reading. The girl was the first to jump up. She gave my evening-clothes a swift, darting look.

'Daddy and Mummy had to go out to dinner, so we're all alone. That's why we haven't changed,' she said.

Then her brother stood up and stared at me in a most discomforting way. I was thankful when we went in to dinner, which was all that had been left from lunch, served up in a different way. I enjoyed the devilled turkey and fried plum-pudding. I think that they were more delicious through being twice cooked. As I ate, I tried to think of things to say to Michael and Joan. They told me, between mouthfuls, that they were out on a short visit to their parents, having both just left school. Michael was going back to England in the spring, to study to become a doctor, but Joan was staying on. They asked me about my uncle, and by their guarded questions I saw that they did not like him at all.

After that there seemed nothing to say. I kept wondering if my uncle would die. I hoped that I would be able to leave before it happened; dreading the thought of being left alone with my aunt. I would not know how to behave with death in the house.

Joan and Michael did not know what to do with me after the meal. We scrambled through a game or two of Mah-jongg, gambling with counters instead of money; then I got up to go.

I hurried back to my aunt's house, breathing in the icy air with relief. Nobody was about downstairs. I went up to Clutterbuck's room and knocked on the door.

'Come in,' she said severely, to guard against being imposed upon. She was sitting on the bed, fully dressed, reading Baroness Orczy.

'Oh, it's you, is it?' she said gruffly, but I saw how relieved she was by the way her face relaxed. I think she had a horror of being told to do something by a doctor or a nurse.

'Why are you back so early?' she asked. 'Didn't you like that Michael and Joan?'

'Oh, they're all right,' I said. 'But how is my uncle, Clutterbuck?'

'He's going on as well as can be expected. It's not quite so serious as they thought at first, but Madam thinks that you'd better go back to-morrow, as she'll be far too busy to have any time to spare for you.'

Clutterbuck always liked making me feel small and insignificant. She got up and went to the door.

'Sit there quietly,' she ordered. 'I'll get you something hot.'

I looked round her room. It was decorated with trophies from many countries. A sandal-wood jewel-box, a work-bag made out of a baby armadillo, some blue Egyptian mummy beads, and on the mantelpiece, photographs of glamorous events in her life and my aunt's.

I wondered why I didn't like Clutterbuck; and looking at the photographs I realized that it was because she would never treat me with respect until I had grown up and done something important in her eyes.

She came back carrying a steaming cup. I guessed before I smelt it, that it was chocolate. It used to be chocolate when I was small, so it must still be chocolate. Nothing changed for Clutterbuck. It gave me a feeling of security and despair. In her company I leant comfortably up against a wall, too hopeless even to think of climbing.

I said good night and went to my own room. There on the bedside table lay the *Tales of Mystery and Imagination*. I took the book up and wished that I could write a story about the mandarin swinging from the scarlet beam, my uncle's sudden stroke, Clutterbuck's sour philosophy, and my aunt's childish, pleasant love of show and her longing for affection.

CHAPTER 33

SNOW was falling when I stepped out of the train. The flakes were big and soft as feathers. No one had come to meet me, so I took a taxi through the muffled streets. The block of flats, starting up from the pure snow, looked yellow and stained. It had seemed so white and glittering in the summer.

Boy opened the door and gave me his wide, mechanical smile.

'Young master come back more early! – Shanghai more better Peking?' he asked archly.

'My uncle very sick, Boy. I no can stay,' I told him.

He made sympathetic clucking noises and carried my bag into the bedroom.

I walked about the flat, enjoying its emptiness. I sat down on the floor in the library and looked at the books. There was an early, pirated edition of *Wuthering Heights*, New York, 1848. It was described as a novel by the author of *Jane Eyre!*

I got up off the floor and settled into one of the arm-chairs. I knew, from the first sentence, that I had found what I wanted for that snowy day.

'1801 – I have just returned from a visit to my landlord – the solitary neighbour that I shall be troubled with.'

I read on, excited and satisfied together. My eyes began to smart. I suddenly felt fiercely hungry. I looked out of the window and saw the crests of roofs sticking through the snow. They looked like the bones of big, rotting fishes, covered with salt. I rang the bell.

'Bring me sponge-cake and tea, Boy, please,' I said. (Cook made it wonderfully, with thick, curdled crust.)

When it came, I poured out the tea and cut into the heart of the cake. I still went on reading, feeding myself without looking up. I found that in my greed and impatience I wanted to be eating cake when I was drinking tea, and drinking tea when I was eating cake. I seemed to have a great need which I must satisfy by taking things into myself.

I read on until the slam of the front door broke the spell. I heard the Boy telling my father that I had come back. I went into the drawing-room to meet him.

'Uncle Edward's had a sort of stroke,' I said. 'So I had to come back.'

My father looked at me with very little expression.

'Is it serious?' he asked. 'Will he recover?'

'I don't think it's quite as bad as they thought it was at first,' I said.

I went back into the library. I didn't want to talk about my uncle in Peking. I wanted to get back to my book.

That night my father said, 'Well, what are you going to do now? You must decide what you want to do.'

'I want to go to an Art School.' I had to say it very quickly, because, for some reason, the words made me feel ashamed.

My father made a face.

'I don't think that's at all a good idea,' was all he said. And after that we talked of other things.

The next day I went to ask Vesta what I should do.

'You should go to a University or an Art School,' she said. 'You can't just play around.'

We walked in the icy garden, throwing ourselves down at last on the pile of leaves where last year's Indian corn had been. I could tell how unhappy Vesta was by the tautness of her body, as I felt it against me, under the leaves.

I supposed that some people would say that she ought to have a baby; but I thought that when people had babies it showed that they had at last given up all hope of doing anything themselves. I was angry with Vesta for being unhappy.

'Have you written anything while I've been away?' I asked severely.

'Yes, but only a few little poems.' Her voice was flat and uncoloured.

'Let's go in, and then you can read them to me,' I said officiously.

The white cat Sal-al was lying on the straw matting in the empty conservatory. She looked at us with a wicked, conceited expression as if all her appetites had just been satisfied. She was beautiful. Vesta and I both said, 'I wish I were a cat!' Before we got to the last word we smiled at each other in annoyance, not liking the idea that most human beings think very much alike.

I sat down in front of the fire with a sheaf of Vesta's poems, and began to read. I thought them very good, almost better than my own; besides, they were typed!

'Which do you like best?' she asked, losing her tired manner.

I held a little one up about a woman and her clothes. The thin filmy paper rustled and curled in the heat from the fire.

'My lord!' Vesta groaned extravagantly. 'Surely you don't think that that's the best thing I've written! Don't you like the long one on Angkor?'

'Yes, but have you ever been there?' I asked.

'That's a very stupid, literal question,' she said. 'Did Coleridge ever go to Xanadu?' She took the poems away from me and locked them in a cupboard. Then her mood changed.

'I wonder what sort of letters you write?' she mused. 'If you go back to England I don't suppose we shall ever see you again.'

She was looking into the fire, with her eyes half closed, and the long fringes of her lashes were mysterious, like the feathery legs of a spider.

I did not want to stay with her by the fire any longer.

'Good-bye, Vesta, I must go,' I said.

'What, before tea!' she exclaimed in mock astonishment, making me feel that I had always arrived just in time for a meal.

'I think I really must go,' I said again, uncomfortably.

As I spoke the Boy carried in the tea-tray, and Vesta, not waiting for her mother, silently poured out a cup of tea and handed it to me.

I sat down meekly and took a sandwich.

I was glad that I insisted on walking home, for I ran into my friend the soldier.

'But I thought you were going away for ever, the last time I saw you,' I said.

We stood at the corner of the road in the cold darkness.

'We were on the boat in the river for three days, then we all got off again.'

He made a spitting noise in his throat, and added, 'That's the Army!'

'Well; now I think I'm going, but I'm not quite sure,' I said.

'What, you going back to England! I don't expect I'll see you again, then.'

Everyone seemed to be saying good-bye. I had an unhappy, mourning feeling which I nursed.

'Shall we leave the road and cut across the fields?' I asked. 'It's nearer.'

'What about having a drink somewhere?' he suggested gloomily.

'No, let's walk across the fields. I need some fresh air.'

I was still self-conscious about going into bars. Besides, I was afraid that he would get drunk.

We turned down a little footpath between high bamboo fences. We skirted a market garden, and after crossing a bridge walked in the direction of a Chinese village.

We walked in silence, feeling the snow crunch under

our feet and listening to the night noises. One of the dogs in the village began to whine and bark.

As we approached we saw that something was happening in front of one of the houses. A woman, outlined against a lighted doorway, wrung her hands and cried, while two men with lanterns stood in the road. Then I saw the small black coffin that lay on the ground between them. It glistened.

The scene was beautiful, but I could not look without feeling ashamed for them and for myself.

With professional groans, the men picked up the coffin. The woman in the doorway set up such a mad piercing screaming that someone from behind caught her round the waist and pulled her in. They had to drag her, for she fell and lay there, a heavy, trembling bundle of quilted rags.

I was fascinated. I gripped the soldier's shoulder tightly in fear. 'Don't they make a row!' he said placidly. 'I suppose that's her kid they're taking away.'

The two coolies passed by, singing whiningly to themselves and breathing out garlic. The smell seemed to make the night thicker, darker. The thought of the coffin being buried in the ground was horrible.

I wanted to see them do it. 'Let's follow,' I said excitedly.

We went to the edge of a field and watched them as they rested the coffin on the ground. They dug no grave but began to raise a pile of earth over it.

We stood there, smoking cigarettes, while they grunted and swore.

Before the end of the week my father said what I expected him to say: 'I've booked your passage back to England.' But in spite of being ready for it, the words came as a shock.

My thoughts buzzed and jumped about as if hot water had been poured on them.

I would have to live in rooms in London or with relations who disapproved of me. Sometimes the English food would be horrible. There would be so little sun. I would belong again to my surroundings and would understand what people said. I would be able to go anywhere without fear, and I would see again the places I loved.

The pros and cons darted one after the other; but, deep down under all my thinking, I knew that I was glad.

When I told Vesta she said, 'Well, don't look so pleased, you toad; do you want to leave us all behind and never see us again?'

Her smile somehow reminded me of a string with a weight on the end of it.

'Won't you ever be coming to England?' I asked anxiously.

'We've only been there once, on a joy trip, and we're not likely to go again. If we go anywhere in Europe I expect it will be Italy.'

'Perhaps I'll come out to China again on a holiday,' I said.

'The Morgans are going back to England in a few weeks too,' Vesta mused. 'Mr Morgan has lost all his money, so he's sending his wife and daughter home to her parents.'

'Wouldn't it be extraordinary if they were going on my ship!' I exclaimed.

'Not so very,' Vesta replied in a governessy voice. Then she added, 'They're having an auction the day after tomorrow; shall we go?'

'Yes, if we don't run into them,' I said.

'Oh, they won't be there, they're staying with friends. They've got some quite nice old English china: rather cottagey but pretty.'

'Then let's go,' I said. 'I love seeing things that aren't Chinese when I'm in China.'

Vesta and I met early and drove off in rickshaws. The mournful hoods and tarpaulin aprons were up, for it was raining.

Although we were early, the Morgans' house was already full of people touching and fingering. They seemed to get a rich pleasure out of it. Their eyes were very sharp and intelligent. Something had woken up inside them at the thought of a bargain.

Vesta and I went into the pantry and marked in our catalogues the lots that interested us. The stuff was mostly Japanese and Chinese, only good enough for Europeans; but mixed with it were the remains of an old English green and gold tea-set, and some ordinary Staffordshire sheep. In the drawing-room were some old blue finger-bowls and a copper lustre jug.

I thought that Mrs Morgan's grandmother must have been a farmer's wife and that these were the remains of her things.

The drone of the auctioneer's voice began, and we grew excited. The wet clothes of the fox-terrier women began to smell.

It was nearly twelve o'clock before our lots came up. Vesta was to bid for the lustre jug and finger-bowls; I for the green and gold tea-set and the sheep.

As the auctioneer called out the number of my lot, something rose up inside me and then sank down again. I suddenly wanted the things fiercely. I felt that they were going to be snatched from me.

The bidding began at a dollar and went up in halves. I kept nodding my head. At six dollars I prayed for it to stop, but it rose to eight. The auctioneer tapped the desk. I wondered if there had been any mistake. Perhaps he had not seen my last nod. The Chinese clerk came up and asked for my name. With a delicious, melting feeling of relief, I paid him on the spot. Then I pushed through the crowds to the pantry.

Some plates and two cooking utensils went with my lot.

The plates were painted with the snow-capped Japanese holy mountain. They were so insipid and common that I decided to leave them behind.

As I bent down to pick out the pieces of the green and gold tea-set I heard someone say, 'Did you buy Lot 63?'

I looked up and saw that a stringy woman with thin fair hair had come into the room.

'Yes, I bought Lot 63,' I said suspiciously.

'Did you want all of it?' she asked.

'I don't want the kitchen things or the plates.'

'Oh, it's the plates I'm after,' she said joyfully. 'They match my tea-set. Will you sell them to me? What do you want for them?'

She looked straight into my eyes, as if she thought that I was about to cheat her.

'I don't know,' I answered, feeling ruffled.

'Would you take two dollars for them?' she asked anxiously, not expecting me to agree.

'All right.' I was only too thankful to be rid of them. 'You can have the kitchen things too,' I added.

'Oh, I don't want to buy those as well, thank you,' she said quickly.

I was pleased with the opportunity for rudeness.

'I didn't mean you to buy them; I meant that you could have them with the plates for two dollars.'

Again she looked at me sharply, expecting some trick.

'You sure?' she asked. 'Well, you never know; they might come in useful some time!'

She opened her purse, handed me two dollars and started to remove her new possessions before I should change my mind.

'So long!' she said incongruously as she sidled out of the door.

I went back to Vesta. She had been able to buy the jug and the finger-bowls, so we decided to pack up our things and go. We found a pile of newspapers under the stairs, and tore large crackling flakes from it.

Outside, the rickshaw coolies closed round us and mobbed us. We shouted at them angrily, afraid that they would break our things.

The rain had stopped. Everything glistened and dripped. We both felt gay and happy as we flew along.

When we got home we paid the coolies and then made a dash for the lavatory. Mr Fielding found us there, washing our finds in the basin. He asked what we were doing.

'We've bought some old china at the Morgans' sale,' Vesta said excitedly.

Mr Fielding looked at us, then turned away and shut the door.

'What do you think is the matter?' I asked Vesta. Her father had made me feel uncomfortable.

'I suppose he thinks it's greedy of us to buy the things that the Morgans have to sell,' she answered.

CHAPTER 34

I STARTED to pack. There was so much that I wanted to take back with me: the old silver, the china, the glass. Quietly I began to put each object in a separate tin, copying the dealers of Kai-feng. The round biscuit-tins at the bottom of my trunk gave me pleasure. I was the only person who cared for the things packed in them.

I took the old table-cloth with the classical design of serpents and quivers of arrows. I tried again to read the four faint names on it. I remembered how it used to be used once a year at Christmas-time. I took some of my great-grandmother's flower-paintings, and sandwiched them between layers of tissue-paper. The silver forks and spoons I wrapped in my socks and vests. Some of the handle edges had been worn to knife-thinness. I went down to the basement of the building. It was divided by strong wire-netting into cubicles for each tenant's trunks and boxes.

I unlocked our own cage door and tried to wriggle my way between the cases. The cubicle next to it was empty, except for a pile of waste paper. As I bent down in my struggles, I noticed a little square envelope which had fallen through the wide mesh. It was not stuck down, so I put in my fingers and pulled out a trembling filmy rubber thing. I did not realize at first what it was; then I grew angry and fascinated. I stuffed it into my pocket, meaning to keep it, but it made me feel anxious and guilty. I hated the thought of anyone finding it on me; so before I left, I poked it carefully through the grille on the other side, where it lay conspicuously on a hat-box labelled 'Mrs S. G. Hay.'

I went upstairs laughing, wondering what she would

do when she found it. Boy met me at the door, he seemed in high excitement. 'Young master,' he said, 'Old master very angry; he talky me, you no can take away anything!'

His words sent a stillness through my body; then I felt my cheeks filling with blood.

'Where b'long Old master?' I asked.

'Have just now go out. He very angry!' The Boy chanted distractedly.

I went into my bedroom. The trunk had been opened and the tins and cotton-wool were lying in a heap on the floor.

The sight made me so angry that I forgot to be frightened. All my careful packing had been spoiled.

I waited for my father to come in; then I walked quickly into the drawing-room. He had already settled by the lamp with his detective story and his whisky-and-soda. He looked up and said:

'Punky, what the devil do you mean by packing up those things without telling me?'

I thought it a strange moment to use my pet name.

'Oh, I didn't think you'd mind,' I said in a futile, casual voice. 'You've got so much stuff here, and you know that I treasure those things more than you do.'

'That's nothing to do with it. You should have asked me first.'

This was so true that it acted like a blow, making me want to retaliate.

'They were my mother's, so they are really just as much mine as yours now,' I said. 'If she were alive she'd give them all to me!' I wanted to hurt him.

He took no notice.

'You must unpack everything,' he said.

'You've done it already!' I answered bitterly. 'There is nothing left to unpack!'

I ran back to my room and locked the door. I lay on the bed, hating the sight of the empty tins and the cotton-wool. I had a longing to be gone, to be on the ship, on the way back to England.

I sat up and decided to go out. I wanted to do something abandoned, to horrify my father. I slammed the front door to show that I had left.

As I ran down the stairs I hated the steam-heated passages and the noiseless lifts: the peach-coloured lighting and the thick blue carpet. The reproductions of old masters on the entrance lobby walls looked cheaper than Christmas calendars.

Out in the street I felt desperate. I wanted to do something spectacular to blot out the silly scene upstairs; and I could think of nothing. I started to run because anger had made me so full of energy.

At Bubbling Well Temple I stopped for breath. As usual, music and light leaked out of the Cabaret which was so strangely named after a saint. I wondered if there were any reason for it; whether the saintly name gave the revellers a pleasurable sense of sin. But I decided that the idea was far-fetched.

I took my courage in both hands and went in. I knew what was waiting for me inside. I remembered the night when the American marine had taken me there. This made me feel a little less nervous.

It seemed strangely empty in comparison with that other night. Only one or two couples were sliding over the dancing-floor. As I stood there, wondering what to do next, a trim, middle-aged Eurasian woman came up to me.

'Are you looking for the other room?' she asked. She seemed so certain that I was, that I found myself nodding my head. She led me across the floor, and having pulled away a curtain, left me in a kind of bar-parlour. Groups of people sat drinking at small tables, but the greater number huddled round the bar, leaning on it, their bodies wedged tightly together like cattle in a byre on a winter's night. Wriggling my way in at a corner, I ordered sherry, the drink I knew best.

The two soldiers next to me seemed very loving. They had their arms round each other's necks. Suddenly I saw one lift his hand and smack the other playfully and viciously on the face. I thought that there would be a fight. I was ready to jump over the bar and escape that way when the rough-house began. But the slapped soldier only looked at his friend mildly, as though he were making allowances; then he took a long drink. The angry red shape of the hand began to glow on his cheek. I wondered if they were the same two soldiers who had been thrown out into the bushes on my last visit.

On the other side stood a short, broad-shouldered man with a pretty silk scarf round his neck and *Les Lettres de Mlle de Lespinasse* tucked under his arm. I could read the title in gold on rich green morocco.

'What a book to bring in here!' I said gaily, knowingly, never having read a word of her letters, but imagining that they were hard and polished and eighteenth-century; not at all like a sloppy public bar.

He grinned at me sleepily and I was glad to see that he was fairly far gone. I didn't want to play a game of 'Have you read?' or 'Do you remember?'

When he spoke, it was with a strong foreign accent, not French, more German, perhaps Dutch.

'How long are you in Shanghai?' he asked, pronouncing the name Shan-Ghai.

I found myself wanting to reply in the same idiom, 'Since one year, nearly.' But I checked myself and said in ordinary English:

'About a year.'

'You like?' He gave me a drunken, earnest look, as if a lot depended on my answer.

'Yes, quite,' I said.

This conversation was too dull to last. He was waving his little glass about, and at last he spilt the whisky all down the front of my trousers. I stood, not doing anything, just looking at the dark little rivulet as it wound its way down to the floor.

Suddenly the man fell on his knees and began to rub my trousers vigorously with his lovely silk scarf.

'Don't do that, don't do that,' I said, stepping back in my agitation, and buffeting other people.

'I so sorry, so sorry,' he clucked. Beads of sweat gathered on his forehead. His shiny face was on a level with my belt. His nose was broad and flattened like a gargoyle's. He looked like an evil devil, about to do me some terrible harm.

'It's quite all right now, please don't bother any more,' I said, still trying to back away, but he held my legs fast with his other hand.

At last he stood up.

'O.K. now?' he asked, his eyes anxiously searching for approval.

He began to tie the whisky-sodden scarf round his neck again. It looked nasty now, and grim, as if it had been stuffed into somebody's mouth as a gag.

He banged on the bar with his little glass and ordered two more whiskies. When they came, he would not let me add any soda-water to mine.

'Bad!' he said, wrinkling his nose and lifting his lip, like a pug dog.

The two soldiers drew attention to their empty glasses by rattling them together. The 'Dutchman' looked at them.

'You want –?' he asked; then he brought his cupped hand to his lips and tossed his head back in dumb show. His fair hair fell over his face and he looked like an albino gollywog.

'Yes, Oui, Ja,' the soldiers said, to show their command of languages. They nodded and grinned when he said the one word, 'Whisky?'

I drank mine in silence, hating the taste. The soldiers could not quite understand why their glasses were not full. Their faces soon regained an expectant look. I decided that it was time for me to buy a round of drinks. Without asking anyone, I ordered cherry brandy. Murmuring broke out when it appeared. The 'Dutchman' looked at me suspiciously and said, 'Grenadine?' The soldiers pretended to use the little glasses of red liquid as eye-baths.

The 'Dutchman' and I went on buying drinks for the rest of the evening. Sometimes the soldiers would show mock surprise and say, 'What! Is this for me?' when we pushed fresh glasses towards them. Then they would toast us solemnly and fall to their affectionate quarrelling again.

When at last we were turned out into the cold, I felt suddenly sick. I could not forget the horrible taste of the whisky. I leant on the 'Dutchman' and said, 'I'm going to be sick!' But I wasn't, which was lucky, for the 'Dutchman,' instead of leaving me, became very protective and almost sober. 'I go home with you,' he said, taking my arm.

We all four of us set out together, and the soldiers began to sing. I joined in and felt better for the deep draughts of fresh air. As we approached the barracks the soldiers grew wily and serious. We said that we would help them to climb over the fence. They wanted to avoid the sentry, as they were so late. The 'Dutchman' patted his broad shoulders to show that they could stand on them, and to prove how strong they were.

We went up a dark blind-alley. On one side were the barracks, on the other the high walls, crowned with jagged glass, of a rich Chinaman's house. Through the darkness I could just see the lumpy shape of the stucco gateway, blocking the end.

The cinders crunched under our feet, but nobody stirred. The men in the huts were fast asleep.

One soldier stood with his face to the bamboo fence, while the other climbed uncertainly on to his shoulders.

The 'Dutchman' and I supported them both from either side. Once or twice all our bodies swayed, and I felt that the whole crazy human tower would collapse. I started to giggle. Someone kicked my ankle viciously.

At last there was a soft thud and we knew that the first soldier had landed on the other side. The next one got up on to the 'Dutchman's' shoulders and balanced himself. I held his legs and felt the hard muscles jumping about under the hairy khaki as he prepared to spring.

We whispered to them through the fence. 'Are you all right? – Good night. – See you again some time.'

We heard them walk off, and then the quiet shutting of a door. The 'Dutchman' turned away and leant dreamily against the fence. Suddenly, as I stood waiting for him, I heard the gate open behind us. There was a stealthy, darting movement through the darkness and someone grabbed the back of my coat so fiercely that the one fastened button was torn off.

In my panic and terror I did the right thing. I stretched out my arms behind me, so that my coat was jerked off and I was free.

Gasping and lurching, I ran for my life over the rough cinders. At first I knew that I was being chased, but the drumming behind me suddenly seemed to stop. Something heavy struck the ground and there were groans and curses. I dared not wait to find out what had happened. I ran on until I reached the end of the lane. There I could hardly breathe. I leant against the fence, waiting for my 'Dutch' friend, hoping that it was not he who had fallen.

He came up laughing between his gasps for breath.

'I fix him!' he said gaily. 'I fix him! I kick him here!' He pointed to his stomach. 'Oh – oh – oh!' He imitated a man rolling about in agony.

'I think he is Indian,' he said. And he wound an imaginary turban round his head to show why he thought so.

Just then we heard shouts, as if someone else were being

297

called. The 'Dutchman' and I looked at each other swiftly; then we joined hands.

'Good-bye,' he said. 'You run this way, I run the other.'

He turned away and shouted over his shoulder as he ran, 'I have left poor Mademoiselle de Lespinasse behind. I hope they treat her well!' The last thing I heard was his laughter at his own little joke. Then I started to run and did not stop until I reached home; although, so far as I could tell, the chase had been abandoned.

I lay on my bed, trying to stop gulping so painfully for breath. Now that I had time to think, I was terrified. My coat was in the hands of the rich Chinaman's Indian night-watchman. He would take it to the police. They would know who I was.

I would have to appear in court and explain that I was helping drunk soldiers to get into barracks without passing the sentry. I thought of my father's face as he listened to me saying this. No one would understand.

I longed to be on the boat, sailing for England. A day was too long to wait. In the morning the police would come to question me.

The rest of the night was horrible. I lay on my back wondering what would happen; and when at last I fell asleep, it was only to awake hot with shame at the remembrance of the quarrel with my father.

As soon as it grew light I got up. I sat on the edge of the bed for a moment, feeling sick and dizzy, then I hurriedly pulled on some clothes and let myself out of the penthouse. I had decided to go back to the lane in the faint hope that my coat might still be there.

In the early morning air the cinders glittered like splintery marcasite. Something white lay in front of me. I picked up and closed the book of Mlle de Lespinasse's Letters. The heavy morocco was a little scarred and battered. I decided to keep it always.

But my coat was nowhere to be seen.

CHAPTER 35

PAUL could not understand why I was so worried.

'I thought you wanted to go back to England,' he said.

'So I do, but this fuss Daddy has made has spoilt it all.' I tried to explain away my anxiety in this way.

'He only wants you to ask him for the things. He's quite right. Ask him to-night and see what he says.' My brother seemed quite sure.

All that day I waited for a detective to arrive and ask me about my movements on the night before. The sight of a peak-capped chauffeur in the courtyard below frightened me. I think my fear had become exaggerated because of the quarrel with my father. My actions seemed to end in covering me with shame. It was like the 'Harlot's Progress'. I began to feel persecuted.

That night I sank my pride and went up to my father. I asked him for the things I wanted.

'Bring the silver chest in and let me see what you take,' he said severely.

I went and fetched the heavy wooden box. It was quite plain; except for my great-grandmother's name under the lock. The oldest silver, which was never used, lay at the bottom. I began firmly to take out the chamois-leather bundles, only stopping when I reached the enormous soup-ladle.

'Surely that's enough!' my father exclaimed.

'All right,' I said, sacrificing the soup-ladle. 'If I can keep these.'

A warmth stole all over me. 'They are really mine now,' I thought. 'They've been given to me.'

'May I have the blue jugs and the open-work Worcester baskets?' I asked next.

'Yes,' my father said.

'And some of the old books?'

'Yes, yes, yes, but don't bother me any more!'

I gathered up the things and took them into my room. In spite of my fear, thrills of pleasure ran through me. I started to pack them again in the biscuit-tins.

Paul lay on the bed, watching me.

'I hope you're satisfied,' he said loftily.

'I don't think they could be coming for me now,' I tried to persuade myself on waking the next morning. I began to sink inside. To-day I was leaving China. I looked at the room, scattered with paper and boxes. It already looked like a tousled, empty cage. Soon I would have to get up and press down the lids of all my boxes. I had eight.

'I hope nothing gets smashed,' I thought. 'It would be awful if anything gets smashed.'

I pictured the unpleasantness of breakfast; the empti-ness inside me, and the porridge and eggs which had suddenly become so difficult to eat.

I got up and went into the bathroom. I could not lie in bed any longer with the awful feeling gnawing inside me.

Vesta was coming to the quay to see me off.

I turned on the taps and waited impatiently for the bath to fill.

'They keep lunatics in tepid baths for hours to soothe their nerves,' I thought.

But the hot water didn't soothe me. It just made my face soft with sweat and steam, and my hair floppy and easy to comb.

I dressed carefully, putting on one of my new shirts, made from the roll of rich silk which Mrs Fielding had given me. The Chinese tailor was supposed to have copied one of my English shirts, but I noticed that the collar and the tails were skimped. I thought that he could only have saved a very little silk by doing that.

Boy came in with my tea. 'Young master very early,' he said. I did not want the tea, but I poured some out before he left the room. Then I drank it and felt glad. I began to stuff my remaining things into the tray of my cabin-trunk. I opened all the drawers and the cupboards, until the room looked as if it had been burgled.

Paul and my father were not yet up, so I hurried into the dining-room. I wanted to eat my breakfast alone. Propping a book in front of me, I started to read, hoping to calm my excitement. A pale squirt of grape-fruit juice shot across the page. Wiping it off, I looked up and saw Cook squinting at me through the service-hatch. I seemed so different to myself, that I was not surprised. People were justified in staring at me. I was going away.

My father came in, smelling of scented soap and tobacco. 'Have you finished your packing, Punky?' he asked vaguely, preoccupied with coffee and the newspaper.

The coolies began to carry my boxes down.

Paul sat down and started to eat methodically and quickly.

I left the table and made a last tour of the penthouse. I stood for a few moments in the little library, watching the silent rows of books. I tried to sniff the lovely, aromatic, deserted smell up into my memory.

Cook waited for me in the kitchen. 'Good-bye, Master Dung-dung' (he never could say Denton), 'I never more see you. By and by, s'pose you come Shanghai, I makey die!'

'What for talky so fashion, Cook?' I said. 'You no very old!'

'You no savvy how old; maybe I b'long one hundred year!' He laughed at the impossibility.

As I left him I realized how charming pidgin-English was. I had a sudden, sharp regret at the thought of never speaking it again after that day.

My father shepherded me into the lift. In the court-yard the servants stood round the car waiting for us. They smiled mournfully and waved as we drove off.

We did not talk. My father busied himself with my passport and money, while Paul looked out of the window.

Even before the car stopped I had caught sight of Vesta, on the quay with her husband. She was dressed in a fur coat which made her look plump and birdlike, and she had on her head a little brown hat, so that she was all one colour. I wished that it had been red.

We walked down the stone steps and boarded the toss-ing, dipping little launch. As the sailor helped me in, I thought how terrible it would be to fall into the black water between the boat's side and the slimy piles, cush-ioned with old motor tyres.

Spray splashed up as the motor-boat cut through the water, and Vesta, sitting beside me, made faces and shut one eye, pretending that she had been soaked. Her hus-band stared at the horizon and smiled without moving his head if someone turned towards him.

Vesta was the first to climb up the gangway, and when I reached the deck I found her talking to a smooth, bun-faced woman.

'Oh, Mrs Morgan, this is Denton,' she said. A plump gloved hand was held out and the fruity little eyes looked into me. They seemed to be searching for harmless amusement at my expense. I told myself that I had this woman's tea-set in one of my boxes. I remembered meet-ing her daughter Megan once. The daughter stood by her now, looking pretty with big brown doglike eyes, full of passive resistance.

We stood for a moment, talking by the rail, then I went down to look at my cabin. I had it to myself and none of my boxes had been put in the hold. Relief flooded over me.

Vesta came in as I was smoothing my hair in the glass. It seemed to annoy her.

'How vain you are!' she said. And the pitch of her voice was queer and rather brittle.

'Isn't going away awful!' I groaned. I was searching desperately for the most normal and commonplace thing to say.

She gave no answer, but gazed contemptuously out of the porthole, with winking eyes.

My brother's face appeared in the circle.

'Oh, there you are!' he said.

Soon they were all crowding round us and my brother had opened the little bottle of Cointreau which he had bought for me. I think he must have remembered something I had once said about liking it.

I poured little quantities into the tooth-glass and we all tasted it, smacking our lips and saying how good it was.

Then the hooter sounded, and everyone jumped up convulsively.

Vesta left with the others, but ran back into the cabin afterwards. Her face, even her lips, were pale, as I had seen them sometimes on cold days. I knew suddenly that she was my greatest friend; and I had the grotesque idea that her husband might imagine us to be in love. It was so funny, I wanted to laugh.

'Good-bye, darling,' she said, kissing me desperately, half afraid, I think, that I might pull away. When she stepped back her hat was a little crooked and some more tight curls had pushed out on to her forehead.

We looked at each other for a moment, then she turned and ran away.

I stood in the empty cabin, wondering what to do; then I too ran up on deck.

She was already in the stern of the bobbing motor-launch. I waved to her, and I saw her face suddenly break into lines. She was crying now. Her mouth was open, showing her white teeth.

Her husband stood behind her, looking embarrassed

and upset. He took her arm and tried to calm her. The launch began to pull away.

I felt my throat thickening and aching. Slow, heavy tears gathered in the corners of my eyes and glistened there until they dropped on to the scrubbed deck, where they made dark patches.

I waved until her face was only a little pink blob; then I turned miserably away and went back to my cabin.

It still smelt of Cointreau. I lay down on the bunk, feeling sick. The woodwork began to creak. I wanted to go to sleep for ever.

There was a knock on the door. A steward poked his head in, saying, 'Lunch will be served in a few minutes.'

Already it was 'lunch', not 'tiffin.'

Once again I washed my red eyes in a shiny metal basin.

Then I went down and sat next to Mrs Morgan and tried to talk as if neither of us had lost anything.

THE END